A VERY SHORT
HISTORY
OF THE
WORLD

GEOFFREY BLAINEY

A VERY SHORT HISTORY OF THE WORLD

VIKING
an imprint of
PENGUIN BOOKS

Viking

Penguin Group (Australia)
250 Camberwell Road, Camberwell, Victoria 3124, Australia
Penguin Books Ltd
80 Strand, London WC2R 0RL, England
Penguin Group (USA) Inc.]
375 Hudson Street, New York, New York 10014, USA
Penguin Books, a division of Pearson Canada
10 Alcorn Avenue, Toronto, Ontario, Canada M4V 3B2
Penguin Books (NZ) Ltd
Cnr Rosedale and Airborne Roads, Albany, Auckland, New Zealand
Penguin Books (South Africa) (Pty) Ltd
24 Sturdee Avenue, Rosebank, Johannesburg 2196, South Africa
Penguin Books India (P) Ltd
11, Community Centre, Panchsheel Park, New Delhi 110 017, India

First published by Penguin Group (Australia), a division of Pearson Australia Group
Pty Ltd, 2004

1 3 5 7 9 10 8 6 4 2

Design by Cathy Larsen © Penguin Group (Australia)
Maps drawn by Alan Laver
Text images by Stock Photos
Author photograph by Irene Lorbergs, courtesy National Council for the
Centenary of Federation
Typeset in 10.5/14 Fairfield Light by Midland Typesetters, Maryborough, Victoria
Printed and bound in Australia by McPherson's Printing Group, Maryborough, Victoria

National Library of Australia
Cataloguing-in-Publication data:

Blainey, Geoffrey, 1930– .
A very short history of the world.

Bibliography.
Includes index.
ISBN 0 670 04202 1.

1. World history. 2. Civilization. I. Title.

909

www.penguin.com.au

CONTENTS

LIST OF MAPS

PREFACE TO THIS
ABRIDGED EDITION

This is an attempt to write a world history that is not too voluminous. It tries to survey history since the time when the first people left Africa to settle the globe. Inevitably, some large themes which I investigated are described so fleetingly that they are like glimpses from the window of a passing train.

I resolved from the outset that I would pay attention to technology and skills, for they have done so much to shape the world. I gave much attention to the rise of the major religions, for they too are attempts to shape the world. I also looked at geographical factors, for they often ordained – until the last century – what could not happen, what could not succeed. Without initially intending to, I gave space to what people ate and how hard they worked in order to earn their daily bread. When the book was far advanced, I realised something that must have once been obvious to everyone: the intense power of the moon, the stars and the night sky on human experience. Chapter Four,

'The Dome of Night' and a section of the final chapter try to remedy that omission.

I found myself also looking at empires and the areas they covered. The size of the territory which one leader, or one state, can rule has grown progressively larger. For the first time in human history, world government of some sort is now possible: whether it is wise and whether it is popularly demanded are other questions. Thus the shrinking of the world is one of the book's recurring themes.

I was conscious, from an early stage, of the risk of making the book too compressed, of trying to pack in too much. To use a cricket analogy, I wished to vary periods of fast bowling – or tight writing – with intervals of slow bowling. To ensure this variation in pace, I sometimes organised the spells of slow bowling in advance of the writing of the main narrative. Even though some of these leisurely episodes occupy perhaps more space than they deserve, they have their own value and symbolism. Amongst such episodes are the bride of the Yellow River, the way of life of the New Zealand Maoris and the influence of the Indian indigo plant on the colour blue.

Europeans are mentioned little in some parts of the book. During the first dozen chapters, Europe rarely appears except as the home of the Greeks and the Romans. The continents of Africa, Asia and Asia Minor, and even the Americas, virtually dominate the story until it reaches the last 400 or 500 years, when

European civilisation has its turn at dominance.

One of the dilemmas was how much space to allot to the last 150 years. Such influential leaders as Garibaldi, Roosevelt, Churchill and Nasser surely deserve a mention; and such profound or symbolic events as the invention of anaesthetics surely call for at least one paragraph; but they receive scant or no attention in this book. My relatively cramped treatment of the 20th century stems from a reluctance to permit that century to be as significant, indeed as self-important, as every century seems to those who live in it. When the history of the world is written in AD 2400, so many resounding events of our time will have receded in relevance, or entered oblivion, just as many of the events which were momentous in Roman or Aztec times no longer raise our eyebrows. So this is the tightrope I have tried to walk.

The previous, larger edition of this book had many readers. Some said the book was not long enough and wrote to request more. Others told me, with some courtesy, that the book was too long: they had no time, they hinted, to read long books. For the benefit of the latter readers I have produced this shortened edition. To retain the flavour and pace of the long edition I have retained many sections of 'slow bowling'. The argument and emphasis of this edition are the same.

The book's defects would have been larger but for the generous help and criticism I have received from many people. I especially thank Dr Jocelyn Chey of

Sydney; Father Austin Cooper of the Catholic Theological College in Melbourne; Mr Raymond Flower of Sarnano, Italy; Dr Barry Jones, Peter Lawrence, Rabbi John Levi and Dr Malcolm Kennedy of Melbourne; Dr Glenn Mulligan and Dr Lotte Mulligan of La Trobe University; and Mr Kage-fumi Ueno, Japan's consul general in Melbourne. Katie Purvis of Penguin Books has been a fine editor. My indebtedness to others is expressed in the source notes at the back of the original edition.

I gained from visits to many museums and art galleries as well as libraries. I especially thank the Deutsches Museum in Munich, the Museum of Natural History and the Science Museum in London, the American Museum of Natural History in New York, and the libraries of the Melbourne, Ballarat and La Trobe universities.

GEOFFREY BLAINEY
MELBOURNE

PART ONE

1

FROM AFRICA

They lived in Africa and, two million years ago, they were few. They were almost human beings, though they tended to be smaller than their descendants who now inhabit the world. They walked upright; they were also skilled climbers.

They ate mainly fruits, nuts, seeds and other food-plants but were beginning to eat meat. Their implements were primitive. If they tried to shape stone they did not carry the shaping very far. Probably they were capable of using a stick for defence or attack or even for digging – if a small rodent was hiding in a burrow. Whether they made simple shelters out of shrubs and sticks to ward off the cold winds in winter is not known. No doubt some lived in caves – if caves could be found – but such a permanent residence would have gravely restricted the mobility needed to find enough food. To live off the land called for long walks to the places where certain seeds or fruits could be found. Their diet was the result of a chain of discoveries, made over hundreds of thousands of years.

A crucial discovery was whether a seemingly safe food plant was poisonous. Scavenging for new foods in a time of drought and famine, some must have died through poisoning.

Two million years ago these human beings – known as hominids – lived mainly in the lands now called Kenya, Tanzania and Ethiopia. If Africa is divided into three horizontal zones, the human race occupied the middle or tropical zone. Probably much of it was grassland. Indeed, a change of climate one or two million years earlier, with grassland largely replacing forest in certain regions, might have encouraged these humans gradually to part company from their relatives – the apes – and spend more time on the ground.

They already had a long history, though they had no memory or record of it. We talk today of the vast span of time since the building of the pyramids in Egypt, but that span was merely a wink compared to the long history which the human race had already experienced. One early record has been uncovered in Tanzania. Two adults and a child were walking on top of volcanic ash softened by recent rain. Their footprints then were baked by the sun and slowly covered by layers of earth. The footprints, definitely human, are at least 3 600 000 years old. Even that is young in the history of the living world. The last of the dinosaurs were extinguished about 64 000 000 years ago.

In East Africa the early humans liked to camp on the shores of lakes and in sandy riverbeds or on the grassy plains: some of their remains have been found in such places. They were also able to adapt to cooler climates and in Ethiopia they preferred an open plateau at a height of 1600 or 2000 metres above sea level. In the evergreen forests of the uplands they were also at home. Their adaptability was impressive.

In the cut-throat contest to stay alive and to multiply, humans were usually successful. In their part of Africa they were far outnumbered by various species of large animals, some of them aggressive, but the humans flourished. Their population became too large for the resources of their area or perhaps a long drought drove them north. The evidence is strong that sometime around two million years ago they began to migrate further north. The longest desert in the world – stretching from north-west Africa and past Arabia – may have temporarily blocked their way. The narrow land bridge between Africa and Asia Minor was easily crossed.

They moved in small bands: they were explorers as well as settlers. In each unfamiliar region they had to adapt to new foods, and they had to watch for wild animals, venomous snakes and poisonous insects. The people leading the way had one advantage. Those other stern opponents of territorial intruders, human beings, were not standing in their way.

It was more like a relay race than a trek. Possibly one group of maybe six or 12 moved a short distance and then settled down. Others came, leapfrogged them or drove them forward. The move across Asia might have taken 10 000 or 200 000 years. Mountain slopes had to be climbed, swamps traversed. Wide, fast, cold rivers had to be crossed. Did they cross them at fords in very dry seasons or cross them in the high country, before the streams became wide? Could the explorers swim? The answers are not known. At night in strange terrain, a shelter or a place of some security had to be selected. Without the aid of guard dogs, a watch had to be kept for wild animals hunting at night.

In the course of the slow and long migration – the first of many long migrations in the history of the human race – these people originating in the tropics moved into territory far colder than any which their ancestors had experienced. Whether they could warm themselves by fires on cold nights is not certain. When a strike of lightning set fire to adjacent countryside they presumably collected the fire by lighting a stick and carrying the fire away. When the stick was almost burned and the fire faded, they could light another stick. Fire was so valuable that, once it was captured, it would be carefully tended. But fire could be extinguished through carelessness, or doused by heavy rain or lost through an absence of dry wood and kindling. While they possessed fire, they must have carried it on their travels as a precious possession, just as the early Australians travelled with fire.

The ability to create fire, rather than borrow it already alight, came late in human history. Eventually humans could produce a flame through the friction and heat caused by rubbing dry wood against dry wood. Or they could strike a piece of pyrite or other suitable rock and thus make a spark. In both processes, some very dry kindling was required, as well as the art of gently blowing on the smoking kindling.

The skilled employing of fire – the result of many brainwaves and experiments during thousands of years – is one of the achievements of the human race. How ingeniously it was used can be seen in the way of life which survived in a few remote regions of Australia until the 20th century. On the flat cloudless plains of the outback the Aborigines lit small fires to send a smoke signal – it was a clever form of telegraph. They also used fire for cooking and warmth, and for smoking out game. Fire was the sole illuminant at night – except when a full moon gave them light for their ceremonial dances. Fire was used in hardening the digging sticks and shaping wood for spears. Fire was used to cremate the dead. It was used to burn a ceremonial pattern on the human skin. It was employed to drive snakes from long grass at a chosen camping site. It was an insect repellent. It was used by hunters to burn the grass in a systematic mosaic at certain times of the year and so encourage new growth, when rains fell. So numerous were the eventual uses of fire that it was the most useful tool possessed by the human race until recent times.

Today humans possess weapons that make the

claw and jaw of a wild animal seem pitiful. For a long period, however, it was the human race that was pitiful. Physically it was smaller and lighter than many of the animals living in the vicinity. It was also hopelessly outnumbered by individual herds of large animals. The entire human population of each region was small compared to that of other fighting species. In Asia the big curved-horn mammoth, a species of elephant, must have far outnumbered the humans whom they occasionally saw nearby, while grazing.

The danger of attack from wild animals was high. Even in 1996 in one Indian state, 33 children were fatally attacked by wolves. In the homeland of Africa the leopards and lions must have been feared by the humans. Obviously, the slow increase in human organising capacity was a vital aid to self-defence, especially at night. Without that ability to cooperate against an enemy, the early humans venturing into new tropical areas might easily have been wiped out by beasts of prey. In a few places the advance guard, numbering less than a dozen, was perhaps wiped out.

About 1 800 000 years ago, the advance guard of this movement reached China and South-East Asia. Little is known about this long series of journeys by the human race, though much more will be uncovered by prehistorians and archaeologists in the next century. Essentially people of the inland, these humans were probably late in settling along the coast and very late in mastering even shallow seas.

A recent excavation on an outer island in the Indonesian archipelago disclosed remains of human habitation dating back more than 800 000 years. The remains, discovered in the ancient bed of a lake in the mountainous island of Flores, proved beyond any doubt that humans had learned to build water craft and to paddle them far out to sea: the sail itself lay far in the future. To reach the island of Flores, a brave easterly sea-crossing was made from the nearest island. Even if the sea levels had been at their lowest, the distance crossed in a small boat or raft from the nearest island would have been at least 19 kilometres. Perhaps this was the longest sea voyage up to that time. It resembled the first journey to the moon in the 20th century, in the sense that it exceeded all previous voyages.

Here and there can still be found glimmers of the daily life of these explorers and pioneer settlers. Near Beijing (Peking), at a camp site of humans, layers of ashes and charcoal were recently exposed by careful digging. Those camp fires had been dead for perhaps 400 000 years but they held the remains of a meal: the burned bone of a deer, and the shells taken from hackberry nuts.

AN AWAKENING

In the space of several million years, humans had become more adaptable, more resourceful. The typical human brain was growing larger. Whereas it occupied about 500 cubic centimetres in the early humans, it occupied about 900 in the human species called

Homo erectus which carried out this long migration. Somewhere between 500 000 and 200 000 years ago, the brain was again enlarged to a pronounced extent. This growth of the brain was one of the remarkable events in the history of biological change.

The brain's structure was also changing, and a 'motor speech area' took shape. The larger brain seemed to be associated with increasing skill in using the hands and arms, and the slow rise of a spoken language. Such a substantial growth in the size of the brain in any species is a remarkable event. How it happened is largely a mystery. One possible cause is the eating of more and more meat. It is unlikely that the human race at this stage possessed either the weapons or the organising ability to kill wild animals of any size. Possibly the meals of meat came from increasing bravery in scavenging the carcasses of recently dead animals, while the main pack or herd was grazing not far away, or from a growing skill in hunting the smaller animals which posed no danger but were not easily caught. It is feasible that in the course of time the fatty acids in the meat improved the brain and its functioning. In turn, that advantage enabled humans to devise better ways of hunting animals. All this is speculation.

The spoken language was acquiring more words and more precision. The fine arts were emerging. The fine arts and the act of communicating by speech both rely on the use of symbols, whether those detected by the ear or the eye. The ability to invent symbols and to recognise them was one result of the slow improvements in the brain. Perhaps a development in the human voice box was also an aid to expressing these symbols in sound.

Despite the advances in studying the mind in the last half-century, the brain and human speech are still far from explored. One medical specialist has suggested that in an intricate activity such as speech, 'the interaction of the parts of the brain will not resemble those of an orderly machine but will more resemble a crazy quilt'. Whatever its origins, language is the greatest of all inventions.

Some 60 000 years ago came signs of a human awakening. Prehistorians and archaeologists, looking back, have pieced together the evidence for a slow-moving succession of changes which in the next 30 000 years merited such descriptions as a 'Great Leap Forward' or a 'Cultural Explosion'. There is dispute about who did the leaping and exploding. Possibly the changes were the work of a new human group that emerged in Africa and then emigrated to Asia and Europe, where they coexisted with the Neanderthals, a species that later vanished. What is clear is the existence of human creativity on many fronts.

The speech of the hundreds of generations of people who were alive during the Awakening is silent and lost, but some of their arts and crafts survive, either in fragments or intact. The arts blossomed in Europe during that long glacial phase which began about 75 000 years ago. Persistent evidence suggests that many humans expected to renew their existence in an afterlife. The journey to that new life required accessories or indications of one's status, and the chosen items were arranged in the grave. In Sunghir in Russia about 28 000 years ago a man of some 60 years of age was buried, his body adorned with more than 2000 pieces of ivory and other ornaments. To reach the age of 60 was to be almost venerable, for most adults died younger.

In another grave was buried, alongside a male, an adolescent girl. She was dressed in a bead cap, and perhaps in a cloak of which the only trace is the ivory pin that fastened it near the throat. Her body was covered with more than 5000 beads and other adorning snippets. The long time spent by friends or the whole tribe in making these decorations, and the care with which they were arranged in the grave, was a sign that death was as important as life.

At many times the people of this nomadic world must have felt an acute uncertainty. They were at the mercy of the seasons, for they hoarded no grains, nuts or other foods with which to face the first phase of a famine. Most of their sheltering places were flimsy. In some regions they lived side by side with tigers, lions, bears, panthers, elephants and other animals of formidable strength or ferocity. Death often arrived suddenly and mysteriously. They sought certainty and consolation. They began to construct religions and to make objects of devotion and homage as well as depictions of the world around them.

The techniques of hunting were slowly improved. Little pieces of stone shaped into spear points, blades and other piercing and cutting instruments – superior to most of those formerly used – were produced in their hundreds of thousands in any one year. Instead of pursuing only small animals, the hunters tried to attack larger ones. Elephants were hunted in Germany. In France the leopard was hunted for its hide and meat. In Italy the wild boar was pursued.

An improved organising ability seemed to come with the improved weapons. The weapons and the skill in human cooperation were part of the same mental awakening. Herds of animals were hunted and trapped, or driven to their death over a precipice, where they provided an extravagant feast of meat. It is now customary to observe that human beings at that time lived in harmony with their environment and did not kill needlessly and recklessly, but the observation has to be treated cautiously due to inconclusive evidence.

In Europe and Asia, wherever the supply of food was favourable, camps and villages were more permanent than before. Houses were usually built on slopes that gave protection from the icy winds. A small circular excavation provided a flat space for the floor made of slate, and wooden posts held up the roof which was covered with the hides of horses and other animals. From the fireplace in the middle of the one large room the smoke drifted up to a small hole in the roof.

Throughout the world, people lived a seminomadic life. Small groups of people, perhaps rarely numbering as many as 20, each occupied a large territory. In the course of a year they moved systematically from place to place, carrying virtually no possessions and making use of the variety of foods that came into season: a grain ripening here, a root crop growing there, a nest of bird's eggs available here, a nut ripening there. So long as the population was small and the natural resources were large the people lived in relative abundance.

Sometimes several groups might come together each year at a place with prolific food, but large gatherings must have been a rarity. In the entire world it is possible that at no time before, say, 20 000 BC did as many as 500 people ever assemble together in the one place. Even then their assembly was temporary. As they hoarded no food and kept no livestock they could not feed a large gathering for very long.

A group or tribe of people that was often on the move could not cope with those who were too sick and weak to walk. Even twin babies were a burden, and one was probably killed. Old people who could no longer walk were left behind to die. A mobile society had no alternative.

THE BLACK COLUMBUS

Each morning, as the sun first rose in eastern Asia, people could be seen stirring themselves – putting wood on the fire, breastfeeding children, setting out to gather nuts or catch wild animals, scraping the inside of an animal skin to turn it into clothing, or chipping away at a rock to shape it into a tool. The same scenes could probably be witnessed at tens of thousands of places as the sun's early rays moved west across Asia and then across Europe to the Atlantic. Similar activity could be seen in Africa, where humans occupied an increasingly large area.

About 100 000 years ago the area occupied by the human race was extensive, but a vast part of the globe still remained empty of people. The animals of the Americas had never heard a human voice or seen a spear. In Australia and New Guinea, which formed the one continent, were no human footprints. Islands far out to sea were inaccessible to the human race. In the Pacific Ocean most of those islands which now are inhabited were unknown to human beings: Hawaii and Easter Island, Tahiti and Samoa, Tonga and Fiji and the large islands of New Zealand were not inhabited. In the Indian Ocean the large and relatively warm island of Madagascar knew no camp fires and on the remote volcanic islands of Mauritius and Réunion the strange flightless bird, the dodo, was not disturbed by human beings. In the Atlantic Ocean, north of the equator, the Azores and Madeira were uninhabited. Greenland and Iceland were covered by ice. The birds of the islands of the West Indies were completely safe from human hunters.

The human race, in effect, was confined to one landmass. The combined area of the empty lands was huge. In total area, the lands which were habitable but empty were the equal of Asia, the Sahara desert and North Africa, all added together.

A succession of voyages of discovery was now being made. Humans were undertaking a second long migration. Between the nearest shores of South-East Asia, which then included Java, and the nearest coastline of New Guinea–Australia were some eight barriers of sea. Most were short gaps or straits, with the opposite shore visible from the point of setting out. The widest gap was about 80 kilometres. Pioneering people on rafts or in tiny canoes occasionally ventured across from one island to the next – so long as one shore was visible from the other. But if the wind blew too strongly, their flimsy vessel would be swamped, and all aboard would be drowned.

The crossing of this mosaic of seas and islands standing between Asia in the west and New Guinea–Australia in the east was spread over thousands of years. On some occasions it was halted, perhaps for as long as 10 000 years. One island would be discovered and settled, and then another boat or raft would find by accident or intention yet another island. Finally, without any idea of the significance of the discovery, the human race came ashore in New Guinea–Australia. There was no reason to think that a continent had been discovered. When the discoverer waded ashore is not known but was almost certainly more than 52 000 years ago.

The new continent was a surprise, a puzzle and sometimes a terror. No dangerous animals existed but many of the snakes and a few of the spiders were highly venomous. Slowly the newcomers explored the continent, every estuary, every mountain, every plain and desert. Walking overland to Tasmania, they cooked in riverbank caves in what was then the tundra but is now the rainforest. These new inhabitants of Tasmania were the most southerly inhabitants of the globe. It was a testimony to the adaptability of humans that they had originated in the tropics, had moved north and then east, and were now halfway to the South Pole.

In the latter phase of this slow movement of peoples, originating in Africa and extending far, the growth of language was one of the triumphs. Dialects and languages multiplied. Even in a large region where everybody, in the era of initial settlement, might have spoken alike, languages diverged. Groups lived in relative isolation from one another, and so their languages evolved. There must have been several thousand different languages when a geographical event began which, permanently separating so many peoples from each other, multiplied even further their languages.

2

WHEN THE SEAS WERE RISING

In 20 000 BC the human race was virtually confined
to one massive continent. Europe and Africa, Asia and
America were not then separated by seas, and this one
landmass was the scene of nearly all human activity.
Australia and New Guinea together formed the second
inhabited landmass but it held less than 5 per cent
of the world's population. There was another curious
facet of this population: it was confined almost entirely
to tropical and temperate zones. The cold areas of the
world were largely uninhabited.

At this time temperatures everywhere were much
colder than they are today. Glaciers were active and
extensive even in the far south of Australia, while in the
Northern Hemisphere a vast area was covered by ice
for most of the year. Finland, Sweden and even most of
Ireland – it was not an island – were wastelands. In the
high country of central Europe an area far larger than
Switzerland was overlaid with permanent ice. Some of
the present sea resorts in western Europe, where now
crowds of people bathe along the beaches on summer

days, were a bleak sight, with ice floating in the water even at the height of summer. Most of the present sea resorts were far from the sea.

North America was mainly a land of ice. Nearly all of the present Canada lay under compacted snow. A huge expanse of what is now the United States – an expanse supporting maybe half of its present population – lay under almost permanent ice. Parts of Central America, which in the 20th century have seen no snow, experienced frequent falls. On the high, western side of South America snow covered a vast area even in summer.

In a majority of the inhabited regions of the world the heat of summer was milder and the patterns of rainfall and evaporation were different from those of today. For human beings as a whole, however, this climate offered one advantage. Dry land spread over vast tracts of territory which now lie under the sea.

As the oceans were at such a low level, a man could walk from southern England to France and keep on walking – if the people along his route so allowed him – all the way to Java. A strong and fit Javanese, at high risk to life, could walk by a most indirect and northerly route to north Asia, and cross by a land bridge to unexplored Alaska. At that period Java was not an island but part of Asia.

Places that are now the world's busy seaports lay on dry land or on the banks of rivers that were far from the open sea. At that time the sites of San Francisco, New

York and Rio de Janeiro could not be reached by ship. People lived near Shanghai and Calcutta, Singapore and Sydney, but had never seen the sea. It was too far away.

Many now-strategic sea straits, which are busy day and night with passing tankers and bulk carriers, were simply corridors of grassland or forest. The Dardanelles and the Bosporus, the straits of Gibraltar and Malacca, Sunda Strait and Torres Strait were only a few of the now-busy seaways which did not exist.

Certain of today's seas and many of the large gulfs did not exist or their shapes were quite different. The Black Sea was a deep lake with no outlet to the Mediterranean. The Baltic Sea did not empty into the North Sea. Such large arms of the sea as today's Persian Gulf consisted of land.

About 15 000 BC a remarkable change began, ever so slowly. The summers and winters became just a trifle warmer. Glaciers retreated a little. Old people, whose memory served as the public library, must have remarked to the young that some kinds of spring flowers and trees seemed to be in bud a little earlier than was usual.

The melting of the ice was rapid between about 12 000 BC and 9000 BC. In many parts of the habitable globe the change in climate must have been remarkable even in one long lifetime. Those people living on the seashores noticed one other change: the sea was rising. It was rising even before the climate became noticeably warmer.

Many villagers near the sea feared that their houses would be swamped one day. Some lived to see that day. Nobody understood the cause of this strange happening, though they would have had their own explanations. They had no means of knowing that vast areas of ice at both ends of the world were slowly melting, and that the melting ice was raising the level of the seas.

With the changing climate came alterations in the flow of big rivers. In Africa, in about 10 000 BC, the water of Lake Victoria began to run into the Nile, and for the first time the Nile became the longest river in the world. In eastern and southern Asia the speeding-up of the flow of the great rivers must have had profound effects. Most of the long Asian rivers depended on the melting of ice in the high mountains of central Asia, and as the summer climate warmed, the flow of some rivers must have been substantially increased by the melt. The flood of silt that came floating along the Ganges, the Yellow and other rivers was partly a result of the increased volume of ice-cold water. These plains, topped with silt, were to be the early cradles of what is called civilisation.

For a time North Africa became attractive to human settlers. In some of the arid country in about 7000 BC, three times as much rain fell as now falls in a typical year. Lakes and marshes dotted the Sahara. People could walk across vast tracts of the region and see nothing but grasslands or park-like expanses where countless trees offered shade. The population of North Africa must have increased rapidly during the more favoured centuries. Then a dryness came and, sometime after 3000 BC, people began to flee from the ever-widening deserts.

The rising of the seas was almost completed by 8000 BC. In all, the seas had risen by as much as 140 metres: a height of 400 feet or more is a common assessment. This was the most extraordinary event in human history during the last 100 000 years – far more influential than the invention of the steam engine, the discovery of bacteria, the landing on the moon and indeed all the combined events of the 20th century. The rising seas were to spur a transformation in human life and an explosion of population.

In South-East Asia, as the seas rose, the old coastline in most places became unrecognisable. It ceased to be a coastline. No coast was altered as much as that of the continent combining New Guinea and Australia. Tropical New Guinea, with its high mountains, was especially affected. In those mountains the snowline in winter used to descend as far as 3600 metres. As the temperatures increased, however, the winter snowline retreated more than 1000 metres further up the mountain slopes. In the highlands the climate became much more favourable for agriculture. New Guinea did not lose from the rising of the seas: the land it lost under the sea was compensated for by the land recovered from the cold snow or chill winds. As the level of the seas continued to rise, New Guinea

Iceland

Baltic Sea

• St Petersburg

Black Sea

Pyrenees

Mediterranean Sea

Madeira

Sahara

Persian Gulf

Beijing • Korea

Hons

Tsushima Strait

Taiwan

South China Sea

Luzon

Nigeria

Rwanda Lake Victoria

Great Rift Valley

Borneo

Sumatra

N G

Java

Flores

Madagascar

Gulf of Carpentaria

Austra

World outline 16 000 BC

Dry land

Ice sheets

Tasma

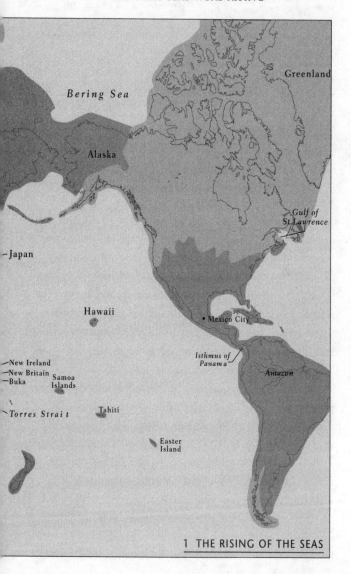

1 THE RISING OF THE SEAS

was finally separated from Australia by the forming of Torres Strait.

Australia was especially reshaped by the rising of the seas, for it was the flattest of continents. Maybe one-seventh of its dry land was slowly submerged while the coastal people watched, quite powerless. Towards the end of this remarkable event, Australian tribes who had once lived as far as 500 kilometres from the ocean eventually heard on stormy nights an unfamiliar and eerie sound, the roar of the surf.

At the far south of the Australian continent the sea created an inland wedge, and Tasmania became an island. The dividing strait became wider and stormier, and the people on the island were marooned. It was to become perhaps the longest-known segregation in human history. Indeed the features of the Tasmanians were much altered during the long isolation. They became frizzy-haired and tended to be smaller than the Aborigines from whom they were descended.

Mainland Australia, unlike Tasmania, was not completely isolated. A stepping stone of islands linked it to New Guinea; and from time to time the two peoples separated by the narrow sea engaged in trade. But in effect the narrow strait, for reasons that are not clear, served as a deep ditch or barrier for thousands of years. On the New Guinea side emerged a way of life based on large gardens, the hoarding of food, a much higher density of population, and a different political and social organisation. On the other side the Australians remained gatherers and hunters, staying in small nomadic groups and living systematically off the land. There can be little doubt that if the seas had not risen, and if Australia and New Guinea had remained part of the same continent with links along a wide front, Australia's later history would have been more in tune with New Guinea's. When the isolation was finally broken by the landing of the British at Sydney in AD 1788, the shock and dislocation for the Australians, their way of life being so different, was acute.

THE LOST AMERICAS

The continent of America had not long been discovered by the human race when the seas began to rise. The first humans probably crossed the gap between Siberia and Alaska sometime before 22 000 BC. The two continents were joined by a cold corridor of land, and in summer the crossing cannot have been difficult. Indeed it is possible that hunters and their families simply crossed the corridor in pursuit of game, found the other side more attractive and decided to stay. In effect they were the discoverers of a new continent, and entitled to a special place in history, but – so far as they knew – they were just doing their normal day's work. Various waves of people probably crossed the corridor and moved down the west coast towards warmer Mexico. Their presence in Mexico in about 22 000 BC can be verified by the precious pieces of shaped obsidian rock that they left in camp sites.

Large animals roamed the grassland, making it a hunter's paradise. Giant bison, mammoths, mastodon, horses and camels ranged across the landscape, and did not know that skilled hunters were arriving. Small game such as rabbits and deer could also be caught in their millions, and new food-plants grew in abundance. When winter approached, the new inhabitants had access to more fur and skins than they could possibly wear.

The population of America increased. Many excavations of human camp sites point to a quicker spread of settlement in about 11 000 BC. The isthmus of Panama was crossed, South America was entered, and few barriers impeded the southward movement of peoples until the permanent ice in the far south came into sight.

Then the rising seas – without warning – began to split America from the world. In about 10 000 BC the land corridor from Asia to Alaska – the only gateway to the Americas – was cut by the rising seas. The Bering Strait was formed. For a time the sea in the new strait was frozen and the ice could be walked over. Even that crossing place was perilous when the climate became warmer. Virtually all contact between the Americas and the outside world ceased, and maybe for another 10 000 years the silence continued. Migratory birds moved between the two continents, but the people lived in isolation. Eventually the inhabitants of America had no knowledge of the place of their origins.

In their prolonged isolation from Asia, the Americas did not stagnate. Humans quickly penetrated every part that was habitable. Slowly the people branched into a variety of ways of life: Inuit hunters in the icy north, gatherer-hunters roaming the cold far south, a variety of peoples combining hunting and farming in various parts of North and South America, while some tribes lived on the abundance of salmon – and the labour of slaves – along the Fraser and Columbia rivers in the north-west. By 2000 BC the Americas possessed a diversity of economies and cultures.

In the late 20th century the idea arose that somehow the rainforest of the Amazon, being isolated and impenetrable, had largely escaped the interference of the human race. With the quickening respect for nature in many quarters of the western world, the rainforest of the Amazon is often marvelled at. Here is primitive nature in all its vulnerable glory: a huge green basin drained by a silent majestic river. Even the Amazon, however, is now known to have had its own remarkable human history during that long period when the Americas were cut off from Europe and Asia. The earliest pottery in the whole of the Americas was made, not in Central and North America, but in the tropical rainforest of the Amazon basin before 5000 BC. There is even evidence that maize, the wonder cereal, was first domesticated by gardeners in this region. Curiously, the biological diversity in this region is usually the most impressive not in the untouched rainforest, but in those areas which were cultivated by the pioneering Amazonian gardeners and now are camouflaged by new growth.

Like the Americas, Japan was also thrust into a prolonged isolation. Its human history was much longer than that of the Americas. It had been settled for tens of thousands of years before the seas began to rise. One of the coldest of the world's inhabited regions, its snowy peaks had for long looked down on vast areas of woodland. Alongside the badgers, hares and wild boar were tigers, panthers, brown bears and bison, a species of elephant and other large animals, though their numbers were diminishing.

As the seas began to rise they cut off Japan's settled, southern areas and converted them into islands. The Tsushima Strait, separating Japan from Korea, was soon formed. When at last Japan was completely isolated, its population was tiny, numbering fewer than 30 000. Most people must have lived on the coast or close to it, and the sea gave them fish, and low-lying valleys and plains gave them wild vegetables in summer. Small groups of people moved about to make best use of the seasons. Prolific seasons were rejoiced in; but lean years were bound to arrive.

For the Japanese in what they call the Jomon period, the expectation of life was low as it was for most peoples. To live for 45 years was unusual, and to reach 70 was a miracle. The bones of a Yokohama man, excavated in 1949, were studied by an X-ray which disclosed that as a child he was sometimes starving.

His teeth, like those of so many nomadic people, were eroded, and the lower molars on one side of his mouth were almost level with the top of the gum. The grinding down of the teeth was accelerated by the practice of cooking meat on hot stones or on an open fire resting on sand, and so a mouthful of meat was often sprinkled with grit.

Already the Japanese made handsome pottery on the main island of Kyushu. One piece, dated at 10 500 BC, is probably older than any pottery in China and perhaps in the whole world. Even older pottery has recently been found. In the course of thousands of years their design became as ornate as the pots of Egyptian, Greek and Chinese civilisations, of which Japan in its remoteness could have no knowledge.

By about 5000 BC, some of the Japanese huts or houses were impressive, measured by the standards of most regions of the globe. A pit was dug, and the walls of the small house of about 4 metres square stood partly in the pit and partly above the surface of the ground. Vertical poles held up the roof of thatched grass and reeds. Within easy talking distance of one another might stand four or five houses which, in all, sheltered maybe 15 people. On cold nights the heat of people's bodies huddled together must have provided much of the warmth, for the fireplace was located outside the house. Small dogs were kept, perhaps for hunting and also for companionship. Occasionally, near the site of the houses, have been excavated small clay figures displaying breasts and buttocks that are unduly inflated. Possibly they were sacred statues which protected a woman when she was giving birth.

Already the Japanese in certain districts were hoarding food. Many groups lived for part of the year near the forests, where a large quantity of nuts could be gathered, part of which was eaten and part hoarded. September, October and November were the months for gathering nuts, the chestnuts falling first. While chestnuts were less nutritious than walnuts, they were more easily preserved on layers of leaves placed in the storage pits near or inside the houses. In contrast, the acorns which fell from the deciduous oak trees required slow treatment in running water to remove the tannic acid. Reduced to fine flour by the action of grinding stones, the acorns were highly palatable. The task of pounding and grinding acorns – and kneading clay for the making of pots – fell largely on the women. The constant exercise had the curious effect of lengthening their collarbones.

With increased ingenuity in producing food, Japan's population in 2000 BC possibly exceeded 200 000, making it one of the most densely populated parts of the world. By present standards, however, Japan was a sparsely peopled wilderness.

THE PARADOX OF ISOLATION

For thousands of years the people living in the territories of what are now Japan and the United States were largely or entirely cut off from the outside world. Their experience was unusual. It would seem that they could have been permanently impaired by this long isolation, at the very time when Europe and Asia were changing rapidly. And yet today these two once-marooned lands are the world's great financial powers.

Perhaps this paradox has an explanation. Geographical isolation, at one time or another, was an acute problem for all peoples. But in the last 150 years, geographical isolation has become a mixed blessing and sometimes an asset. In a shrinking world, ideas and goods and people can cross with ease a sea barrier that was impenetrable 10 000 years ago. But the sea is still a barrier for invading armies. For Japan and the United States the sea barrier ceased to be a disadvantage and became a major strength. It largely saved them from invasion. The sea made them reluctant to become entangled in costly wars fought far from home.

Europe has been weakened again and again by wars fought on its soil and seas in the last 150 years. It has always revived, but the extent of its revival and global influence has been impaired by its own divisions. In contrast, in the United States during that time, only one war has been fought on its soil – a civil war and not a war against invaders. If the United States in 1800 had been situated in Europe it probably would never have been able to rise to its ultimate power. It would never have succeeded in a policy of isolationism. Likewise, Japan's main islands, facing a desperate military situation during the final months of the Second World War, were not invaded even then. Indeed, recognising the sheer difficulty of invading Japan, the United States in 1945 had little alternative but to drop the first atomic bombs in the hope of frightening the Japanese into surrendering. In essence, the geographical factors which had penalised and isolated Japan and North America after the rising of the seas were to be an advantage in certain situations.

3

THE FIRST GREEN REVOLUTION

In Syria and Palestine, soon after the seas had reached their new high water, a minor revolution seemed to be taking place. Unlike the better-known industrial revolution it was incredibly slow, and the force of its impact would not be felt for thousands of years. But human life was on a course from which there was no retreat.

The village of Jericho was a showcase of the revolution by about 8000 BC. Consisting of little mud-brick houses, it grew wheat and barley on tiny patches of garden. These cereals, originally growing wild, were selected for cultivation because the grains were large compared to those of other wild cereals; and a large grain was more easily collected and ground down into a rough wholemeal flour. The villagers must have prepared the ground, selected a firm kind of seed which did not shatter once it ripened, and sown the seed in a more concentrated way than nature did. The grain, harvested with stone knives or scythes, was stored in the village. Today half of the world's calories come from a small variety of cereals, the first of which were cultivated by these villagers of the Middle East.

At first the people of Jericho and similar villages possessed no domesticated animals. Much of their meat still came from wild gazelle and other beasts and birds which they diligently hunted. But within about 500 years of first taming wheat and barley and certain peas and pulses, they were keeping goats and sheep in small herds, presumably near the village. Here was yet another hoard of food: indeed a herd is a hoard. Evidence suggests that the early species of animals were first domesticated in different regions – sheep on the borders of the present Turkey and Iraq, goats in the mountains of Iran, and cattle on the Anatolian plateau. Sheep and goats were especially gregarious and so were more easily tamed: to tame one was to tame many.

The people who first domesticated sheep and goats and cattle and kept them together in flocks and herds were not likely to be the same as those who began to domesticate plants. To grow wheat or tame the first goat required at least a dozen sharp-eyed observations, each one coming from a different man or woman. It is probable that men, being normally the hunters, were the domesticators of animals, and that women domesticated the early cereals. The cereals and the livestock did not initially coexist in harmony. Early gardeners did not want animals grazing near their young crops and eating them or trampling them down.

On the little farms and gardens the daily work had to follow a timetable more rigid than in nomadic days.

If it was the time for weeding or for digging or for sowing the seed, the opportunity had to be seized – or it might be lost. The new way of life called for a discipline and a succession of duties that contrasted with the freedom of the gatherers and hunters.

It is far from certain why this double breakthrough should have come in the same corner of the Mediterranean, but that region did offer advantages. Its countryside possessed two wild cereals which yielded very large grains. It was also inhabited by sheep and goats, which, being small and gregarious, were more easily tamed than most of the world's large animals. But these lucky advantages in themselves are not enough to explain change. In the history of the world, opportunities and luck have been relatively plentiful but the people who grasped them have been rare.

Other factors had moulded the beginnings of this new way of life. The rising seas drowning coastal land had driven people inland, where, as a result, a mingling took place of peoples, ideas and habits. Furthermore the climate was becoming warmer, thus making certain plants and animals more prolific. Cereals, certainly, grew over a wider area than hitherto. The big animals, traditionally a vital source of food, were becoming fewer; and that provided an incentive to tame wild animals.

For long periods the pioneering tribes who were setting up gardens and keeping flocks had to coexist with nomadic peoples. To live side by side imposed a strain. In times of near-famine the hungry nomads were tempted to raid the neighbouring villages which kept a store of grain and a flock of animals. The villagers in turn fortified themselves and kept constant guard. With larger numbers and better organising – to farm was to organise – they were usually a match for the nomads in any fight.

The future lay with the new farmers and flock-keepers. To have access to the granary in a time of starvation was to own an asset such as no tribe in the nomadic era could possess. During a drought the village which possessed a store of grains and a flock of sheep or goats could survive longer.

The people might own the sheep but the sheep in a sense owned the people, virtually enchaining them. Therefore, the traditional way of life – the scavenging and foraging and the joys of the successful hunt – still carried an appeal. It also provided food, especially in spring. Several thousand years after the origins of farming, many villages relied more on hunting and gathering food in swamps, forests and plains than they did on the new output of cereals, milk and meat.

The spread of this new way of life along the shores of the Mediterranean was slow. By 7000 BC, crops were grown, and sheep and goats were feeding under the close watch of their owners in Greece and Serbia and in the short Italian valleys sloping down to the Adriatic Sea. By 5400 BC the farmers with their digging sticks were in western Scotland and Ulster. By 3000 BC in

Scandinavia, patches of crops and herds and flocks could be seen.

At least 2000 years separated the first farms in Greece from the first farms near the Baltic. In marvelling at such a slow spread of farms and flocks across Europe, one obstacle should be remembered. Dense or spaced forest covered 80 per cent of Europe. To fell much of that forest with stone axes – the iron axe was unknown – and a million little fires called for patience and sweat. To forage was easier.

Meanwhile, cattle had been driven by their herders into many parts of North Africa, ranging from Egypt and Libya to Algeria. While Africa largely imported its first domesticated animals and crops, it domesticated the ass – a beast of burden – and the small guineafowl, which was to be a favourite dish on the tables of ancient Egypt and later of Rome. The first domestic cats were African, and later they became dutiful guardians of the grain storages which were so attractive to mice. Africans were also the first to domesticate and grow millet, which was usually viewed as an inferior grain, and the first to grow sorghum and its luxuriant heads of grain, along with wild rice, yams and palm oil.

Everywhere the tilling of the soil began in the most primitive way. The main digging tool was a wooden stick with its end sharpened and then made harder by fire. The fire-hardened stick must have been one of the vital inventions in the history of the human race – more important than the tractor – and it served gardeners in many parts of the world for thousands of years.

To sow the seed called for experiments. It is easy to assume that early farmers carried a woven bag full of seed, sprinkling it with a wide movement of the hand as they walked over the freshly dug soil; but in many places that way of scattering seed was unknown. In some African regions, women dug thousands of holes with a digging stick or hoe, or even with the quick stab of a toe in soft soil, and dropped a few grains of millet in each hole. Others filled their mouth with grain and spat it out, a few grains at a time, after each hole was dug. In some parts of southern Africa the grain was actually sprinkled on the grass and soil before the simple ploughing took place.

Greece, not long after 3000 BC, developed a distinctive kind of farming centred on the olive tree and the grapevine. On the steep slopes which hitherto had been fit only for sheep and goats, the vineyards and olive groves increased the yearly calories available to a village by as much as 40 per cent. Olive oil was used not only for cooking but to fill lamps and clean the body. Wine and olive oil altered the diet in the eastern Mediterranean.

Whereas every nomad had once spent the main part of each day gathering and hunting food, the new order fostered such specialists as brickmakers, house builders, bakers, brewers, potters, weavers, makers of garments, soldiers, shoemakers, tailors, keepers of granaries, diggers of irrigation ditches, and of course farmers and shepherds. Perhaps 90 of every 100 people in a region were still engaged in the growing of food and foraging for food and allied tasks, but the other 10 people took up a variety of specialist callings. The new specialists lived in villages, and the larger villages grew into towns. The town and the city were impossibilities before the development of farming.

The capacity of a district to feed people was being multiplied three or six or even more times by more efficient use of soil and grasslands, minerals and fisheries: a set of achievements which was beyond the skills of nomadic peoples. The population of the world, hitherto tiny, increased dramatically. Perhaps only 10 million people had lived in the whole world at the time when the first experiments in the farming of crops and the keeping of flocks were made. But by 2000 BC the population of the world was probably approaching 90 million. Two thousand years later, at the time of Christ, it was close to 300 million.

At times the expanding population was cut back by epidemics. The nomads, without knowing it, had possessed advantages in health. Being on the move they left their sewage behind. Wearing few or no clothes in tropical climates they were more exposed to germ-killing sunlight. Owning no animals, they were a target for fewer diseases. In contrast, in the new order the crowding of people into towns increased the risk of infection.

So, while the new way of life provided more food and thereby increased the population of the world, it also fostered viruses which periodically cut back the population. The daily handling of the newly domesticated livestock probably exposed people to diseases which hitherto were confined to those animals. One form of tuberculosis came with milk from cows and goats. Measles and smallpox were transferred from cattle to the people who herded them, milked them and ate their flesh. One form of malaria probably came from birds. Influenza came from pigs and ducks.

THE HUMAN SACRIFICE

A new form of political organisation was emerging. Whereas in nomadic societies the power had been shared mainly by the older men, the new farming order was increasingly controlled by a small elite of rulers or by a chieftain who was usually male. While defending his town and farmland, the chieftain took the opportunity to repay his enemies for old slights or wounds. He captured some and enslaved them. Whereas a nomadic people rarely had a use for slaves, a sedentary ruler could employ slaves or forced labour in making irrigation canals, temples, fortifications and other projects. The new rulers could collect taxes in the form of grain, meat or other goods whereas the lands of the nomads had been tax-free zones.

The new rulers ordained priests. The priests in turn gave legitimacy and moral support to the rulers. While religion itself was an ancient ally of the human race, full-time priests and priestesses were a novelty. They helped to bring down the rains that ended the drought; they paved the way for a plentiful harvest; they helped to defeat enemies in war; and they probably provided a feeling of inner peace for those who might otherwise have felt troubled. By 3500 BC many of the rural villages and small towns of Europe and the Middle East were building religious monuments of impressive size.

The new religions reflected a sense of wonder at the universe and its workings and also the fears and hopes felt towards the immense powers of nature. Nature had to be worshipped and placated. The population of a region could be decimated by a hailstorm that flattened or bruised crops, diseases that killed livestock, a plague of insects or fungus that attacked the harvest, a spring which passed without rain, the decline of wild game because of disease or drought, and an unexpected flood. To ensure that the soil was fertile, or that the annual harvest would be prolific, gifts might be offered to the gods. The greatest gift was the sacrifice of a human life. That sacrifice might open the gate through which abundance could flow.

THE PUZZLE OF NEW GUINEA AND THE AMERICAS

The highlands of New Guinea were so remote that they were little explored by Europeans until the 20th century. In another sense they were not remote but one of the pivots of the green revolution. As early as 7000 BC, when agriculture had not yet reached Europe, New Guineans cultivated various yams and other root crops, the shade-loving taro, the sugar cane and the native banana. Drains dug by hand improved the soil and aided this simple form of farming. That the idea of gardening came to New Guinea from South-East Asia is unlikely but not impossible.

In New Guinea the trees were cut with stone axes, the cutter using the short, sharp blows typical of the tomahawk rather than the long-handled swings of the modern axe. Eventually the wood and under-growth were burned, a surrounding fence was built, and edible roots were planted with fresh fire-ashes serving as nutrient. Weeding was a vital task, and performed usually by women. After a couple of crops the soil was temporarily exhausted, and some distance away a new patch was reclaimed arduously from the forest. It was pioneering, with an abundance of muscle and stamina and sweat. This shifting form of cultiva-tion, sometimes called 'slash and burn', required large tracts of forest, of which only a fraction was tilled and planted in any year.

The Americas, like New Guinea, developed their own gardens. Plants such as squash and cotton and chilli peppers were being cultivated in Mexico by the year 6000 BC, and later emerged maize and beans. On the east coast of what is now the United States, gardens appeared in about 2500 BC. In due time, agriculture became the basis of the American civilisations which the Spanish eventually discovered.

The prevailing view is that American agriculture and its distinctive civilisations arose largely in isolation. It is widely assumed that the rising of the seas permanently isolated the new settlers who crossed from northern Asia to the Americas; but the possibility of a recurring cultural influence from eastern Asia, Africa or Europe cannot be eliminated entirely. Perhaps a new wave of settlers occasionally reached the American continent.

A few pieces of evidence favour the theory that Asia and the Americas remained in contact. Thus the Chinese melanotic chicken, with its black bones and dark meat, existed in the Americas, where it was treated in the same way as it was in China, being sacrificed for magic and healing but shunned at mealtimes. Did this chicken arrive later from China in the boats of second-wave colonists? Likewise, a few scholars argue that the distinctive Mayan calendar of tropical America probably came from Taxila in the present Pakistan, and that four of the 20 names given to the days of that calendar were borrowed directly from Hindu deities.

The flow of ideas and plants and animals across the Pacific was perhaps in both directions. Nonetheless, one farming region arose earlier than the others and was more dynamic in its effects. The Middle East was like a fire which, once blazing, gave out more and more light.

Hand-shaped pots – whether baked by the sun or by a red-hot fire – were a vital part of the new way of life. Whereas nomadic people moving frequently had no use for pots, people living in the same place for much of the year gained enormously from the invention of pottery. In the western world it is now difficult to comprehend why pots once were all-important, so little are they used today, except for ornament. Pots were especially valuable for lighting and cooking, and efficient in using fuel. There were pottery lamps, or bowls in which candles stood upright. Large pots, some of which were equipped with lids and handles, held water and beer inside a house. An unglazed pot was favoured as a receptacle, for it seemed to keep water cool. In the Cameroon grasslands huge pots were used for the making of palm wine while others held kola nuts. Nigerians played pottery drums at funerals. Women were the potters in some regions: they ran what was then the main manufacturing industry.

A sedentary society skilled in making pots was able to move towards a new menu of food and drink. It was far, far more likely than nomads to brew fermented drinks, for heavy pots were needed in which to store them. A society owning pots was able to make yeast and then employ the yeast in baking bread in a pottery oven. A society which boiled its meat in pots rather than heated it on an open fire or hot rocks was, curiously, more likely to crave salt. Indeed, salt was the first food to become a regular item of trade in the Middle East and Asia.

The potter was the step-parent of the metallurgist. Potters and their clay were to be the forerunners of the metalworkers and their ores. While the making of pottery under intense heat did not lead automatically to the smelting of metallic ores, it served as a vital step. How to make the best use of fuel, how to increase the heat by a blast of fresh air, how to handle the burning sides of the pots, how long to allow them to cool – answers to these problems served as guides and pointers to the treating of metallic ores with an intense heat.

One of the momentous days in the history of the world was when almost-pure metal was first extracted, with the aid of a very hot fire, from lumps of hard and rich copper-bearing rock. The earliest furnaces and workshops for smelting copper have been unearthed at Timna in southern Israel, in sight of the bare mountains of Jordan. The furnace, first operated around 4200 BC, was a little hole in the ground, oval in shape and scooped to the depth of maybe an adult's hand. To prevent too much of the heat from escaping, a simple wedge of rock was placed flat over the fire like a loose lid. It was a backyard enterprise. Even to say that is to exaggerate its scale.

The smelting of copper eventually led to the discovery of how to make bronze. Possibly it was an accident, but only an alert mind is capable of seeing the significance of what arrives by accident. Bronze was made by fusing 90 per cent pure copper with 10 per cent tin; the resultant alloy was tougher than copper and easier to cast into shapes. By about 3500 BC, bronze was being made by the metal smiths in the city-states of

Mesopotamia. Where they found the tin, an essential ingredient, remains uncertain.

Miraculously, a man of this era of copper was recently glimpsed in the flesh. His body – the flesh still on the bones – was discovered about 5000 years after he set out on a risky walk in the Tyrolean Alps, near the present borders of Austria and Italy. He was crossing a mountain gap which at 3200 metres was higher than the highest roads across those mountains today. The season was probably autumn, and he was warmly clad. His head was covered by a cap consisting of many pieces of fur sewn together. His shoulders were protected from snow and cold wind by an outer cape neatly woven from reeds or strong grass. His coat, of deerskin, must have kept part of his body warm as he walked, but it is not certain whether the coat had sleeves. Certainly his legs were clad in leather leggings, while his feet were covered by calfskin shoes.

That he was making a long rather than a short journey is suggested by the equipment he carried: an axe with a copper blade, a knife with a cutting edge made of flint and a handle of wood, a quiver with 14 broken or used arrows, and a half-completed bow with which to shoot arrows. Of importance to a mountain man, in an area where fuel and kindling were not easily found for the fires so necessary on cold nights, he carried an ingenious birch-bark container capable of holding the embers of a past fire. Thereby he could light his own without undue trouble.

He vanished in the snow. Perhaps, when his return home was long overdue, friends or family searched for him. He could easily be identified, for his skin displayed several small tattoos and his prized copper axe must have been familiar to friends. The search ceased, and the blanket of ice covered him, century after century. Only in AD 1991 did the melting of the ice expose his body.

4

THE DOME OF NIGHT

In big and brilliantly lit cities – the headquarters of today's world – the power of the night sky can hardly be appreciated, for the sky is dulled by the city lights. Moreover, new explanations of human events, both secular and religious, have largely superseded explanations based on the stars and moon and sun. But for most of the years of human experience, whether recorded or unrecorded history, the night sky possessed a splendour and a magic. And when the first civilisations arose, the 'heavenly objects' increasingly possessed a powerful symbolism.

THE MYSTERY OF LIGHTNING AND THE SHOOTING STAR

In nomadic tribes and in farming villages, deep fear was stirred by meteorological events. In Tasmania numerous Aborigines were frightened by severe storms. 'Heavy rain during the night,' wrote a white observer in 1831, 'accompanied by loud peals of thunder and vivid flashes of lightning, at which the natives evinced considerable fear'. On the following evening the sight of 'an electric spark' in the dark sky inspired calls of dismay. Perhaps the thought of being struck by lightning heightened the fear. Glancing nervously at a tree which had been shivered by lightning, they refused – like rural Germans on the other side of the world – to touch the exposed wood.

The night sky was the domed roof during all those years when people largely slept under the stars. Children were taught to observe the regular marching of the stars across the night sky. On rare occasions, they saw the dark sky crossed by swift-moving lights. Some lights were shooting stars and visible for only a second or two, and others showed an arresting tail of fire. The nomadic hunters and gatherers were remarkably observant of the night sky, and so they possibly learned by observation that shooting stars were twice as numerous in the early hours of the morning as in the first hours of night. When a strange happening was visible, the night sky was believed to be speaking.

All over the world, people devoted mental activity to the comets and stars. Few events were more exciting to them than the sight of a burning meteor falling in the night. Most of the meteors disintegrated while falling, and most which reached the globe fell into the ocean, but a few hit the earth. A meteorite is a meteor that reaches its destination, usually in the form of a black piece of rock; and such rocks, seemingly falling from the home of the gods, were treated with wonder when they were found. In Mexico the precious stone of the pyramid of Cholula, and in Syria the stone worshipped at Ermesa, were probably meteorites. In Mecca, in the holy building, was a sacred stone said to have fallen from the heavens. It was worshipped by Arabian tribes and by Mohammed himself.

The idea that a meteorite or shooting star was a message from the gods seemed to be confirmed by its noisiness – as well as its incandescent brilliance – when it plunged to earth. It sounded to some like the rumbling of thunder. To others, in the era of steam, it sounded like a train roaring past. In some societies a falling star was viewed as fortunate and in others as evil.

The nomadic people who lived under the stars, and the settled people who lived under the cloudless skies of the first civilisations in the Middle East, had every reason to observe the night sky. On a moonless night the sky was a wonderful tapestry set out above them. It also altered from hour to hour, and the pattern of alterations was observed and talked about. In the dryness of Central Australia, where no permanent river existed, some Aboriginal groups saw the Milky Way as a wide river flowing across the sky. In the eyes of many peoples, powerful creatures lived in the sky. To some, a dark gap in the Milky Way was the home of a demon.

The early civilisations flourishing along the rivers Tigris and Euphrates were to continue the enthroning of the stars. Skilled in astronomy, their people could predict many of the movements of major planets and clusters of stars, and in turn believed that these movements enabled them to predict human events. The Babylonians even learned how to predict an eclipse of the moon long before the eclipse occurred.

The rise of astrology, and the study of the possible influence of the stars and planets on human events, is now dismissed in intellectual circles as make-believe, but there was a tentative logic in this intellectual discipline that was to attract some of the best minds in the early civilisations in China and the Middle East. If the sun could shape summer and winter, and the moon could determine the high tides and shape the calendar, why could these powerful forces not also shape human destinies? This question intrigued scholars for thousands of years. Physicians were also taken with it, and until the 20th century those persons suffering from mental illness were called lunatics, meaning that their sickness was influenced by the moon.

The moon, small or large, was usually a commanding presence. The largest object in the night sky, rising and setting some 50 minutes later on each successive day, it moved majestically. A new moon was invisible, for it marched in step with the sun across the day sky. In contrast the full moon could be seen throughout the night. Alive and powerful and personal, the moon was a female to some peoples and a male to others. It was a symbol of life and death, and was said to determine when the rains would fall. It was believed to influence the growth of vegetation; and for thousands of years it was a rural rule that farmers always should plant during the new moon. At a later time, in India and Iran and Greece, it was believed that people after death journeyed to the moon. The cycles of the moon were to constitute the first calendars, after the art of astronomy appeared.

'I HAVE DREAMED A DREAM'

Night was the time when people had dreams – jubilant, terrifying, peaceful, familiar or strange. Night was seen as a mysterious realm by a variety of tribes, and humans were admitted to that realm while they slept. The dream was the evidence of their visit. In northern Canada the native peoples near Hudson Bay believed that, when they were asleep, their soul slipped away from their body and temporarily entered another world. In Central Australia the Arrernte believed that each person had two souls; and that during sleep the second soul actually left the body. They understood that their own dreams were really themselves seeing the simultaneous activities of that second soul, taking place outside the body. The dream was almost an eerie form of television. If a terrible event happened to the soul which had left the body, the terror was instantly conveyed to the person who was asleep and dreaming.

Tens of thousands of years before the rise of priests and soothsayers, vivid dreams must have been recounted with awe. The importance of the dream was a reflection of the importance of night, when dreams took place. In a simple camp, in a nomadic society, the presence of night and the intensity of the darkness was almost overpowering. Today, a huge brilliantly lit city almost overpowers the night.

In the modern era the dream quietly changed its meaning. Dreams ceased to be interpreted simply as forward-looking. The psychologist Sigmund Freud saw a dream not as a glimpse of the future but as a mirror of the personality and past of the dreamer.

It is impossible to say when human beings first read a meaning into the moon, sun, stars and comets. But to ignore the night and the night sky because they are recorded so sparsely and fleetingly would be to neglect a vital and tantalising part of human history.

THE HIDDEN MONUMENTS

Nomads built no grand monuments, no pyramids and lofty columns of stone, no temples and no lighthouses. They were incapable of hewing heavy blocks of stone and carrying them far, but in a sense they did not require monuments. A monument is a proclamation of what is important; but to the people living 15 000 years ago the sky and earth were crowded with monuments, some visible only to those with trained eyes.

For some nomadic societies the sky was a monument created by their own ancestral beings. Their land was created in the same way. Every hill and rocky ridge, every detail of the landscape, had been created by these beings when they first lived on earth. In the eyes of the early Australians, the hills, cliffs, animals and everything vital in their own tribal territory were virtually sacred monuments to their ancestral beings, and the original act of creation had to be periodically repeated through the religious rituals, ceremonies and dances left behind by those creators. Thus the living people maintained their contact with those who long ago had created this life-giving landscape and skyscape.

It is jumping ahead of this story but it should be said: the later religions were also profoundly affected by the night sky. The Jewish calendar was based on the moon; and the commencement of the religious year was determined by the juxtaposition of two distinct events – the sight of the ears appearing on the crops of barley and the first sight of the crescent new moon. Buddha was born at a special point in the cycle of the moon, while a bright guiding star was said to pinpoint where Jesus was being born. In Hinduism and Jainism one of the sacred events is a festival of lamps, and it takes place on the full-moon day of a certain month. The holiest day in the Christian calendar is determined by the moon. In Islam the calendar is still based on the moon; and Ramadan – the month of fasting – officially begins at the moment when the new moon is visible to the naked eye. Chinese civilisation honoured the moon and stars. Even the first universities, rising in the Middle Ages, gave emphasis to astrology. To be a professor of astrology in one of these universities, or to be the consulting astrologer to a Christian king or a general in the 12th century, was to possess real power. It was Copernicus who, four centuries later, was to shoot astrology from the academic sky – but not from the people's sky, where it remains powerful.

5

CITIES OF THE VALLEYS

If a tireless traveller had lived in the Middle East in 4000 BC, and had performed the unusual – perhaps impossible – feat of journeying overland all the way from the shores of the Black Sea to the upper Nile, they would have found no breathtaking monument. They would have found no city. They would have found no temple of learning and no royal palace of luxury. If, some 1500 years later, their footsteps had been retraced by another traveller, grand sights would have been relatively common. They would have existed, however, mostly along the big rivers of the region. In the rise of civilisation, four impressive rivers in this corner of the world and several great rivers in other remote lands were central.

The big rivers of the Middle East crossed dry plains whose soil was enriched each year by floods. Tens of millions of tonnes of silt were carried downstream and spread thinly on top of the exhausted ground like a new layer of fertiliser. Likewise in the dry seasons canals carried water from the rivers to irrigate the parched

2 VALLEY CIVILISATIONS

farmlands. On the flood plains more people could be fed within a small area, and bigger towns could be nourished, than almost anywhere else in the world at that time. In an era when land transport was primitive, the wide river was also the super-highway, along which boats could cheaply carry grain and building stones to distant parts of the kingdom.

THE VIEW FROM THE PYRAMID

The banks of the Nile nursed Egypt's civilisation. The river threaded its way along a narrow valley, which near Aswan in upper Egypt was only 2 kilometres wide. The sand of the desert actually trickled into the river here and there. Further downstream the valley was often 30 or more kilometres in width, while in the delta the mosaic of rich low-lying land and river channels was over 200 kilometres wide. At floodtime the delta countryside, the main source of Egyptian wealth, became a sweeping lake which lapped the edges of the permanent villages perched on their low mounds. Indeed the delta villages were known as 'islands'. The earth, freshly top-dressed with new soil carried down by the flood, was ready for another harvest of barley and wheat after the floodwaters subsided.

The river was not always a wonderful asset. If the flood was too high or flowed too fast, all kinds of earthen levy banks and water channels were destroyed. More-over the water did not flow effortlessly to the higher fields. As farming became more developed, people or roped animals had to be employed to lift the water in buckets or baskets from a lower to a higher level.

Egypt had a long line of powerful monarchs, impressive cities, a vigorous religious and economic life, granaries jammed with grain in the years of prolific harvests, and royal tombs in which rich treasures lay in permanent darkness. Here lived army generals, bureaucrats and priests who showed considerable powers of organising and of record-keeping. Their picture script, an early form of writing, served as a method of communication along the river.

Here were architects setting out their fine schemes, and builders capable of implementing the plans in massive stone, and thousands of artists working in precious metals, copper, wood, textiles and precious stones. Here were designers of canals for transport and irrigation, one canal even linking the Nile and the Red Sea. Here lived scientists who increased the knowledge of the moon and stars and devised the pioneering calendar dividing the year into 365 days. Here paraded influential priests who formulated a view of the afterlife in which princesses continued to be honoured as princesses, while even commoners might have a taste of eternity. The king, being a god hiding inside a human body, merited a tomb to match.

The annual flooding of the Nile was not taken for granted. Everywhere, even amidst the oases in the desert, costly temples were built in honour of the divine ruler, without whose blessing there could be no 'annual rise of the Nile'. In return, tribute or taxation was paid to the temple in the form of barley and wheat or even land. Eventually the temples owned about one-third of all the arable land along the Nile.

The tall reeds waving in the wind were a familiar sight in parts of Egypt – and also Mesopotamia – where the rivers overflowed into marshes or fanned across a delta. A host of labourers gathered the reeds for the thatching of houses. The sharp end of the reed also served as the pen or stylus with which pictures and syllables were cut in damp tablets of clay. Ultimately clay was challenged by another writing material from the rivers. The papyrus plant grew in the marshes of the Nile – or, as the Book of Job expressed it, 'Can papyrus grow where there is no marsh?'. As early as 2700 BC, clever Egyptians were converting papyrus into a thick form of paper or parchment, ready to receive markings from the reed pen. Paper, which is almost the essence of a bureaucracy, was Egypt's own invention.

Perhaps the Egyptians were the first people to treat dogs and cats as pets. Cats were depicted on tombs; in death their bodies were mummified in readiness for the afterlife; and they were mourned by families, who showed their grief by shaving off their own eyebrows. As early as 2000 BC the greyhound was also kept, especially to participate in the sport of hunting the hare.

In medicine the Egyptians probably led the known world. Magic and knowledge were mixed: a potent mix in the mind of the believer. Much of the knowledge of human bodies came from the custom of preparing them to be mummified. In anatomy, surgery and pharmaceuticals the Egyptians had their triumphs, and possibly they were the first to use bandages and splints. In their cures they used the fat of such creatures as mice and snakes, as well as herbs and vegetables, each ingredient being carefully weighed or measured. The Greek classic by Homer, *The Odyssey*, referred to Egypt's physicians as the best, and by that time their medical reputation for skill and flair and bravado was close to 2000 years old.

In 2600 BC the Egyptians were the first known bakers of a modern style of yeast bread. In shape, their loaf of bread was more like a flat omelette than the taller loaf which was eaten in Greek times. A baking stove, with a firebox at the bottom and an oven at the top, was their invention.

The flood plain of the Nile normally produced a surplus of food which not only fed those who worked the fields but also that one-tenth of the population who lived in the cities and served the monarch and his attendants and priests. It was this surplus of food, this small overflow of wealth, that enabled a succession of the kings to plan some 80 pyramids as royal tombs.

As the country along the Nile was fringed only by low foothills or escarpments, the pyramids could attain a dominance impossible in a mountainous landscape. The first pyramid was built about 2700 BC. The Great Pyramid, 200 years later, was designed to be 146 metres high, or equal to the height of a modern 50-storey skyscraper. It called for the efforts of some 100 000 workers, including slaves and those farmers who were idle when the annual floods were at their height. Heavy blocks of limestone and granite had to be cut in the quarries and transported to the site without the aid of wheeled vehicles or pulleys. It was the most remarkable structure so far built in the world. That it was built by a kingdom with a total population barely exceeding one million is even more remarkable. Egypt's population was to rise, and in the time of the New Kingdom some 1500 years later it reached maybe four million.

Egypt, more than any other of the river civilisations, enjoyed long periods of stability. Its continuity in language and culture was remarkable. Its monarchy lasted for some 3000 years – one of the most durable institutions in recorded history. While Egypt's defects were conspicuous, so too were its virtues.

WHERE THE WHEEL FIRST TURNED

A rival civilisation flourished in Mesopotamia. There, the world's first known state, with its accompanying secular and religious bureaucracy, arose in about 3700 BC. The state occupied a warm plain between two rivers, the Tigris and the Euphrates. Indeed, it was a creature of the fertile valley.

Fed by melting snow in the mountains of Turkey, the twin rivers had covered about two-thirds of their journey to the sea before they reached the edge of the plain, and were close to the sea when they finally merged. They occasionally changed course or were filled with silt, but for centuries they were used by small boats or by rafts made of skins, which carried much-needed timber down from the wooded hinterland. The lower valleys of the twin rivers were prolific when planted with barley and wheat. Whereas in most other regions the farmers were digging with sharpened sticks and simple spades, here they actually ploughed the ground, thus enabling a large area to be cultivated by a small number of servants. Part of the barley was fermented into beer, possibly the first beer in the world.

In the south of Mesopotamia, known as Sumer, fine cities arose on the banks of the rivers and canals. Several of the Sumerian cities were in sight of each other. In about the year 3000 BC, 18 cities were flourishing in an area no larger than the present Republic of Ireland. Uruk, standing in the present Iraq, was said to hold as many as 50 000 people, all of whom were fed by the farmlands close by. The cities tended to be the capital of a small surrounding territory or state, but warfare reduced the number of states. To be conquered was a common experience for the peoples of southern Mesopotamia.

In these cities the temple was as vital as the cathedral was to be in Europe more than 3000 years later. The priests with their rituals, sacrifices and prayers called on the rain-bringing winds to blow from the right direction and shower the parched ground.

The priests also pleaded, when their prayers were answered too readily, for the floods to subside. They proclaimed the wonder of the universe too.

Whether these cities of Mesopotamia were more inventive than Egypt is a question not easily answered. Almost certainly the solid wooden wheel was invented here. One cart with solid wheels could, if drawn by an ox, exceed the carrying capacity of a short procession of men. Later the devising of a light wheel, with radiating spokes, transformed peacetime transport and also led to the extensive use of horsedrawn chariots in warfare. The wheeled vehicle, in war or peace, was especially suited to the plains.

The arts of writing and reading arose at one of these cities in about 3400 BC, though Egypt is also a contender for this honour. The early writing took the form of pictures. These writing-pictures were drawn with a sharp instrument on damp clay, which was then allowed to dry and harden. An orchard was depicted as two trees in a tub. A container of grain was symbolised by an ear of barley. The head of an ox, accompanied by the numeral 3, signified three oxen. One of the purposes of writing was to record the foodstuffs and textiles carried into the temples, which also served as storehouses.

The art of counting also made headway. The more advanced of the river-cities devised two distinct numeral systems, one using 60 and the other using 10 as its base. The 10s or decimal method ultimately won; but the 60s method had a more lasting victory.

As a result of the calculations of the mathematicians of Babylon, the 60 survives in the 60 minutes that constitute each hour.

In these lands of the twin rivers, the rival cities and empires fought for the right to exist. Eventually the empires close to the Persian Gulf were superseded by those whose home was in the foothills. One empire of the hills was the Assyrian. Its name echoes in the modern nation of Syria, but its heartland lay in the present Iraq; and its first capital city, Assur, stood on the fertile plains of the winding Tigris River. Rather late in the course of a long history the Assyrians were vigorous enough to capture their rival, Babylon, and bold enough to attempt the conquest of Egypt. The most powerful empire in the western world, its rule extended to within a few days' horseback-ride of both the Caspian Sea and the Persian Gulf.

Members of the royal family were enthusiastic hunters, either in the wild or in the game parks and zoological gardens kept for their pleasure. The king himself rode to the hunt in a chariot drawn by three horses, each wearing blinkers to prevent it from being distracted as it ran. The driver stood in an unroofed cabin and a hunter or two stood beside him, ready to fire arrows.

The Mesopotamian lion, which was smaller than the African lion, was the target of countless hunts. It is easy to guess why this species of lion became extinct. A baked tablet surviving from 1100 BC records that one royal hunter while on foot killed a total of 120 lions.

When he was hunting from the relative safety of the chariot he killed another 800 lions.

In Assyria the sciences – especially astronomy – and the visual arts flourished, along with engineering. Here the masters of irrigation designed canals to carry water across the plains to large cities and so create a green carpet of irrigated fields. Fine palaces and temples stood in their cities. In the art of warfare they were not backward.

Early glassmakers worked here in about 1500 BC. For centuries they made glass vessels by surrounding with molten liquid a smooth core which was later removed, leaving behind the shaped glass. In the British Museum the delicate Sargon vase, of light green, still responds to different lights. Whether it was created in Assyria or made its way there through trade or conquest is not known. Glass was only for the rich.

The houses, meadows and orchards of Nineveh, the most impressive of Assyria's capital cities, were supplied with water flowing down a canal from mountain ranges. As the canal had to cross a valley, a bridge of five pointed arches was designed to carry it. Teams probably made up of thousands of prisoners of war were assembled, and they began to quarry chunks of limestone and neatly shape them into heavy blocks. Two million stones were cut and carted to the site of the long bridge or aqueduct. If this bridge of about 700 BC had lasted until the railway age it would have allowed three trains to run side by side, such was its width.

On the wide plains where two large rivers wandered, various cities were born during a period of 2000 years. They left behind oblong tablets of clay on which were recorded lists of their kings and the earliest dictionaries. They left behind tiny sunbaked or fire-kilned barrels, with writing circling the barrel, one line on top of the other. The script is impressively neat, straight lines having been lightly ruled on the wet clay to guide the writing.

How eagerly many of these messages, in tiny hand-writing, must have been read. Here is a tablet from an astronomer or astrologer warning the king that the approach at sunrise of a crescent moon is a special warning for his soldiers fighting far from home. Here in burned clay, baked in 667 BC, is a prediction that an eclipse of the moon will occur. The Assyrians believed that movements in the sky profoundly affected human events. Even the activities of thieves were so affected.

The rival empire ruled from Babylon was no less advanced in astronomy. Its calendar was based on the moon, the moon god being in charge of the night just as the sun god was in charge of the day and all its events. Of these competing gods the moon was the more powerful. A new moon was believed to be a boat in which the moon god travelled in a slow and stately way across the expanse of the night sky. That same crescent moon was to be revived many centuries later by the new religion of Islam.

The moon determined the calendar. The new moon marked the start of the month. Ultimately Babylonian astronomers could predict to the minute when the new moon would be seen on the horizon. The prediction was important because the calendar month formally began not at midnight, but at the moment when the tip of the new moon peeped above the horizon. In Babylon's calendar, 12 lunar months equalled 354 days, thus giving each year a shortage of 11-and-a-quarter days. The shortage was solved by adding a 13th month to the calendar in every third year.

Bold steps in the advancement of knowledge had been made on these wide river valleys and their uplands, sometimes called the Fertile Crescent. Eventually these wide valleys knew decay. Rise and decline are normal processes in human history. Here the bruised environment also hastened the decline.

The miracle is that some of the green farmland on the lower Euphrates and the Tigris lasted so long. In their hilly hinterland, more and more trees were felled for firewood and for building materials. Meanwhile the topsoil eroded, the valleys became silted, and the rivers tended to overflow their banks.

On parts of the plains the constant irrigating of the soil, and the destruction of the trees with their deep network of roots, forced the underlying salt to creep towards the surface. Freshwater ponds became salty. It was observed that the crops of wheat – unlike those of barley – could not tolerate salt in the soil, and that in some regions wheat became a rarity. The plains were a foretaste of what would eventually happen in the irrigated zones in numerous arid lands extending from Australia to California. In the dozen or more centuries after 2000 BC the population of certain regions in Mesopotamia slowly declined.

These city-states, so mighty in their day, were also weakened by periodic wars. With their bows and spears and javelins, they turned warfare into an art form. Many of the soldiers also carried slings – maybe as long as their arm – and used them to hurl stones at an enemy upwards of 100 metres away. To protect themselves they wore caps coming down to the top of the ears and a light armour on the upper part of the body.

The Assyrians became masters of another weapon: this powerful weapon was called terror. When they finally entered a city which had refused its opportunity to surrender peacefully, they would murder, torture and mutilate people on a large scale as a warning to other cities. To be defeated in war was a painful experience in nearly all the early civilisations, but it was especially painful for those defeated by Assyria. And yet Assyria could also be constructive. It moved large numbers of rebellious or defeated peoples to a distant region, there to cultivate the soil or build monuments and public works.

A WELL-SCRUBBED CITY OF THE INDUS

Egypt and Mesopotamia had been flourishing for 1000 years when another valley civilisation emerged not far to the east. The wide Indus valley was watered by rivers that tumbled out of the snowy Himalayas and glided down to the Arabian Sea. Nearly all of the valley lay outside the tropic zone. While the Indus River eventually gave India its name, most of it now lies inside the Republic of Pakistan.

The Indus valley was generously endowed by nature. Jungle originally grew along its fertile river-banks, and when cleared away, revealed a rich soil. The river was wonderful for agriculture, for the annual floods, larger than those of the Nile, inundated the low-lying areas from about June to September. Each year they spread a layer of life-giving silt. The evidence suggests that the monsoon came further inland and that the climate was unusually moist by today's standards. So extensive was the flow of muddy water that today some of the sites of this civilisation are covered by 10 metres of silt.

Farmers were at work in the valley as early as 6000 BC. From time to time they were invaded by people who, coming from the present Iran, had seen or heard of one or other of the valley civilisations. They began to create a distinctive Indus civilisation. Emerging by about 2500 BC, it was to flourish for seven or more centuries. Covering an area perhaps five times the size of Great Britain, and ruled by priest-kings, it gave rise to large cities. One city, Mohenjo-Daro, possibly held 40 000 people and was therefore one of the world's largest cities. Dominated by a citadel at one end and laid out in rectangular streets, it was well drained and amply provided with fresh water. Even the private houses were fitted with a brick-paved bath.

Skilled in the arts, the people of the Indus cities left behind images of their daily life. Many of the inhabitants so depicted were of a tall distinctive build with a big, domed head and a very broad nose. The women wore a kind of miniskirt with a belt around the waist and nothing above. They liked to see their own face in copper mirrors, to shape their hair into a bun with the aid of a comb made of ivory, and to decorate their lips or eyes with a red pigment. At night, lamps or candles consisting of vegetable oil lit up their houses.

Wheat and barley in several varieties, field peas, sesame and mustard seed were grown. The fruits included dates and watermelon. It is likely that sugar cane and cotton were first cultivated here, later spreading to the Middle East and eventually to the Americas. That two notable crops should come from the Indus was a measure of its importance.

Amongst the animals grazing along the valley were pigs, sheep, goats, camels, asses and humped cattle. Some of the animals were used for transport, and bullock carts carried a canopy to provide shade for passengers. Cats and dogs were kept, and the egg-laying hen was possibly domesticated here. Pottery was mass-produced, and toys made for children included imitation cattle that nodded their heads.

The river and its annual floods served as the artery of this civilisation but the arteries must have become clogged. More and more forest was removed by the farmers, and then isolated trees were cut down to provide wood for the kilns that baked the mudbricks. The floods eroded some areas and filled others with silt. The big towns had to sit themselves on mounds in order to escape the floods which, as the valley silted, rose higher and higher. The city of Mohenjo-Daro was rebuilt about nine times, often after floods damaged or endangered it.

The life of the Indus, as a centre of power, was much shorter than that of the Nile or the rivers of Mesopotamia. By about 1800 BC, long before the arrival of the new techniques of working in bronze and iron, its cities were beginning to decline. The climate was becoming drier. More significantly, the valley was penetrated by the Aryan invaders who for centuries had been increasing their domain in north-western India.

The creating of large villages and the domesticating of plants and animals had been a vital step in the history of the human race. The early valley civilisations formed another step. Sitting in the silt-rich valleys of the Middle East and the Indus, they borrowed from each other and sometimes stimulated each other. A clear geographical advantage, apart from the river and the silt, was that the flanks of each civilisation were partly protected by desert, thus providing a defence against attackers. The climate of the river valleys was another asset, for they could grow cereals which in turn were especially easy to preserve for long periods.

The effective hoarding of grain was vital if cities – far larger than the world had yet known – were to survive. That the other civilisation of Asia arose in the warm silt valleys in China is further evidence of the influence of the big snow-fed rivers on human history.

6

AMAZING SEA

No stretch of salt water exerted such a pervasive influence on the rise of today's world as the Mediterranean. Without that sea and its peculiar qualities and unusual position, the world's political, economic, cultural and social life would have veered in another direction.

In an age when the sea – so long as it was calm – was cheaper and swifter than land for the carrying of cargo and passengers, the Mediterranean offered advantages. It extended from the Atlantic Ocean in the west almost to two inlets of the Indian Ocean in the east: the protruding Red Sea and the Persian Gulf. The long arm of the Mediterranean, the Black Sea, stretched towards the interior of Asia. Two shorter arms, flanking the Italian peninsula, extended almost to the foothills of the snow-clad European Alps.

This sea united Africa and Europe and Asia. A maritime freeway, it linked diverse regions that each produced something different – copper and tin, gold and silver and lead, wine and olive oil, grain, timber, livestock, dyestuffs, cloth, weapons, spices, obsidian and other luxuries. It was a swift conduit for ideas and religious faiths. If Asia or Africa had themselves possessed a sea as large and central, the history of those continents would have been profoundly different. In essence this sea was a strategic lake, with the crowning advantage that, at the Strait of Gibraltar, its narrow throat opened into the wide ocean.

The Mediterranean, being almost surrounded by land, could be astonishingly smooth for long periods. On some days it was a flat mirror, and in summer it was relatively free from storms. Here the large rowing boats known as galleys were in favour, partly because of the absence of wind at certain times of the year. In calm weather, oars were the only motive power. The oars enabled galleys to enter narrow harbours which, if the wind were blowing from the wrong direction, were too risky for a sailing ship to approach.

When storms did arise, and whitecapped waves pounded the pebbly beaches, galleys could be sunk in the space of minutes. Whole fleets could vanish, with few sailors surviving. In 480 BC, when the Persians were attacking Athens, the outcome of the war was partly determined by a rising wind which dashed Persian ships against the rocky Greek coast. Century after century, famous lives were to be influenced by these occasional Mediterranean storms.

The Mediterranean experienced no heavy rising and falling of the tides. The level of its water changed little during the course of 24 hours, and so ships could

3 THE MEDITERRANEAN

Boundary of Roman Empire
c. AD 100

tie up to piers and docks and be unloaded with relative ease. In only a few shallow ports did ships have to wait for high tide before they could enter or leave. The city of Venice, with canals instead of streets, was only practicable because the tidal range was low.

The advantages of this long attenuated sea, and its deep gulfs, meant that a strong military power could command a large area. In turn, the Phoenicians, Greeks, Carthaginians and Romans made use of it. Here, too, the wonderful invention of the sail was first seen. The earliest record of a sail is a decoration on a vase made in Egypt about 3100 BC. The sail is square and resembles a big blackboard on an easel, and no doubt was employed in a ship sailing along the busy River Nile. Leather or skins might well have been used for the early sails, but by 2000 BC they were being replaced by linen which was woven from the strong fibres of the flax plant. A sure supply of flax was to remain an ingredient of naval power until the age of the steamship.

The hoisting of sails on masts, and the more skilled use of ropes, went arm in arm with an improved knowledge of the winds. By the time of the poet Homer, the Greeks knew much about the winds and their prevailing directions; indeed a knowledge of the winds and stars was virtually the only compass when at sea. Thus sailors far out to sea on a dark night could ascertain their bearings partly by noting the direction from which the wet, cold and blustery wind came. Known as the Zephuros, the source of that wind usually signified the west.

The galleys carried a sail. When the wind was blowing from a favourable quarter, a square sail was raised; but if the wind was only light the crew plied the oars. Eventually small galleys gave way to large galleys, which were especially favoured for fighting at sea. Oarsmen were now stationed on two decks instead of one. Later the trireme had three decks and maybe 170 oarsmen. Those oarsmen seated on the upper deck had to ply very long oars so that the blades could reach the water far below.

The combination of sails and oars enabled ships to attain a speed which the sails alone or the oars alone would not have achieved. Thus a light tailwind enabled the galley, when fully manned, to increase its speed from 4 to 6 knots. Sometimes a powerful wind pushed the ship up to 10 knots and the oars were not even needed. If sails were raised on two masts, the ship sometimes heeled over so far that use of the oars was impossible.

In Athens the naval galleys relied more on the effort of free men, but the galleys which carried cargo relied more on slaves. On any calm day, tens of thousands of slaves must have been at work at the rowing benches of ships owned by Greek cities and colonies. Their ankles carried fetters which prevented them from leaving their position beside the oar. If their ship suddenly went down during a battle or storm, they had little hope of escape.

The Mediterranean, especially its northern shores, was to become the centre of power and creativity. Its rising influence was aided by the landsmen's slowly increasing mastery of ships and by another slow-moving event: the advent of cheap iron.

Iron items had long been a luxury. Early iron did not come from the rocks, where it was abundant, but as a rare gift from the skies. For long the meteorite provided the only kind of iron in use. Being heavenly in origin it was often set aside for sacred rituals. Eventually, iron ore was detected in the rock; the heavier and richer pockets were mined in a primitive way, and attempts were made to separate the iron from the barren materials permeating it. Copper smelting offered guidance. In about 1500 BC, unknown but brilliant metallurgists learned to smelt iron ore by raising the temperature of the furnace to more than 1500 degrees Celsius, which was 400 higher than the temperature required for the smelting of copper ore. Quickly iron from the earth became cheaper than iron that dropped from the sky. Nonetheless, metallic iron was still so expensive that most Europeans did not even own one fragment of this metal that was capable of transforming the ploughing of the ground and the axing of trees.

By about 1000 BC iron was challenging bronze in central Greece as a precious metal to be buried with the dead. Two centuries later, iron wares and weapons were widely used along the Aegean. Though wood remained more important, even for the making of work

tools, iron's special strength and sharpness were changing warfare, agriculture and some of the crafts.

THE BRIGHT LIGHT OF ATHENS

Every few centuries in relatively modern times there
have been brief periods of vitality which, long after they
are over, seem to stand like a light along a lonely coast.
These eras have usually been confined to a small part
of the world, though their light might shine far around.
The Greeks lit such a light. Day and night it burned on
the high headlands overlooking many stretches of sea,
and for centuries it could be seen from afar.

The Greek colonists spread wide. Today on the
Black Sea, tourists in the coastal pleasure boats in
the Russian harbour of Sukhumi are told that they pass
over rippled sand covering the ruins of an ancient Greek
city. By the sixth century BC the Greek colonists occupied a strip of coastline in southern France and Spain.
Their cities were sprinkled along the coasts of southern
Italy, Sicily and North Africa, the islands of Crete and
Cyprus, as well as a long belt of what is now the coast
of Turkey. These cities were small, but most were bubbling with vitality. Part of their vitality was reflected in
vigorous quarrels with one another. If they had combined instead of clashed, they would have conquered
most of the western world.

Athens emerged as the most impressive of the
Greek city-states. Its territory of dry hills, known as
Attica, was no larger than the present urban area

of greater Los Angeles. Its total population rarely exceeded 300 000, and yet it was the most influential pocket of territory the world had so far seen. After it was burned or looted by Persian invaders in 480 BC, the Athenians fought back and trounced the enemy. Defeat and humiliation gave them opportunity and incentive. Bold dreams were set in stone. The Parthenon, begun in about 447 BC and completed in less than 10 years, housed the elegant statue of the goddess Athena, carved by Phidias and adorned with gold and ivory.

Athens and a few other city-republics of Greece led a bright flowering in the history of art. Learning from the Egyptians, the Greek artists gained too from their own exciting and confident intellectual climate. Possibly the finest period was between 520 and 420 BC, when grace and fluency marked so many of their buildings, paintings and sculptures.

The expansion of trade called for something less clumsy and cumbersome than the bartering of one set of commodities for another. In 670 BC the Greek island of Aegina was one of the first to mint coins. Made of silver, they were recognisable because their face had the imprint of the sea tortoise. Money eased the trading of goods, for a merchant accepted money when there was no trade item he desired.

Objects as small as the nail of the little finger, as well as stately temples, displayed the skills of the working artists of Greece. Two tiny scaraboids, carved from rock crystal late in the sixth century, can be seen in the Getty Museum in California. One depicts a horse swishing its tail while being led by a young man. Another is a tiny ring, almost the colour of a ripe red-currant, depicting a naked youth scraping oil, dirt and sweat from his leg with a curved blade.

In the art of luxurious living the elite of the Greek cities, especially in Sicily and southern Italy, were per-fectionists too. Delicacies came from afar. Fresh fish, including such small species as the sea squirt, were a familiar sight and smell in the markets. Poultry was introduced from India about 600 BC, but the popular bird of the Greek farmyard was the little quail.

For slaves and poorer citizens the main foods were wheat, barley, beans, and the acorns that fell to the ground. Beef was a rarity. At times even olive oil – used as 'butter' on bread and oil for cooking – was almost too expensive for the average household, and indeed most olives grown near Athens were crushed, squeezed and then shipped as oil in large pottery jars to faraway ports. For the poor a drink of wine – and it was always diluted with water – was not a daily pleasure.

THE WRESTLER OF CROTON

The Greeks were the first people to become obsessed by an activity so characteristic of the present era: com-petitive sports. Their Olympic Games, open only to citizens of the network of the Greek world, became a red-letter event every fourth year. Usually said to have commenced in 776 BC, they were a minor carnival at first. Whether competing as runners, throwers, wrestlers or chariot-drivers, the Greek athletes originally wore clothes but eventually nearly all preferred to be naked in the thronged arena.

A few ambitious cities recruited athletes and paid them handsomely if they won. Professionalism quietly permeated a festival which was later hailed as the heart of amateurism by those Europeans who revived the Olympic Games in AD 1896. A Greek city named Croton, at the foot of southern Italy, displayed the modern desire to win whatever the cost. Rich and large – to walk around its walls was a journey of perhaps two hours – Croton was able to entice athletes from other cities. In the hundred years beginning in 588 BC, the runners of Croton were victorious again and again.

The athlete Milo brought more glory to Croton by winning the Olympic wrestling six times in succession. His massive shoulders were strong enough to carry a live ox around the stadium. Once he devoured an ox in a single day. When he walked through his city, breathing the evening air, his presence must have been the focus of more civic pride than was aroused by the presence of another of that city's immortals, the eminent mathematician Pythagoras.

Envy and rivalry weakened the Greek cities. It is sometimes predicted that international sport will become a happy substitute for international war, but the experience of the cities of Croton and Sybaris, which were Greek-speaking rivals, casts doubt on this prediction. Sybaris, jealous of Croton's prowess in athletics, set up its own sporting carnival in about 512 BC. Croton was not impressed. Ultimately it despatched to Sybaris an army under the command of none other than Milo the wrestler. Greek fought Greek, with blood spilling on the temple floors and the grassy arena. The city of sensuality was virtually destroyed.

The Greek city-states learned to excel in the sport of popular politics. Experimenting in democracy, they carried it further than perhaps any other early society. In Athens the property owners, assembling almost every week, made speeches and gave instructions to those who were briefly in power above them. Nobody was long in power. Even the influential council – consisting of 500 men, all over the age of 30 – was always in flux. Its members were chosen by lot or lottery, and no member could serve for a lifelong total of more than two years. Above the council sat another group, one of whose members was selected – again by lottery – to preside formally over the city and its hinterland. His term of office was astonishingly brief. He ruled simply from sunset to the next day's sunset. In effect the assembly of citizens leased out its power in tiny morsels to the higher officials and then summoned back those morsels and inspected them.

How could a small state, often engaged in war, be effectively governed in this way? The chief of the armed forces was partly exempt from the short-term rule. In the fifth century, at the height of Athens' democracy, the military chief was personally elected, not chosen by lot.

Greek democracy was vulnerable in time of crisis or war. It was slow to make decisions and, like most democracies in modern times, reluctant to impose the necessary taxes. Aristotle, one of the remarkable Greek minds, detected the virtues and failings of this rare mode of government. He regretted that if too many of the poorer property owners attended the assembly, their clamour for subsidies to be paid to themselves might milk the country dry. In his opinion, 'the poor are always receiving and always wanting more and more'. And yet he supported the idea that all who held land should share in the right to govern their country and the duty to pay taxes.

In Athens public decisions were made directly by the people and not at arm's length, as is now the practice in every mass democracy. But the democracy of Athens, like the roadway running from the city to the port of Piraeus, was hemmed in by walls. Only those classified formally as citizens were eligible to speak and vote; and after the year 451 BC, an Athenian citizen who married a foreign woman thereby deprived any of their ensuing children of the right of voting. The poor did not vote. Women and the numerous slaves did not vote. Only owners of property could vote, but many farmers were too poor or lived too far from Athens to be able to halt work and attend the vociferous debates.

The Athenians believed in democracy, though not

in equality. In their opinion, people were born unequal and never would be equal. In a fighting speech in 330 BC, the orator Demosthenes directed disdain against a rival orator, Aeschines, accusing him of coming from a humble background: 'As a boy you were reared in abject poverty, waiting with your father in his school, grinding the ink, sponging the benches, sweeping the room, doing the duty of a menial rather than a freeborn man.' It was as if one's humble past could never be forgiven.

An ability to speak grippingly – whether as a story-teller or poet, prophet or persuader – had been prized by a thousand different tribal and illiterate societies over the space of countless years. The Greeks called it oratory and converted it into an art form. Oratory was also a tool of power, because the open-air assemblies of rowdy and moody voters, sometimes numbering 6000, could be swayed by a magnetic speaker.

Masters of debate, the Greek cities dotting the Mediterranean shores were also masters of violence when a need arose or was imagined. While Athens was listening to the honeyed tongues of orators, Greeks in Sicily were slaughtering and torturing one another. Agathocles, ruler of the powerful city-state of Syracuse, killed 4000 in one day. The Romans were to improve on that record.

These remarkable Greek harbour-cities, even after the death of democracy, buzzed with intellectual energy. Today, many discerning scholars suggest that

Plato of Athens was the most gifted of all philosophers, while Aristotle is revered in what is now called political science. In architecture and the arts the Greek cities, while indebted to Egypt, laid new paths. In medicine, a doctor on the small island of Kos was foremost in the western world; and his name lives on in the Hippocratic oath – the ethical vow of modern medicine. In physics, ethics, linguistics, biology, logic and mathematics, the finest of the Greek thinkers and investigators were like a succession of lights flashing in the darkness. History, stemming from a Greek word, was another field in which the Greeks were pathfinders. Their vitality and genius also went into theatre, sports and democratic politics, as well as difficult abstract ideas.

Engineering was another of the Greeks' strengths. On the island of Samos in the sixth century BC a tunnel was driven 1 kilometre through a high limestone hill in order to tap a supply of fresh water. At about the same time, Greek stonemasons were the first to use the claw chisel, so useful in working marble. Their builders were possibly the first to use a crane to lift materials to rising walls, but slaves were preferred to the new crane.

Overall the Greeks excelled more in Science than in technology. Even their most ingenious weapons called for physical labour on a massive scale. During the siege of Rhodes in 304 BC, a portable tower and stone-thrower, running on wheels, was built to aid the attack, but several thousand men were required to haul it into place.

A new city in Egypt, named Alexandria, was to become the chief inheritor of the Athenian tradition. Founded in 331 BC, the rising city became the intellectual dynamo of the western world. A remarkable library and museum were built. Brilliant Greek scholars such as Euclid arrived to pursue their thinking; medical research was advanced by the anatomist Herophilus, who dissected the human brain and eye in the year 285 BC; and a quarter-century later a famous medical school was born. Jews came to the city in numbers to trade, and Jewish scholars accompanied them and translated their Old Testament from Hebrew into Greek. It was known as the Septuagint, for it was the work of more than 70 translators.

If there had been Nobel prizes for science, medicine and literature in that epoch, Alexandria would have been the home of more prize-winners than any other city. And yet all this ingenuity did not transform the daily work of a civilisation in which the slave served as the all-purpose machine. Alexandria and other Greek cities were probably capable of making many of the steps which constituted, just over 2000 years later, the industrial revolution; but they had no need for an industrial revolution.

The powerful Hellenistic civilisation, now centred on Alexandria as well as the old Greek heartland of Europe and Asia Minor, was not lacking in self-esteem. It was often imitated. More than 2000 years later the map of the world, including lands never known to the Greeks, was sprinkled with Greek echoes and reminders. In the United States the early capital city, Philadelphia, carried a Greek name. In upper New York State arose Syracuse, Ithaca and a cluster of towns with names honouring ancient Greece. In Australia in the 1850s, the gold-diggers setting out from Melbourne to the new goldfields passed two mountains, Mount Macedon and Mount Alexander.

An archipelago in Alaska and an island opposite Antarctica both carry the name of Alexander. In the 19th century the three largest empires in the world were for long periods presided over by monarchs bearing Greek names: Queen Alexandrina Victoria of England, Alexander II of Russia, and Louis Philippe of France.

Perhaps the most powerful influence exerted by Hellenistic civilisation was on the Roman Empire. The Romans, especially after 200 BC, happily imitated much that was Greek. They admired the literature, theatre, food, politics, visual arts, oratory and much of the style and culture that had first flourished and taken shape in Athens. This process of imitation has been likened to the worldwide imitation of America in popular culture today.

Athens was pervasive and persuasive in ways which were almost impossible to predict. It had long passed its political prime when it became the quiet teacher of the Romans.

7

LORD OF THE YELLOW, KING OF THE GANGES

A highway of grassland ran nearly all the way – interrupted sometimes by mountains and lakes – from central Europe to eastern Asia. It ran from the banks of the River Danube to the forests of Manchuria. Measured from coast to coast, the grass highway ran almost from the Adriatic Sea to the Yellow Sea. The land along that wide corridor embraced poor soil and rich; and in southern Russia, where the soil was rich and the climate more gentle, it was called the steppe. Here, soon after the year 2000 BC, people were beginning to make an important conquest. They were taming or domesticating the horse, which hitherto had been simply hunted for meat.

Not as tall as today's typical pony, these small native horses were an asset. When trained, they were loyal and intelligent allies. When they lost their rider they could find their way home. They supplied milk for infants and so enabled mothers to cease breastfeeding a baby at an earlier age. In turn the gap between pregnancies became shorter, and so the population of the steppes was likely to increase more rapidly. The horse could provide meat, especially in winter when food was scarce; and its dung, when dry, served as a fuel on those grassy steppes where trees were few. Thanks to the horse, the sparsely settled grasslands eventually supported more people than before: perhaps too many.

Many centuries later, especially after 700 BC, the riders learned how to ride horses into war. Riding long distances, they could take an enemy by surprise or retreat swiftly when necessary. About 500 BC the invention of the stirrup – in effect a metal footrest suspended by a leather strap – enabled riders to stand up on a fast-moving horse and use their full strength to thrust a spear at an opposing foot soldier.

Horses made up for the lack of people when the raiders of the steppes had to face a more numerous enemy. One warhorse might often be worth 10 foot soldiers fighting on the opposite side.

BIRD'S EYE ON CHINA

Around the year 1500 BC, China lagged some way behind the river valleys of the Middle East in political organisation, in the art of producing metals, in writing, and probably in agriculture and astronomy. But as makers of pottery in kilns, China and Japan were well advanced. These fire-based skills paved the way for advances in metallurgy. The casting of bronze became a Chinese speciality, and their hunting chariots were decorated with bronze, almost like the chrome on large postwar American cars. Then a few Chinese began to make cast iron, and by 400 BC they were learning to specialise in the manufacture of ploughshares – the strong cutting edge that turned over the soil. The production of the high heat needed in the furnace was achieved by a blast coming from sophisticated double-cylinder bellows. Some of the bellows were later driven by power derived from water rushing down narrow streams.

In the 500 or more years before the start of the first Christian millennium, the Chinese were, for a time, the most inventive of the peoples for whom early records survive. In metallurgy they were kings. In handling water for irrigation they devised new methods. In mathematics and astronomy they sought new knowledge. With looms they made silk for fine garments. They became skilled in haulage and transport, using wheelbarrows pushed by humans, carts and ploughs pulled by oxen, and carriages drawn by horses.

The rulers of the larger states inside China lived in luxury and helped themselves to a generous share of the wealth produced by the toiling peasants and artisans. While many Chinese owned their own small lot of land, they had to devote part of their time to the needs of their ruler, either in building public works or fighting in local wars. In death the rulers also helped themselves to the peasants. When a king died, as many as 40 people might be entombed with him. In earlier centuries they were buried in the belief that they could serve him in the afterlife with the help of some of the thousands of jade and bronze items that were buried with them, but later the workers who constructed the elaborate tombs were buried so that they could not disclose to others the secret of how to enter the carefully locked burial chambers and steal the treasures.

China consisted of a galaxy of more than 100 small independent states; but between about 700 and 464 BC, most of these were eliminated, largely as a result of warfare. Seven major kingdoms now ruled most of China. The succession of wars reduced the number of kingdoms to two and then to one. By 221 BC, China was united.

The strongest influence on the training of the new Chinese bureaucracy was Confucius. He was a scholar of a kind more likely to be found in Athens than perhaps in any other state along the Mediterranean. He came to the view that the good life was more important than any afterlife.

Born in 551 BC in the heartland of China, in a minor principality near the Yellow River, he belonged to a poor and mouldy wing of the aristocracy. Initially he held rural posts such as managing a horse stable and keeping records for a granary: the kind of minor tasks that ambitious young people now recite in their curriculum vitae in the hope of persuading future employers that they have not been idle. Eventually Confucius became a full-time teacher, a profession which was not then important.

He believed that the nobility should govern, wisely and humanely. He believed in a hierarchy rather than equality. He tended to believe in the old rather than the new; and he thought that the ancestors had much to teach the present. He praised courtesy and loyalty, humility and kindness. Once, in answer to a question about the kind of person he was, he charmingly described himself in the third person: 'he is the sort of man who forgets to eat when he engages himself in vigorous pursuit of learning, who is so full of joy that he forgets his worries, and who does not notice that old age is coming on'.

He died at the age of 73, having created no church or institution. But his ideas lived on, being reinterpreted by different generations. No other secular thinker who is influential today has exercised that influence for a total of 2500 years.

THE GREAT WALL

China had remarkable linguistic and cultural unity, but its political unity was precarious. It was much closer to those grasslands which nurtured the riders so skilled in fighting, and it was to suffer even more than Europe from their invasions. Significantly, a great wall to defend the Roman Empire from the inland invaders was never built, but China at an early stage had to plan such a wall in order to keep in check its enemies living in the dry and sparsely peopled lands to the north-west.

The Great Wall of China was completed in 214 BC, though in another sense it was never completed because it often had to be extended or enlarged. It reflected the organising ability of the rulers and the stamina and strength of the hundreds of thousands of labourers who were compulsorily assigned to national tasks. They had less reason than their rulers to admire the wall. They had been taken far from home, perhaps never to see their families again, in order to work long hours in the brickyards and quarries that served the wall. They soon learned that the country near the wall was rugged and at one point the wall had to make a long detour to avoid the big bend of the Yellow River (Huang He). In total the wall and its loops extended for 6300 kilometres. If a similar wall had been built across the widest part of Australia, from east to west, it would have been no longer than the Great Wall of China.

In times of danger the Chinese armies guarding the wall must have been huge by the standards of the time. To keep a constant watch, day and night, from most of the towers, when an invader was expected, would have called for tens of thousands of eyes. In addition the wall required a big number of soldiers whose main task was to fight rather than watch.

In the long term, another factor helped to promote China's political unity. Whereas Europe was dissected by large intrusive seas and long peninsulas, China's coastline was more regular in shape. Many European states could be independent for long periods because they were islands or peninsulas, and so the sea defended them. The sea in all its unpredictability does offer a defence against enemies sailing in what are unfamiliar waters. Very often, in the history of Britain and Greece, for example, invasions were thwarted by storms. A strait offers a stronger natural defence than does a land border.

The Chinese population was comparable to that of Europe. In the six centuries between 300 BC and AD 300 it is doubtful whether the population of Europe surpassed that of China for more than a few years. Most Chinese lived in the basin of the mighty Yellow River. At that time it was the Nile of China but less tameable than the Nile. The Yellow River tumbled, glided and rippled for days before it approached the lowlands of China. Unable to make up its mind where to go, it flowed north and then for about 800 kilometres it flowed south – as if it had no intention of ever turning east and flowing to the China Sea. Those who fly over this wayward part of the river can see it far below, a brown streak in the gorges, with forests on one side and parched terraced farms on the other, and no bridge to link the two riverbanks.

Once the trees were more numerous than they are today. As the population of China increased, the felling of trees for firewood or for the making of charcoal led to massive erosion in the hill country. The silted Yellow River became a torrent of thick brown soup. The people of China had no means of knowing that this river was the leading silt-carrier of the world, besides which the Amazon and the Nile were poor relations.

The river was so vital but so tempestuous that it had to be wooed by a human sacrifice. In the 400s BC it was the annual custom to placate the invisible Lord of the Yellow River by giving him a human present. A pretty girl was dressed as a bride and placed on a wooden raft shaped like a marriage bed. The marriage bed was pushed into the rushing river where soon the bride slipped from sight.

To tame the river called for ingenuity and the conscripting of an army of labourers to build and rebuild the embankments and training walls. In 109 BC the emperor erected a pavilion to honour all the people who plugged holes in the dykes and so saved villages from the raging waters. In each decade the bed of the river continued to rise, and therefore the artificial embankments had to be raised even higher. In many places the bottom of the river was well above the level of the surrounding plain. It is a measure of the might and flexibility of the Yellow River that in different centuries it has rushed into the sea either to the north or the south of the mountainous Shandong (Shantung) Peninsula.

Whereas the Nile was confined to a narrow plain, the Yellow River refused to be confined. Its valley was possibly the most densely settled place in the world during the five centuries before the time of Christ. Even in 500 BC, a time when the Greek port-cities and the Persian empire were both flourishing, a line of large towns prospered along the valley of the Yellow River. Its valley or plain was the hub of China and held well over half of the population: the movement of people to the Yangtze in central China and to the warm south commenced later.

As the production of millet and rice became more efficient, and as irrigation channels were dug, the farms could support larger cities. A few were defended by long walls made of rammed earth. One wall was a massive 36 metres in width at the base and extended so far that it encircled a small city. The moving of the earth to construct these walls would have occupied some 12 000 people for about 10 years, and they in turn would have been fed by a procession of carts carrying grain. Along the Yellow River several cities grew to a size which must have impressed all travellers who passed through their gates. The new capital city of Loyang (now Luoyang), founded in AD 25, held a population of close to half a million: perhaps only Rome was larger.

China had some of the characteristics of the Roman Empire, and the marching army was as important for China as for the Romans. Spaced along the Chinese highways were hundreds of official rest houses, with beds and places for washing, and feed and stables for the horses. Along the highways came couriers on horseback, carrying secret despatches written on thin strips of wood and enclosed in bamboo tubes which were then locked, so providing maximum security. At well-spaced points along the roads stood beacons, which in times of emergency could transmit simple signals of smoke to the next beacon, which was then set alight. In 74 BC the news of the death of the emperor was relayed some 1300 kilometres in the space of 30 hours, largely by the smoke rising from the beacons.

China was rather like the United States in the 19th century, when an abundance of unused forest and marsh could be taken up for farming, thus serving as a safety valve for the press of population. In southern China, the vast areas of forest, scattered woodland and semitropical river flats supported few people. But hundreds of thousands of northern Chinese peasants were migrating south in search of land. Rice was being planted as the main crop of the south and it was heavy in its demand for water. Here, too, the tea bush was first cultivated, giving China a commodity which, more than 1000 years later, was to outshine silk in the eyes of Europe.

Korea and Japan lay in the shadow of China and its new ideas and techniques, but flashes of light shone in their direction. The new metallurgy arrived, and iron began to replace stone in the heads of axes and in the sharp edges of the sickles which reaped the grain. A new kind of pottery was made with a potter's wheel and placed in an oven to be fired at a high temperature. Earlier than 500 BC, a new food-crop, rice, crossed from China to Korea and Japan and began to transform daily meals.

THE ISLAND OF INDIA

In Asia at this time the only potential rival to China was India. In fact they were too far apart to be real rivals. They knew little of each other. The fact that both were in Asia meant nothing to them. Asia was a European concept in geography; and for long the concept was unknown to the more learned of the Chinese, who thought China was too pivotal to be part of any other geographical unit.

India, unlike China, was virtually an island. Cut off from most of Asia by the Himalaya mountains, which ran east for almost 2500 kilometres, India could be approached more easily from the north-west. There the mountain passes encouraged traffic. India lay closer to the civilisations of the Middle East and Greece than to the heartland of China; and the exact position of the mountain passes increased the likelihood that its links would favour the Mediterranean world. India's main language was of the Indo-European family, not of the Chinese. Its invaders arrived more from the direction of Europe. Its external trade, whether by sea or land, also favoured that direction.

Of the countries in the tropics and the temperate zones of the world, India holds a larger area of ice than any other. It also embraces a very large area of hot country. Fortunately the high mountains, with their melting snow and ice, sent a flow of water to the parched plains in summer. The melting water from the high mountains helped to make up for the deficiencies and irregularities in the rainfall, which came mostly with the south-west monsoon from the Indian Ocean.

The Ganges River was a child of these whitecapped mountains. It normally ran for the whole year, carrying water across a huge plain. After 1000 BC, the Ganges replaced the Indus as the populous part of the Indian subcontinent. Cities multiplied along the valley, and the farms had to multiply in order to feed the cities. By 400 BC, India probably held 30 million people. In the whole world, only northern China could surpass this press of people.

At this time it is probable that China and India between them held one-third of the world's people, perhaps more. The silt-strewn plains and the snow-fed rivers were the secret of their capacity to support such large populations. The Yellow River carries in a typical year a suspended load of about 2100 million tonnes of soil, far more than any other river in the world. Second is the Ganges with about 1600 million tonnes. About half of the silt of these rivers is deposited at the delta and the river estuaries, though much comes to rest in farms and irrigation channels. These mighty, muddy rivers of India and China are unparalleled. Without the vast volume of silt, the population of China and India would have been much lower.

Whereas China's special talent at this time was in technology, India's was in religion. Hinduism, which arrived with the Indo-European migrants, held its high priests or brahmans in almost godlike esteem. It was a flexible religion, given to producing branches and off-shoots. Its devotees ranged from rich priests and lonely threadbare wanderers to crowds who combined newer Hinduism with their old idols. The religion was never static. At an early stage it sacrificed animals on impor-tant occasions while later it tended to sanctify most living things. It ranged from a belief in many specialist gods to a belief in the supreme god, Brahma.

Hindus believed that every creature had a soul and that after death it migrated to a new body. The idea now is seen as essentially that a human being could be reborn into a variety of insect or animal species. Therefore cows and goats, mites and insects had to be treated with respect. Why the cow, alone of the meat-providing animals, was especially venerated in India is a puzzle.

Hinduism did not depend on its followers assem-bling in large numbers in a temple: its wooden temples were not assembly halls but statements of faith. The creed was full of rules for daily life and eternal life. It also came to emphasise the recycling of lives. This idea implanted some hope, while blessing the miseries of the status quo. The consolation for living in poverty and being humble in status was that one's life, if lived virtuously, might be rewarded at death by the passing of the soul into a worthier being. On the other hand, the dead person's soul might pass, on returning to earth, into a lesser animal.

It is remarkable that India became a democracy in modern times, because the long-lasting Hindu civilisation at first sight was innately hostile to the ideas that all adults should have an equal vote, irrespective of their caste, and that all adults should be able to share in the social mobility which was part of the democratic spirit. But to graft exotic new trees onto old, when there seemed little hope of success, and to watch them grow vigorously, is not a rare experience in human institutions.

THE PRODIGAL SON BECOMES THE BUDDHA

In the 6th century BC, Hinduism, tolerant of diversity, gave birth to new religions. It gave rise to Jainism and to the more influential Buddhism. Siddhartha Gautama, the founder of Buddhism, had similarities to Christ. Born at the time of the full moon, his arrival was greeted not by three wise men but by one.

Gautama's father was a Nepalese prince living near the border of India, in the steamy lowlands which are one source of the River Ganges. He owned three palaces where Gautama, when older, enjoyed the entertainment provided. Showing no early sign of that sense of duty which he later preached, he was constantly entertained by female musicians; and when the music stopped he was further entertained. He supped at the fleshpots, a kind of prodigal son. He married his cousin and they had one son; but this brought no sense of responsibility to Gautama.

Then, to the surprise of his friends, he sought salvation. He left home at night, on horseback, and his life changed forever. Following that strong Indian tradition of asceticism he tried to punish his body, eventually losing so much weight that his ribs protruded 'like rafters' in a shed. After enduring much pain and spending time in the wilderness, he found the light. He became 'the Enlightened One' or the Buddha.

Henceforth, Buddha pursued holiness. He thought it was essential to annihilate the self: the ultimate goal was *nirvana*, an ideal condition in which he would virtually extinguish himself. Pursuing the goal of quiet self-extinction, he was rewarded with inexpressible happiness. He won the admiration of many of the poor, for he did not accept the Hindu idea of caste. He also attracted the rich, who established, in cities and towns along the Ganges, Buddhist monasteries for those men who wished to perfect themselves. He set up a religious order for women, and his aunt was the first to enter the nunnery.

In the dry season the Buddha moved about, begging for food and teaching the word. Those who gave him food felt that they shared in some of his holiness. Like Francis of Assisi, who was to tame a wild wolf in central Italy during the Christian era, Buddha succeeded in taming, with his calm presence, a mad elephant. His teachings were later summed up by the Indian politician Mahatma Gandhi in the words: 'Life is not a bundle of enjoyments, but a bundle of duties.'

At this time the dynamic parts of the globe were India, the eastern Mediterranean and China. Far apart, they had few links with each other; and yet each was simultaneously living in a seedtime. In the 480s BC, Buddha in old age was preaching his word along the Ganges, Confucius was writing down his precepts in northern China, and the Athenians, having just defeated the Persians at the Battle of Marathon, were cultivating those arts and that democracy on which their fame was to rest.

Buddha died in about 486 BC, when he was close to 80 years of age. His death was widely mourned in the region but his creed did not seem likely to win converts far from the banks of the Ganges. A little more than two centuries after his death, his creed received a lucky break. It so happened that King Asoka became the first ruler to govern nearly all of a land which in Buddha's lifetime had been fragmented into many kingdoms.

Ruling from a city on the Ganges, this powerful king – perhaps the most powerful in the world – became a devout Buddhist and even erected shrines to honour the ashes of Buddha. At a time when Buddhism might otherwise have been pushed aside by the central and versatile creed of Hinduism, the king quietly spread its religious message. A king with absolute power is the most persuasive of all missionaries, in the short term.

At first it was Hinduism which attracted foreigners. Renewing itself from time to time, it spread along the coast of South-East Asia and to a cluster of islands. The phase of strong Hindu influence in South-East Asia lasted for centuries, and then, almost everywhere, the Hindu gods retreated. The small island of Bali, far from the mouth of the Ganges, remains a lonely Hindu outpost.

In the history of the world's religions, northern India rivals the Middle East as the most fertile birthplace. Curiously the Indian religions made little headway to the west. Their recruiting grounds lay to the east. Buddhism proved to be the most successful recruiter, and its victories were to be won in lands where India had possessed virtually no cultural or commercial influence during Buddha's own lifetime.

8

THE RISE OF ROME

Rome was built, its historians and legend-makers liked to proclaim, on the seven hills. Not all the hills, however, were peopled when Rome was young. The town was too small to require such space. Past the walled town ran the Tiber River, flowing at last into the Mediterranean less than 40 kilometres away. Sometimes yellow with mud washed down from the steep hills after heavy rain, the river was used by small boats carrying cargo to and from the river mouth. At first a monarch ruled the town and the small territory nearby, but in 509 BC the landed families were victorious and their republic was to last nearly five centuries.

The small city of Rome was still struggling to survive. In 390 BC it was besieged for seven months by an army of Gauls who finally entered and half-wrecked the city. Rome did not yet command even half of the Italian peninsula. In 300 BC it did not even control Milan and the site of Venice, which was not yet a village. Rome ruled none of the islands of the western Mediterranean, virtually all of which were in the rival sphere of influence of Carthage, the powerful city on the coast of North Africa.

Rome's talent was in producing generals and soldiers, admirals and sailors. These fighting men, having subdued the neighbouring Sabines, Etruscans and the Piceni, began to challenge the land and sea empire based on Carthage. By 240 BC the Romans controlled the rich island of Sicily, once part of Greek civilisation. In the following year they captured the Carthaginian island of Sardinia. But then Hannibal, the great general of Carthage, seemed likely for a time to crush Rome, for he led a victorious army through Spain and over the French Alps and far into Italy. His forces were finally defeated in 207 BC. It was the Romans who now extended their overseas empire, easily penetrating Carthage's domain in North Africa. From these new possessions in North Africa and Sicily came a procession of ships whose cargoes of grain were needed to feed the expanding city of Rome.

For the Greeks the sea was a natural highway but the Romans built their own highways. In 312 BC Roman engineers began to build the first of their arteries, the Appian Way, which ran all the way from Rome to the southern port of Tarentum, on the inner heel of Italy. Soon that highway was extended to the back of the heel – the Adriatic port of Brindisi where today can be seen the ancient stone column celebrating that feat of engineering. Ultimately, well-built Roman roads extended along much of the coast of North Africa, around much of the northern coast of the Mediterranean, and to the remote rivers the Danube and Euphrates. They were not mere roads. Where they survive they are still known as 'Roman roads', as if they are a distinct species, which indeed they are. Cutting through hills, and crossing marshes on stone or earthen causeways, they were described by the English novelist Thomas Hardy as like a parting line in a head of hair – thin and straight.

The Roman roads for their time were more remarkable than the super-highways built in Europe for the motor era. Fast couriers could travel along the roads and, as in China, feel certain that, unless floods or snow intervened, their horsedrawn vehicle would adhere to its timetable. In many parts of the Roman Empire a message sent by road arrived long before a message sent by sea. Along the Roman roads went fast horsemen, tramping soldiers, merchants, slaves and babes in arms.

The Roman bridge was a work of art, though the Romans had gifted predecessors in the building of roads and bridges. To see a Roman bridge still bearing traffic is to feel a sense of awe. The engineer, the people who quarried the stone and the stonemasons who built the bridge have long been silent but their bridge stands in all its strength and elegance. The Roman bridge at Rimini, within sound of the Adriatic Sea, consists of dressed blocks of whitish limestone, with shells and the remains of a fish or two still embedded in the white stone. Built about the year 5 BC, it consists of five barrel or semicircular arches beneath which a river, now shrunken, briskly flowed in floodtime. Even today the bridge is a one-direction crossing, used by Italian cars and motor scooters, and enhanced by a ledge on which pedestrians can walk with a narrow margin of safety.

INSIDE THE MARBLE CITY

All roads did lead to Rome, and it grew to an almost unmanageable size. It was probably the first city in the world – though China too had large cities – to support a population approaching one million. It was the goal for drifters and the destitute with nowhere else to go, for those who wanted work and excitement, and for the fiercely ambitious who wanted the top chance. Rome's stone-paved streets were crowded with wheeled traffic and people, some pouring in from Italian farmlands and others arriving as prisoners from the latest war. The growing city relied on aqueducts; and the long arched bridges conveyed from the foothills the continuous flow of water that filled the public baths and the water pots and jugs in countless homes, and flushed away the sewage. Some public baths were huge marble halls with numerous lesser rooms and many baths, both hot and cold. Places for gossip and pleasure, they multiplied. The city of Rome alone held about 800 public baths.

Many of the ships which carried stone and timber and grain to Rome were larger than any built in the western world in the following thousand or more years. They could be longer than 50 metres and as wide as 15 metres, making them appear rather tubby or even ungainly by present standards of design. A fleet of ships, almost like today's bulk carriers, was especially built for the carrying of building stone. These large Roman ships relied on the wind instead of oars. Their task was to carry cargoes cheaply rather than quickly, but occasionally they made fast passages. One cargo ship is reported to have sailed from the Italian port of Naples to the Egyptian port of Alexandria in a mere nine days.

If European sailors at the time of Columbus had chanced to be shown the wreck of a big wooden Roman ship, uncovered by shifting sands, they would have been surprised by her length. Columbus's flagship, *Santa Maria*, was only about 30 metres in length, much smaller than those Roman ships which had been engaged in carrying grain or building stones from Egypt. Even the eye-opening steamship of 1843, the *Great Britain*, with her one funnel and six masts, was to be no wider and not quite twice as long as the big Roman cargo ships sailing the seas 2000 years previously.

Roman writers left for future generations a detailed picture of daily life and its fun, anguish, pleasure and pain. We can almost taste the meals of the common people: the coarse bread, the 'fresh hand-pressed cheese, and green figs of the second crop', and of course that tiny but popular fish, the whitebait. We can walk around Roman farms, thanks to the poetry of Virgil, and hear advice on how to farm. Thus the seventh day of the moon was considered lucky for roping and taming wild cattle, and in summer the hay of a parched meadow should best be cut after dark: a haymaking rule which was often followed in Italy even in living memory.

In almost every phase of Rome's history there were crises. Thus in the last century of the pre-Christian age came severe setbacks. In 86 BC many members of patrician families – once so powerful – were massacred by their rivals. In the following decade Spartacus the slave led a rebellion, attracting rural slaves to his banner in their tens of thousands. When he was finally defeated in Italy in 71 BC, some 6000 of his followers were captured and crucified along the Appian Way.

Civilising strands were intertwined with the violent strands. Even in slavery there could be civility and compassion. Early in the second century AD the son of a slave died; and the slave-owners commissioned the carving of the dead boy's head from a block of marble, adding this simple message in Latin:

> To the dearest Martial,
> A slave child,
> Who lived two years, ten months, and eight days.

The child wears an innocent look, with his long elegant ears, short mouth, neatly clipped hair raked halfway down the forehead and – just above the right ear – an Egyptian good-luck charm. The insignia did not denote that the child was living in Egypt, which was then a Roman colony. Rome's was a cosmopolitan empire, and ideas and religions and fashions flowed with ease across the Mediterranean and along its coasts, just as ideas and objects at present flow with ease: indeed the child's head can be seen today in a museum in Los Angeles.

Rome began as a republic in which a small number of families shared power. Later the electorate of citizens living in Italy and entitled to vote was increased to hundreds of thousands: in the end they numbered more than one million. Of course it was pointless for Rome to imitate Greek democracy and the public meetings of citizens voting on the spot; and so the secret ballot was the Roman alternative. For several centuries Rome ran a form of representative government which virtually every leader in Europe, 300 years ago, would have condemned, by their own standards, as dangerously democratic. The heads of state were elected. No politician or general could hold the reins of power for long. Much of the decision-making rested with the representative assemblies.

Rome's distant and ever-expanding empire was not easily governed. Where could new taxes be found? Citizen armies could no longer carry the brunt of the military service and so mercenaries and even slaves were recruited, and some were likely to be loyal more to their general than to Rome. Even the generals fighting on far frontiers were not easily kept in check. They needed some independence in order to fight successfully, but if they were too victorious and too popular with the Roman public they were indirectly a challenge to those civic leaders holding power in Rome.

The perpetual tension in Rome seemed to find a solution. To people proud of their republic an emperor was unthinkable, but the unthinkable was now thought aloud. In 63 BC, Augustus became the emperor, while contending that he was simply first citizen of the old republic. He held military control and he held a firm hand on the senate. Slowly the Roman emperor became all-powerful in life and venerated as a god in death. Each emperor now named his own successor.

The transition from republic to monarchy, while drastic, breathed new stability into the Roman Empire. It continued to expand and to hold on to what it had won. As the citizens no longer voted for or against those wishing to lead the empire, citizenship could safely be extended. The climax came in AD 212, when all free men could become Roman citizens, enjoy the protection of the remarkable and evolving system of Roman law, and pretend to enjoy that other privilege of citizens: the right to pay taxes to an empire which was often short of revenue. Rome was such an incredibly successful empire, its political history and its modes of government were so well recorded, that when London became another Rome in the 18th century, its political and cultural leaders were to be obsessed with Roman history.

ALONG THE SILK ROUTE

Between the two major civilisations of the world, those of Rome and China, lay a wide geographical gap. The land route between western China and the nearest ports of the Black Sea was, even before the time of Christ, the longest in the world. It crossed mountains and plateaus, stony plains and salty deserts, fast streams and gorges, and immense pastures. The route was more like a relay race than a procession, for the goods being exchanged were handed from merchant to merchant, from bazaar to bazaar, and so they made their slow way across the continent in carts or on the backs of horses and camels moving in long convoys.

The main cargo carried from the east was silk. The rich of Rome and Alexandria craved silk garments, and for long China was the only supplier of them. The humble silkworms, feeding on the leaves cut from millions of Chinese mulberry trees, lived for only 45 days; but during a short life each worm produced a cocoon of slender strands which, unravelled, might run to 900 metres. The thin strands were woven into a thread from which the silk was manufactured by hand in many Chinese towns.

A roll of silk was a magical textile. Light in weight, capable of being stretched without breaking, easily dyed with bright colours such as Tyrian purple, and soft when rubbed against human flesh, silk was prized by the few Romans who had a chance to wear it. Being expensive, it was not worn by the average person in China; and being far more expensive by the time it reached the Mediterranean it was regarded as a high luxury when landed in Rome.

As the silkworm was a living spinning machine of tireless energy, it was certain to be captured by merchants from other nations. Silkworms were smuggled to India, where silk fabric, not of the highest quality, was produced. Silkworms eventually reached Sicily and France, but the skills of the Chinese spinners and weavers remained at home. China continued to manufacture the superior silk.

China's economic life was so advanced and so versatile that it wanted little from the west. China was pleased to acquire small amounts of the fine glass which was made in Lebanon and Egypt and carried along the trade route across Asia: a fragile cargo to be perched on the swaying back of camels. China also accepted occasional parcels of wool and other cloth, and precious metals.

Along the silk route, into the setting sun, came not only silk but other items valued highly in the west. Such prized medicines as preserved rhubarb and cinnamon bark came from China. Even more important were seeds and living plants. China was a botanical garden from which the outside world, century after century, borrowed seeds and cuttings. The Chinese were probably the first to cultivate the peach tree and pear tree, which eventually reached India about the second century after Christ.

It was in China that the orange was first cultivated, bringing wealth to the owners of orchards. The orange tree was valued not only as a source of fruit but also for its wood, which was often selected for making the bows that shot the arrows. Just before the time of Christ the first Chinese oranges and lemons reached the Middle East, having come part of the way in ships using the route from India to the Red Sea. An orange is clearly depicted in a mosaic at the town of Pompeii, which was buried by volcanic ash in AD 79.

The Chinese and Romans held one view in common. Each of their peoples believed that their own civilisation was superior to any other. While China possessed an extent of territory that vied with Rome's, its emperor did not hold sway over as many languages, cultures and peoples as did the Roman emperor.

At the time of Christ, Roman ships were in command of nearly every major port in the Mediterranean. Wherever the Greek sea-cities had prospered, whether in Sicily or Egypt, the emperor was now in control. The tramp of Roman soldiers, the systematic splash of the oars of the galleys, could be heard from the eastern to the western shores of the Mediterranean and even beyond the Strait of Gibraltar – a region into which Greek influence had never extended. Roman coins were the currency along the west coast of the

Atlantic from Spain to Brittany, and north as far as the sandhills and salt marshes along the coast of what is now Holland.

Rome's rule extended from the Black Sea to the north of England. Roman regiments were quartered as far down the River Rhine as the town of Cologne where that stately river was crossed by a Roman bridge. Likewise the Danube River in the present Hungary was crossed by a Roman bridge whose stone piers and semicircular wooden arches were designed by the notable builder Apollodorus of Damascus.

These outlying cities, harbours, garrison towns and provinces were important to Rome. Outposts, they protected the inner empire. They also contributed food, soldiers, slaves, raw materials and, not least, they provided revenue. From time to time they also brought vexation to the Roman rulers. One source of vexation was a new creed that would outlive the Roman armies.

9

ISRAEL AND THE ANOINTED ONE

The coast of the present Israel was fringed with sand dunes and not welcoming to a strange ship. It was meagre in those inlets and natural harbours where a ship could anchor. Indeed the city of Jerusalem, compared to most of the other famous cities of the Mediterranean, lacked easy access to a natural harbour. The Hebrews – or Israelites or Jews – originally owned flocks rather than ships, for they were people of the pastures and not the sea. Lebanon, to the north, possessed the natural harbours; and there the Phoenicians traded and flourished.

The word Hebrew signified a wanderer, or one who 'crossed over'. For most of their history – and they probably originated from the headwaters of the Persian Gulf or the nearby deserts – the Hebrews had no secure home. These wandering people knew times of prosperity, when their flocks and tents occupied fine pastures, but they also remembered times of humiliation, captivity and exile.

Enslaved in Egypt, they eventually escaped with

their leader Moses towards a land they believed God had promised them, the present Israel. According to one version of their history, preserved in scripture, they were almost trapped by their pursuers on the western edge of the Red Sea. Then suddenly the sea parted, allowing them to proceed. The event seems miraculous; but perhaps it was not. For the early name of the Red Sea was the reed sea or the marshy sea, and in many places it was shallow. Such is the shape of the shore that unusual tides can occur. Indeed in 1993 a team of oceanographers observed that when a wild wind has blown at about 70 kilometres an hour for about 10 continuous hours, the sea virtually recedes. It is conceivable that the Hebrews, with the Egyptians not far behind, crossed the sea on such a freakish day. Then the sea rose, drowning the pursuing Egyptians.

Around 1000 BC, the Hebrews under King David had their years of glory, for he captured Jerusalem. His son and successor, King Solomon, built the magnificent temple atop the city's hill; and in that building of almost unparalleled splendour, his people worshipped God, who had guided them to this promised land.

After the death of King Solomon, in about 935 BC, his kingdom was divided into two states, Israel and Judah. It is from Judah that the Jews take their name. Eventually these two pocket-sized states became too weak to fend off ambitious outsiders. In 587 BC soldiers of the New Babylonian empire looted and destroyed the noble temple at Jerusalem and the Jewish leaders went into exile for nearly a century. On returning home, they lived under a succession of foreign rulers: the Persians, Alexander the Great, and the Greek-speaking Seleucids. For much of this time the spiritual life of the Jews blossomed. Prophets were heeded, scholars of theology were encouraged, and the idea took root of spiritual survival beyond the grave.

THE TEN COMMANDMENTS AND
100 LESSER RULES

The Jewish God was all-powerful and everlasting. His name was rarely spoken, such was the awe and majesty surrounding him. He was eventually to be called 'Jehovah' by the Protestant reformers 2000 years later. Jehovah protected the Jews on condition that they obeyed his precepts, his commandments.

The first of the Ten Commandments proclaimed that there was only one god in the whole world. At a time when the typical religion had many gods – the temples of the Middle East were crowded with gods for each season and each purpose – the Jewish religion was unusual. Its members were instructed to bow down before no other god.

The Ten Commandments instructed the Jews how to conduct their lives. An underlying rule was that they must respect their neighbours and show them sympathy. They were commanded to honour their parents. They must not kill, they must not commit adultery. They must not tell lies about their neighbour, and not even think of stealing the neighbour's ox and ass. It will be observed that the ox and ass, but not the sheep, were so mentioned. Vital as beasts of burden and high in price, the ox and ass were widely used for ploughing the fields and for carrying and hauling heavy loads.

The rigid practice of Jews was to work only six days in each week and to worship and rest on the seventh day, which, according to their reckoning, was Saturday. One of the first wide-ranging laws of social welfare in the world, the Sabbath day of rest extended not only to householders but also to their servants, female and male. More than 20 centuries later the most advanced of the world's social democracies were to introduce, for many employees, a working day limited to eight hours; but that recent experiment in social welfare was less significant than the six-day working week religiously adhered to by these children of Israel.

The Jews were more obsessed with their own history than any other people the world had known. They busily recorded their trials and tribulations, their defeats as well as their victories. Along with their sense of history was an emphasis on fairness and ethical behaviour in daily life. At times they were almost overwhelmed by rules and guideposts.

Constantly probing the nature and mission of human beings, the Jewish spiritual leaders were to become as influential as those Europeans who, in the scientific and industrial revolutions some 2000 years later, immersed themselves in the task of mastering the material world. But if a history of the world had been written in 200 BC, the Jews would not have merited many sentences. So far they had been no more influential than hundreds of other states and monarchies, peoples and tribes, in Africa and Asia, Europe and the Americas.

Israel, after centuries of vicissitudes and few victories, experienced a miracle in the second century BC. It enjoyed 80 years of near-independence. The miracle did not last, and Rome's ever-expanding empire arrived in 63 BC. But many of the Jews still living in their own homeland became wary of Roman rule. It was their intuition that Jehovah would intervene and save his favoured people. Jesus was foremost amongst these prophets.

Jesus was born in about 6 BC, according to the Gregorian calendar used today in the West. Growing up in a village that was tucked away in the hills, he followed his father's trade as a carpenter or builder. A skilled trade, it probably earned an income well above that of most workers in Palestine. At a time when few people could read and write, he also possessed the advantage of literacy.

Imbibing the intensely religious and political atmosphere of Israel, then under Roman occupation, he mastered the teachings of the Old Testament. He was especially inspired by the urgent preaching of John the Baptist, a wandering preacher who shunned all the outward comforts of the cities and showed his distaste for comfort by eating the simplest foods and dressing in a coat made from the hide of a camel. His message to all who listened was 'Repent'. His symbolic gesture was to baptise, or to immerse in water, those who deeply repented their sins. Jesus was eventually baptised by John in the waters of the River Jordan.

In his early thirties Jesus put down his hammer, saw and chisel and left his village – he had no wife – and took up the same calling as John the Baptist. He began to preach and teach in villages, in the countryside and even in synagogues. He could now reason and preach and persuade with what can safely be called genius. The sick were brought to him; and to everybody's astonishment he seemed to heal them with a touch of his hand or a quietly confident command.

That such an extraordinary young man should come from a rural village caused no surprise. Indeed he was known simply as the Nazarene, meaning a native of the village of Nazareth. Later he would be called the Christ, meaning in Greek 'the anointed one'. Today he might well be called a faith healer.

His sayings flew on golden wings. His preaching could be mysterious but was also down to earth. He would tell a simple story about daily life, fix to it a moral message and conclude with a plea for his wayside listeners to adopt his new way of thinking. Indeed his preaching and his parables have left behind a wonderful record of daily life. He spoke about the hiring of labourers to work in a vineyard at a penny a day, and told of the vineyard owner who was perplexed that his fig tree yielded no fruit, or discussed, in passing, the sensible way to bottle the new season's wine: 'Neither do men put new wine into old bottles,' he said. No doubt his rural listeners nodded in agreement.

Huge crowds assembled when it was announced that he would preach and heal. He must have been a fine orator with a distinct voice that could float to the most distant member of the crowd, but in the course of a hectic month his voice would reach only a fraction of the people of Israel. As he needed the help of other men to preach in all those villages that could not be fitted into his busy timetable, he gathered fulltime volunteers or disciples. The first were fishermen from a nearby lake. Soon there were 12 disciples, gripped by his magnetism. Even more disciples were needed. As he explained with his homely rural reminders: ' The harvest truly is plenteous but the labourers are few.'

Jesus displayed a deep feeling for the underdog: for those who were poor, those who were sick, and those who mourned. He seemed to uphold the old Jewish values and the authority of the Old Testament, but he also had a revolutionary streak. He announced that the day would come when 'the last shall be first' and the humble would be the most powerful. This was not reassuring news for those holding positions of civil and religious power in Jerusalem.

The main Jewish sects and synagogues were not sure how to regard this prophet. Some felt threatened by his swelling influence on the crowds. Some were understandably alarmed because he disputed the rigidity of their teaching and their cementlike adherence to the hundreds of ancient Jewish rules and rituals. That he would take the fight into their synagogues and challenge their moral credentials was an additional threat. He was not frightened by rebukes. He was looked upon by the Roman rulers as potentially subversive.

His life as a preacher and healer was to be short. In about AD 30, when still in his thirties, he virtually beckoned his enemies to lay their hands on him. He resolved to come to Jerusalem with his followers at a holy time of the year. He celebrated a last supper with his disciples and, in their presence, foretold his own death. Arrested at the demand of his numerous enemies, he was tried for blasphemy in a Jewish court and then sentenced by the Roman rulers to die by a humiliating procedure from which Roman citizens were exempted. He was flogged and then his body was nailed to a tall cross-shaped structure of timber, with two common criminals placed on smaller but similar crosses on each side of him. A placard written in three languages – Latin and Greek and Hebrew – proclaimed what was viewed as his dangerous pretension: 'Jesus of Nazareth, King of the Jews'. He died slowly, in acute pain.

It is said that an eclipse of the sun then occurred, as if the heavens knew that an event of magnitude was taking place. That afternoon he was taken from the cross and buried by loyal friends. On the third day his body disappeared from its grave. In the following days his disciples believed that they had briefly glimpsed or heard him, here and there. They were convinced beyond a flutter of doubt that he was the son of God, to whose presence he had now returned.

Nothing did more to make his whole life seem momentous than the ascent into heaven. There, it was said, he would wait until the day of judgement when he would appear on earth again to punish the wicked and reward the good.

10

AFTER CHRIST

If Christ's message was to stay alive, it could do so only with the help of the Jews. They were a scattered people, mostly living far from their homeland and thus offering a network through which the Christian message could spread.

At the end of that period now known as BC or 'Before Christ', most of the Jews had never set eyes on the land of their ancestors. Many Jewish families, having gone into exile as captives, became part of their new land. Other Jews went as traders or soldiers to distant ports and lived there, generation after generation. A census conducted by the Romans in AD 48 indicated that seven million Jews lived in the vast Roman Empire. Maybe as many as 9 per cent of the empire's population was Jewish – a proportion of Jews higher than that inhabiting Europe on the eve of the Second World War. Another five million Jews lived in parts of Asia Minor and Africa that lay beyond the empire. As political conditions deteriorated in Palestine, and as more and more Jews decided to leave, the city of Babylon became home of spirited Jewish theologians.

Jewish synagogues could be found all the way from Sicily to the Black Sea, southern Arabia and Ethiopia. The synagogues in Rome alone served about 50 000 Jews. In many of the remote Jewish settlements the synagogue remained the hub of social life, with a library and perhaps a hospice. These faraway synagogues were often a testimony to the generosity of congregations, many of whose members donated one-tenth of their annual income.

The Jewish religion, though initially for the Jews, had long ago widened its appeal. Many gentiles or non-Jews attended a synagogue and accepted its ethical code and its view of the world, though did not necessarily submit to the minor surgery and major ritual of circumcision. In many synagogues in the eastern parts of the Roman Empire during the first century BC, the Hebrew language was superseded. The congregation prayed in Greek and heard the scriptures read aloud in Greek.

The chain of synagogues along the Mediterranean and in the interior of Asia Minor became an early forum for the spread of Christ's teachings. St Paul was the first notable convert. He had not spoken with Christ or heard him preach, and at first he opposed his cult following, seeing it as a danger to mainstream Jewish religion. Paul's attitude was transformed, however, by a mystical experience on the Damascus road. He became an ardent Christian missionary. Some 14 years after the death of Christ, he began to reshape the infant church. He possessed unusual qualities. He felt at home in a synagogue: his parents were Jewish and he himself had once trained to be a rabbi. He held Roman citizenship, which gave him a passport to official circles; and he spoke Greek, the tongue of the cultured.

While the early converts to Christianity were mainly Jews, others were equally attracted. Soon, many people who had no connection with a synagogue heard the Christian message and began to meet together in private houses or public rooms. The question of who could become a Christian was increasingly debated within the new congregations. Many Jewish Christians objected to outsiders, for they saw Christianity as simply a branch of their own religion. It was in the city of Antioch, in the south of the present Turkey, that this dilemma was first debated with vigour.

In Antioch, a decade or two after the death of Christ, the question of who should be allowed to be a full member of the Christian church was resolved in favour of the internationalists rather than the Jews. Everyone who came in a state of repentance could become a Christian. This inevitably led to a widening rift between the synagogues and the new Christian churches. Each competed for the same worshippers, whether Jew or gentile. While many of the Christian congregations consisted exclusively of Jews, more and more of the new congregations attracted people from all races and backgrounds. St Paul emphasised this all-welcoming strand when he wrote his powerful letter to the Galatians: ' There is neither Jew nor Greek, there is neither slave nor free, there is neither male nor female, for you are all one in Christ Jesus.'

In the first century after the crucifixion of Christ his followers lived mostly in the towns rather than the villages and countryside. Women probably were the majority of Christians. Those who clung to the church in these difficult years had to be brave. The emperors in Rome occasionally turned against the Christians, and Emperor Nero Claudius blamed them for the famous fire in Rome in AD 64. In a kind of match of the day, many Christians were gored to death by wild beasts in the presence of a crowd of spectators.

In their inward tussles on the question of how far to follow the rules of the synagogue, the early Christians were not sure whether to discard the strict Jewish rules on food. Many of the early Christian converts no doubt followed the Jewish prohibitions on pork, shellfish and other foods. Paul himself, though Jewish, was more relaxed towards food. In response to the argument that some foods were innately unclean, he decreed that 'nothing is unclean in itself'. Paul was seen by numerous Jews as a traitor to their faith. He was harried and persecuted by them.

Ultimately most of the early Christians, knowing that Christ's last supper in the presence of his disciples was a momentous event, adopted a positive attitude to food. As wine was part of the last supper, it was enthroned along with bread in the special ceremony known as the sacrament or Eucharist. To eat a meal together became the symbolic custom at early church services.

Those who had known Christ became the first leaders of the church and of course they were Jewish. Peter, once a fisherman, was the senior disciple after the death of Christ; and he is said to have led the early church in Rome. Eventually native-born Italians came to the fore. Linus, said to be a native of Tuscany, was the bishop of Rome, or the pope, not long after Nero's persecution of the Christians.

In Rome itself and in far-flung cities of the Roman Empire, mobs – with Jews sometimes taking part – rampaged against Christians. The list of martyrs grew long. As it was rare for Christians to form a majority of the population in any city or large town in the empire, they depended on the toleration accorded them by others. They would have been more tolerated if they had been less assertive. At times they did not pay sufficient homage to those Roman emperors who increasingly saw themselves as godlike.

Christianity became like a shoe in the hands of a hundred shoemakers, taking on many shapes by the year AD 300. From province to province the expanding church differed in its beliefs and rituals. A merchant and his wife who transferred from a congregation in Asia Minor to one in Italy might blink when they first saw their new pastor perform the rituals or explain his theology.

SUNDAYS, SALT AND SCRIPTURES

The present form of Christianity, the observances and holy days, emerged slowly. Sunday at first was not necessarily the Lord's day. The Jews had honoured Saturday as their day and at first the Christians tended to honour that day as the heart of their week. St Paul began to accord the place of honour to Sunday, that being the day of Christ's resurrection. When Emperor Constantine became a Christian and made the Roman Empire conform to his new faith, his law of 321 declared Sunday to be the day of worship in the city but not in the countryside. There the cows and goats had to be milked, the harvest brought in and the ground ploughed, irrespective of the day.

Easter soon became the special time in the calendar of Christians, but its exact date was not easily chosen. Along the coasts of Asia Minor, the early heart of Christendom, Easter Day was not at first on a Sunday. For years Christian theologians argued about the day when Easter should ideally fall. Their disagreement was strident in 387. In that year, in Gaul, Easter Sunday was celebrated on 18 March, in Italy it dawned exactly one month later, and in Alexandria it was even later, being celebrated on 25 April. In the seventh century one region of England was celebrating Palm Sunday on the same day that another part was celebrating Easter. The unity of Christendom was often precarious.

Many of the special days in the Christian year were latecomers. For three centuries the early churches around the shores of the Mediterranean did not celebrate Christ's birthday. Eventually the Christians sensibly seized upon the popular festivals which had long been set aside to mark the shortest day of the year in the Northern Hemisphere. Thus in Rome, 17 December had been celebrated as the pagan day of merrymaking known as Saturnalia, but that day of rejoicing was eventually commandeered by the Christians and moved to 25 December, where it was proclaimed as the birthday of Christ. Even when Rome definitely decided to celebrate the present Christmas Day, the Christians in Jerusalem adhered instead to 6 January.

Like Christ's birthday, the special day set apart for Mary, the mother of Christ, was slow to find its place in the Christian calendar. In 431 the Council of Ephesus gave Mary an honoured role; and her own day, 25 March, increasingly became known as Lady Day. As the cult of Mary grew, a minor cult developed around her own mother, Anne or Hannah; and a day called 'the conception of St Anne' was eventually honoured in the Italian city of Naples. For hundreds of years Mary was given more veneration in the eastern than in the western churches.

Christianity, a borrower as well as an initiator, slowly adapted some of its rituals from the everyday life of the Romans. For example, when a Roman baby reached its eighth day, a few grains of salt were placed on the tiny lips in the faith that the salt would drive away the demons who might otherwise harm the child. When the early Christian church was baptising new followers, it blessed a small morsel of salt and, in imitation of the Roman custom, gave it to the baptised ones. This was in keeping with the teaching of Jesus who, knowing how sparing in the use of salt were the poorer people, selected salt as a symbol for the precious and the rare. When he went into the mountains he had told his disciples: 'Ye are the salt of the earth.'

In many of the places where large numbers of Christians assembled, they sparked debates amongst themselves. They argued because they came from various parts of the Roman Empire. They argued because Christ sometimes spoke in parables and did not quite make his meaning clear to those who heard his message secondhand. They argued because they relied on those who, after Christ's death, wrote down his teachings and offered conflicting accounts of the same sermon or miracle. And sometimes Christians argued with each other because they each read into Christ's words what they themselves wished to read. And yet a thread of unity was unmistakable. Travellers usually felt at home, at least in spirit, when they entered a Christian church far from home.

For at least four centuries Christianity was like hot metal being poured from furnaces into moulds of varied shapes. Sometimes a furnace almost exploded or the fire was put out. Often the furnaces were remodelled and many times they were enlarged. The moulds were changed again and again, so that the early followers of Christ, if they had come alive again, would not have quite recognised many of the beliefs and rituals of the church which they had helped to found. They would also have been mystified by another fact: the end of the world – so imminent in their eyes and such an urgent spur to their deep beliefs – still lay in the future.

Meanwhile, the city of Rome was ceasing to be the heart of the vast empire. The empire's armies, and their procession of famous generals, were replacing the old institutions of Rome as the hub of power. Moreover that city was situated too far towards the western end of an empire whose real wealth and balance of population lay at the opposite end of the Mediterranean Sea. Accordingly in the year 285 the empire was divided for administrative ease into two: a Western Empire ruled from Milan, and the main or Eastern Empire ruled from the city of Nicomedia: it lay on the Sea of Marmara, about 100 kilometres east of the present city of Istanbul, and soon it blossomed with grand buildings.

In history many vital events are shaped by underlying forces, movements and factors, but occasionally one person almost alone changes the direction of the world. A boy who lived in the city of Nicomedia in its proudest years, when the battalions of stonemasons were almost tumbling over one another, was to be such a shaper of great events. Constantine was the son of an army officer who was to rise swiftly to become the emperor of the western half of the empire. When Emperor Constantine was killed in battle at York in England in 306, the son, barely into his twenties, was acclaimed by the army as his father's successor. Constantine proved to be a fine general. To the surprise of many, he was intensely sympathetic to Christianity. In France six years later, he was converted. In his military campaigns he henceforth carried a portable chapel which his servants could quickly install inside a tent, thus enabling divine service to be held for him and his comrades at a few minutes' notice.

Constantine believed that Christianity was intrinsically suited to be his ally. It did not wish to take over the state, having been long accustomed to a humbler role. Tending to be internationalist, it did not display the ardent nationalist strand sometimes visible in Judaism. It could fit neatly into a multiracial empire. By treating all peoples as equal, Christianity seemed well suited to an empire which consisted of Greeks, Jews, Persians, Slavs, Germans, Iberians, Romans, Egyptians and many others. Its only blemish was that it did not always pay respect to the emperor and his claims to divinity. But once Constantine became a Christian, even that blemish was automatically erased.

In the history of Christianity no single event since the crucifixion of its founder was as influential as the change of heart of the young Emperor Constantine in the year AD 312. He offered civic toleration to Christians. He restored properties that had been confiscated from them. With his mother he began to build grand churches, one of them as far away as Jerusalem.

Hitherto, Christians had constituted probably no more than one in 12 of the inhabitants of the vast Roman Empire, but now – suddenly seated in a privileged position alongside the emperor – their adherents quickly multiplied. For the first time more people within the empire attended Christian worship on Sunday than attended the synagogue on Saturday. City residents who might have once sneered at Christians found themselves wondering whether in the new religious climate they might gain secular favours or promotion if they were seen attending a Christian place of worship.

In contrast the synagogues, which sometimes had been in favour with Roman rulers, were now despised. In less than a century Jews lost the right, unless they changed their religion, to marry Christians. They lost the right to serve in the army. They could not seek converts for their religion. Here and there mobs destroyed synagogues. The godfather of Christianity was in effect declared to be illegitimate. In the earlier era, some Jews in some cities had tried to harm Christians, turning the Roman authorities against them. But now the boot was on the other foot and used more frequently and more ruthlessly.

Constantine was hardly an orthodox Christian – he

arranged that his own son be put to death – but he did not deviate from his belief that God was on his side. There was only one religion in his eyes, and those who did not subscribe to it were a threat to the empire. He became more fervent in his faith.

Constantine died in 337, and was buried in the baby city of Constantinople which he had planned. The heyday of Rome had clearly passed, and it had lost its supremacy to this new city of the east.

Neither empire, east or west, was in full control. The fighters advancing from the steppes were increasingly capable of victory. The Huns, who were probably Turkish in speech, first reached the River Don in Ukraine in 370. Eighteen years later they were camped close to the Mediterranean. Rome, accustomed to these raids by ever-changing 'barbarians', had a long history of successes against them; but now it was incapable of repelling them. Enemies coming from the far interior had no trouble entering Italy and even approaching Rome. The famous city was half-destroyed in 410 and again in 455. People fled the city which for so long had been the mecca for migrants. Rome declined with sobering speed.

The Roman civilisation was mighty, but how mighty? It inherited much from Greece and was not as imaginative as Greece. Rome was more skilled in warfare than the Greeks and more successful in imposing the first vital ingredient of a civilisation: law and order. Rome set up the vast free-trade zone or common market, and for a long period it maintained on its frontiers a relative peace, measured by the warlike standards of human history. The Romans shaped what is still called Roman law, the legal system adopted by most peoples of Europe and South America. They were probably the world's finest engineers up to that time, building impressive aqueducts that provided a safe supply of water for cities, and constructing highways which lasted for centuries.

The Romans left behind a superb literature. They handed on Latin, which remained Europe's shared language for close to 2000 years. Even at the beginning of the 20th century, Latin remained the language of prayer and ritual for the world's main Christian denomination and a second language within European lands. Furthermore, Latin is alive and eloquent through the Romance languages which dominate Central and South America, the existence of which was unknown to the Romans. Even in eastern Europe, the Romanian language uses a grammar based on Latin. Above all, the last phase of Roman history gave the official blessing to Christianity. Here was a launching pad more powerful than that available to any other major religion in the world's history.

Why did the Roman Empire eventually decline? It is one of the fascinating questions of history and open to a combination of answers, ranging from lead poisoning in Rome itself and soil exhaustion in the countryside to the rise of Christianity. The Huns and other outside raiders were significant, but their raids were successful partly because they were meeting weaker resistance. The empire largely decayed from within. Almost certainly the more important question – and just as elusive – is why the empire lasted so long. Rise and decline form the normal pattern of human institutions. It is easier to rise than to remain on top.

How remarkable that a city which by 200 BC was becoming the most powerful of the states along the Mediterranean should still be dominating western civilisation more than five centuries later. The sheer length of its dominance can be assessed more easily if transposed to a modern chronology. It is the equivalent of a nation which was dominant in most of Europe during the heyday of Columbus and still supreme in the presidency of Bush and Castro.

THE RIVAL

Constantinople was a new city arising within the old city of Byzantium. Founded by Greek colonists in the eighth century before Christ, the old town had sometimes been captured by enemies and sometimes ransacked, but it was always rebuilt. It stood on a superb triangle of land with the sea washing two sides. Commanding a vital trade route and the only entrance to the Black Sea, its position was symbolic as well as strategic, for it was on the very edge of Europe and within a short rowing distance of Asia.

To enlarge the living and building space of this

new city, outer walls were built at some distance from
the previous walls, and later the perimeter of these
walls went out even further, such was the city's swift
growth. Thick walls were needed, for the city was to
be besieged nine times between the years 600 and
1100. Meanwhile it became a marvel of the western
world – only China possessed larger cities.

Constantinople was the first city so designed as
to provide prominent sites for Christian churches.
Soon the churches were numerous. Visitors especially
wished to pray in one of the noblest buildings in the
world, the Hagia Sofia or 'Divine Wisdom'. Its dome
was rebuilt after the earthquake of 559 and the church
was to be converted nearly a millennium later into a
mosque capped by minarets.

A bishop or patriarch was consecrated in the new
city, and soon his spiritual status rivalled that of the
pope of Rome. As Constantinople held the palace
of the Roman emperor, that heightened its bishop's
status. Even in language the western and eastern
churches were separate. Greek was the language of the
eastern church, and Latin of the church of Rome. As
Rome and Constantinople were separated by a voyage
which could occupy up to a month when seas were
rough or the winds unkind, they did not always keep in
touch. Moreover Constantinople now held more than
500 000 people, whereas Rome, at the mercy of the
incoming barbarians, had so dwindled that it held no
more than one-tenth of that population.

In the course of many centuries the western and eastern churches, or the Catholic and the Orthodox, would grow apart in their theology as well as their organisation. Thus the Catholics, but not their rivals, believed in purgatory – a halfway house on the path to heaven where the more deserving of the dead received such punishment as they merited. In Orthodox churches the division between the layman and the priest was not as sharp as in Catholic churches, and moreover a married man could be ordained as a priest. In their congregations laymen could even preach, but Catholics were allowed no such privilege. In that sense the Orthodox churches had close resemblances to the Protestants who were to arise in northern Europe.

So Christianity slowly lost its unity. But diversity, in the long term, was perhaps one of its strengths. Christianity was adaptable. Easily understood but adaptable to different cultures, it brought hope – and sometimes fear – to hundreds of millions of people. Its new rival, Islam, showed those same qualities.

11

THE SIGN OF THE CRESCENT

Islam is often a puzzle. The West tends to cloud its origins in mystery. It is assumed that Islam, arising out of the land of camels and nomadic pastoralists, must be a mirror of the ideas of a simple people for whom anything larger than a tent was an unfamiliar sight. In fact Islam arose less from the desert than from walled towns. It arose less from the herders and shepherds than from merchants who were in weekly contact with the outside world. It arose less from the red windblown sands and the arid loneliness of the interior than from towns shadowed by rugged bony mountains and standing close to the sea, or towns in the centre of irrigated oases. Some of the towns of Arabia were busy ports, and many Arabians piloted a seagoing ship with as much ease as others guided a caravan of camels. They traded with India and East Africa by sea and with Asia Minor by land.

Mecca, which became the birthplace of Islam, was situated just over 60 kilometres from the Red Sea. It relied on long-distance commerce, for it stood astride the overland route which ran from the more fertile south-west of Arabia across the desert to the Mediterranean Sea. This route, served by strings of load-carrying camels, was a vital stage in one of the trade routes linking lands as far apart as India and Italy. Two of southern Arabia's traded products were the expensive myrrh and frankincense, which were used to make incense, perfume, embalming fluids, and the anointing oils used by Jewish priests. It could well be that the valuable gifts of myrrh and frankincense presented to the baby Jesus had actually been carried by camels along this desert trade route traversing the birthplace of Mecca. On the eve of the founding of Islam this overland route was flourishing, perhaps because it was a safe alternative during the long wars between Persia and Byzantium.

Mohammed, the founder of Islam, was born in Mecca in AD 570. When he was young he lost both his father and mother. Arabs, being seafarers of the desert, sometimes sent their boys or young men as apprentices with the camel-caravans that traded in far-off cities; and Mohammed went in one such caravan. At night the orphan boy learned to identify many of the stars in the brilliant night sky, and to know the hour when the moon would rise above the desert edge: the new moon would be a symbol of his faith.

Mohammed was highly intelligent and impressed his rich employer, a widow. They married when she was 40 and he was 25. She bore him two boys, who died as infants, and four daughters. It is curious to contemplate that the founder of a religion now singled out for its subjection of women owed so much to a woman. Mohammed probably could not have launched a new religion but for her financial backing at a time when he was buffeted by opponents.

As a trader and courier Mohammed travelled to distant cities where he learned much about the ideas of that outside world. He inhaled ideas from Judaism and Christianity – not in one deep breath but in many short breaths. In 610 he experienced an intense religious awakening during which he received the message that there was only one god – an idea not supported by the tribal religions of his land.

Mohammed felt that he was filled with the spirit of God. He preached his ideas with fervour: he was a powerful persuader. He made enemies too. When he began to criticise the pagan pilgrims who idolised the black sacred stone at Mecca, he was bound to make enemies. Mecca was a pilgrims' town as well as a trading town, and its economic life depended on religious tourism as well as trade. Many who came as pilgrims stayed on to trade for a few days. For Mohammed to criticise idolatry and the worship of the black stone was rather like today's mayor of Venice calling for a ban on the entry of tourists.

Mohammed knew that his prospects in Mecca were limp. In 622, after making careful plans, he fled across the coastal mountains and dry watercourses to Medina, a town less than 400 kilometres to the north. Standing amidst a large oasis of date palms and fields of irrigated cereals, it became his home. The day of his arrival, 24 September 622, was to become the first day in the new Islamic calendar. In Medina he became the secular and spiritual ruler. Whereas the early Christians had been, generation after generation, a minority possessing no political power, Islam was soon the dominant religion in its chosen town and district and the possessor of all political power.

HOLY WAR

Mohammed quietly declared war on Mecca's main merchants. He sent out forces to raid their richly laden processions of camels that passed nearby on their way to and from distant towns. In 626 he planned to attack a caravan said to consist of 1000 camels. Though Mecca learned of the plan and applied superior forces, it suffered a surprising defeat. Mecca, the larger and richer town, should have been capable of trouncing Medina; but Mohammed was a skilled general, many of his troops were enthusiasts, and he increased his military strength by making alliances with nomadic tribes, several of which were Christian. In the year 630 he captured Mecca with ease.

His creed took shape with speed and precision. Its rules were simple. The believers had to pray five times daily, facing Mecca as they prayed: the first man to call the muezzin or summons for prayer was to be a black man. The holy day was Friday, which marked out the

Mohammedans from the Jews with their worship on a Saturday and the Christians with their Sunday. Devout believers had to try to make a pilgrimage to Mecca once in their life. They had to give generously to the poor. And they had to fast between daylight and sunset in the lunar month called Ramadan. The fasting rule now seems strict, but at that time most Christians also fasted during the 40 days of the season leading up to Easter. Other rules protected worshippers of Islam from moral danger, though women were more protected than men. Women wore veils in public so that their face could not be glimpsed. On the other hand, richer men could each take four wives, and Mohammed himself in his last years also slept with Māriya, a Coptic concubine.

Islam retained, perhaps more than any other of the world's five powerful religions, a strand of the ancient pagan religions. It retained a sense of wonder at the universe and the heavens; and indeed the moon held a more distinctive place in Islam than in the other main religions. The crescent moon was often a symbol of Islam and today appears on the flags of many Islamic nations. The Islamic calendar was based on moon rather than sun; and that is why the feast of Ramadan moves on and on, and never stays for long in the same month. Perhaps the moon also had a special place in the imagination of people living in or close to desert. At night the clouds rarely hid the moon, and on a typical night the moon was the main spectacle in the night sky.

Mohammed's preachings were to be brought together in the one book, the Koran, which was written in Arabic. Poetic and often inspiring, simple and emphatic, it was the Bible of the new religion. It was far shorter than the Old Testament of the Jews and a little longer than the New Testament of the Christians, running to a total of 78 000 words. It painted the joys of the heaven waiting for true believers.

When Mohammed captured Mecca in 630 he was well on the way to unifying the long-divided Arabia. He died two years later and was buried at Medina. A mosque arose over his grave, and as a place of pilgrimage it is second only to Mecca.

Mohammed was not yet seen as the saviour of surrounding countries. But his armies began to win victory after victory far from home. The early victories were resounding. The enemies abroad began to fall just as easily as those at home. The city of Damascus was captured in 635 and Jerusalem a year later. Many Christians hoped that the loss of Jerusalem to the new and militant religion would only be temporary; but this holy city of Christianity was to be held by Islam for about 1100 of the following 1300 years.

Less than 20 years after the death of Mohammed, his religion and his sword ruled from the fringes of Afghanistan in the east to Tripoli in the west, a distance of some 5000 kilometres. The loud call to prayer could be heard on the shores of the Mediterranean, the Black Sea and the Caspian Sea, the Persian Gulf

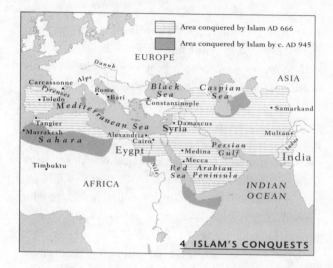

Area conquered by Islam AD 666
Area conquered by Islam by c. AD 945

EUROPE
ASIA
Danub
Carcassonne Alps
Rome
Drôme
Toledo
Mediterranean Sea
Black Sea
Caspian Sea
Bari
Constantinople
Samarkand
Tangier
Marrakesh
Sahara
Alexandria
Cairo
Damascus
Syria
Multan
Timbuktu
Medina
Mecca
Persian Gulf
Eygpt
Red Sea
Arabian Peninsula
Indus
India
AFRICA
INDIAN OCEAN

4 ISLAM'S CONQUESTS

and the Red Sea. The spearheads of Islam continued to probe in all directions. They soon reached the Strait of Gibraltar, at the gateway to the Atlantic. Far to the east they reached the mouth of the River Indus, on the Indian Ocean. The towns of Multan in the present Pakistan and Samarkand in central Asia were taken in 712; and one year later, far to the west, Seville in Spain was held by Islam.

In the ninth century nearly all the large islands in the Mediterranean became Islamic citadels – even Sicily and Sardinia, Malta and Crete. For a time the south coast of France and the heel of Italy were Islamic. Far into the Sahara desert rode the conquerors. Even the western frontier of China seemed in their grasp. Late in the 10th century the message penetrated far into

India, and eventually the skyline of the north-west and the Ganges valley – but rarely the south – was dotted with mosques. The spread of the creed into the islands of Indonesia and the Malay Peninsula was slower, and in the year 1200 nobody could have predicted what eventually came to pass: that Indonesia would be the most populous Islamic nation in the world.

Amidst almost continual triumph, one devastating blow fell on the heart of Islam. In the year 930, Mecca was entered not by the faithful but by invaders who carried away the black sacred stone to Bahrain, where it rested in exile for several decades.

Islam was not a centralised empire on the Roman pattern, but everywhere its adherents worshipped the same God and revered the same book. Moreover Arabic was its unifying language in much the same way as Latin or Greek had been for a large part of the Roman Empire. Given the communications and arms of the time, Islam's empire was too extensive to be ruled from one central city. But its creation was an extraordinary achievement and, seen in its context, dwarfed even the remarkable spread of Communism in the first half of the 20th century.

TRIUMPH IN AFRICA

Penetrating into Africa, Islam extended beyond the outer reaches of the Roman Empire. It quickly crossed the Red Sea to the shore opposite Arabia, while the prophet himself was still alive. At the same time it

penetrated but did not dominate the Christian kingdom of Nubia, which held the territory on both sides
of the upper Nile. As early as the eighth century, ports
in East Africa resounded with the call to prayer from
the little mosques. South of the Sahara desert a long
band of dry territory extending to the Atlantic Ocean
received its first Islamic merchants in the eighth
century. The Koran was spread in Africa mainly by
persuasion and example. In most of the ports and
inland trading towns it won initial converts from only a
fraction of the citizens.

The people of the desert with their herds of camels
and their moving camps were more sympathetic than
the farmers of the fertile land to the new religion. The
desert nomads found that the religion could not only
give their life a new meaning but fit neatly into their
wandering ways. In Islam a group did not necessarily
need a permanent mosque for its Friday services and
it did not need access to a priest even for a burial. For
wanderers a religion requiring no priest and no church
was highly practical.

The diffusion of the new religion and way of life was
conducted through an alien language. Arabic was the
only language of worship for Islam. Converts learned
by heart the key passages of the Koran, understand-
ing them as best they could while reciting them with
fervour. With the religion came new taboos on food.
African villages which voted a roast pig as a meal to
remember soon abandoned this delight; and some

villages where home-brewed beer was a pleasure abandoned it forever. With the religion came a host of commercial contacts. Islamic traders did business at open-air markets as far apart as Mombasa, Canton and Timbuktu.

Islam proclaimed the kinship of all peoples, but the idea did not extend fully to slaves. Islamic traders escorted female and male slaves on long journeys to the point of sale, though they rarely enslaved people of their own faith. Many of the slaves who, centuries later, were shipped to the Americas belonged to lands where Islam had long been a force; but relatively few of those slaves were fervently Islamic. So in the American plantations, Islam did not gain a firm footing, leaving the ground clear for Christianity.

12

THE WILD GEESE CROSS
THE MOUNTAINS

China was far more an importer than an exporter of religions. The new religions travelled on the silk route across Asia but not in the same direction as the silk. Rarely in the history of the world did the one road carry in the same direction, in quick succession, such a long procession of missionaries of new religions. Thus, Syrian monks and missionaries carried east the version of Christianity which was known as Nestorianism. In the Chinese city of Xi'an (Sian), the terminus of the silk road, is a handsome slab of stone which records that a Nestorian Christian missionary arrived in China in the year 635.

Jewish merchants travelled along the grass highway, and in the Chinese city of Kaifeng set up their own synagogue. It was flourishing as late as AD 1163, long after the Christian churches in western China had vanished. It was rebuilt four times in the following 500 years. By that time its small band of adherents must have lost all personal contact with the land so vividly described in the Old Testament.

Islam came along the silk route, travelling with caravans and armies. Half the road was in Islamic control by the early 700s, when even the walled city of Tashkent was an Islamic stronghold. Some Muslims in their caravans traded all the way to western China, where they eventually had more success than Christians, Jews or miscellaneous Persian sects in winning converts.

It was the Buddhists who, coming out of India, penetrated the furthest into China. A few walked up the valleys of the Ganges and Irrawaddy rivers and then passed through high country and so to the border of China. Others possibly went to China by sea. Many walked north of India and took the route through a pass in the Hindu Kush, at a height of 4000 metres, and so on to Bactria where they joined the silk route.

At first Buddhism did not expand dramatically. It was long confined to India and Sri Lanka. Then in India's north-west, centuries after the death of the Buddha, the creed recycled itself. Known as the Great Vehicle or Mahayana version of Buddhism, it was more saleable abroad and gave Buddhism a missionary appeal. It increased the prospects of ordinary people finding salvation through devotion to Buddha.

The creed did not expand in eastern Asia until the time when the young creed of Christianity began to expand in Asia Minor. Indeed the first Christian possibly reached India at about the same time as the first

Buddhist reached the river-cities of China. By AD 65 Buddhism had won a tiny foothold in China. It was so different to the prevailing Confucianism in its attitudes, so revolutionary in its belief in the reincarnation of human beings in another body at the instant of their death, that the two creeds seemed unlikely to coexist. But the Indian creed sat down quietly, as a rule, alongside the older doctrines of Confucianism and Taoism. In the following three centuries, millions of Chinese were happy to accept the precepts taught by Buddhist monks as well as those handed down by Confucianism and the popular Taoism. It was as if Buddhism were simply the new, expanding department in the religious supermarket of China.

Early Buddhists in India did not wish to move mountains: they mostly accepted the mountains. In China the new version of Buddhism was more activist. At their new monasteries the Chinese monks used slaves – slavery was an accepted institution in China as in India – to clear away forests and cultivate new soil. The monks' willingness to teach the rudiments of reading to the villagers, and even their inclination to act as pawnbrokers and banks, altered social and economic life in many regions.

Buddhism not only generated economic energy but also inspired contemplation and mysticism. Chinese nature-poets emerged. Hsieh Ling-Yun, an aristocratic playboy and bureaucrat who was virtually sent into exile in AD 422, settled down on his rural estate, almost surrounded by rivers, about 500 kilometres from Nanjing. A student of Buddhism, he now had time to ponder problems in theology. He also began to absorb the spirit of the countryside as he climbed the rock faces in his special walking boots. Alternating between melancholy and jubilation, he spelled out his moods in verse. That his poetry was revered in China some 1400 years before Wordsworth and the nature-poets became famous in England was a sign that many Chinese already viewed the landscape as a kind of mystical temple. Into that mood Buddhism fitted with ease.

The devout Buddhists erected grand monuments. Along the wide rippling river at Luoshan (Lo-shan), opposite dangerous rapids, one comes across a gargantuan statue of the Buddha, carved in the red face of the cliff and standing 71 metres in height, or as tall as a 20-storey building. The carving, begun in 685, was probably intended to be the largest in the known world. Seen from the river on a day of autumn mist, it resembles the face of a huge pilot, ready to guide the riverboats.

In the western city of Xi'an can still be seen the tall octagonal tower sometimes known as the Big Wild Goose Pagoda: in early Chinese poetry the migration of the wild geese was treated as an auspicious sign. European traders arriving in Xi'an for the first time must have mentally compared the pagoda with some of the noble triumphal columns which had survived from the Roman Empire: in height and ornamentation the Big Wild Goose Pagoda was the more impressive.

In China the largest of the Buddhist pagodas displayed that same soaring quality as the later Gothic cathedrals would exhibit in western Europe. It was as if the builders had delicately raised one umbrella, and then unfurled another smaller umbrella and placed it on top, and so, floor after floor, the tower rose, reaching a height of 11 or even 13 storeys. In fact some pagodas were built from the top down, a wooden frame having first been constructed. The interlocking beams used to support the tall building were a Chinese invention. To worshippers walking home from a day in the rice fields, a tapering pagoda must have been an inspiring sight.

The creed made more headway in China than any other outside creed, and was the most influential teacher of the Chinese for an unbroken period extending for about 800 years. Buddha was not always in favour but his influence was enduring. The last of the Chinese emperors, early in the 20th century, was a follower of the Tibetan branch of Buddhism.

BUDDHISM ON THE MARCH

During its first millennium as a religion, Buddhism extended further from its birthplace than did Christianity in a similar span of time. Buddhism reached lower Burma before AD 300, and Java and Korea before 400. By the 600s one of the kings of Sumatra was a Buddhist and the town of Palembang, a centre of Chinese trade, was much influenced by Buddhists coming from both China and India.

Japan, not yet a united country, was almost like blotting paper in the way it absorbed a variety of Chinese influences, including architecture, painting, poetry, law and religion, but it was also quick to modify them when appropriate. Buddhism became dynamic in Japan at the very time when Islam was dynamic on the far side of Asia. By the end of the seventh century Japan was becoming a Buddhist land.

Nara, a new capital city built in imitation of Chinese cities, became virtually a city devoted to Buddha. Emperor Shomū was already sympathetic to the religion when in 737 his country was hit by an epidemic. The smallpox proved to be more devastating for the Japanese than the Black Death was to be for the Europeans. The emperor, turning for comfort and guidance to the Enlightened One, ordered the construction of a magnificent bronze statue, the Great Buddha of Nara, which still stands upright.

The emperor instructed every province to build a monastery and a nunnery. Temples spread to every corner of the land. In 749, after surrendering his throne to his daughter, the emperor himself became a priest. Although the local Shinto shrines did not easily surrender their domination to Buddha, by AD 800 the two creeds were becoming allies, and Shinto shrines even carried echoes of Buddhism in their architecture.

In eastern Asia, Buddhism depended, like any

imported religion, on royal approval. In China, Japan and Korea that approval was sometimes withdrawn and then it was renewed. In the ninth century in China, Buddhists, who for long had been the favoured ones, were often persecuted. A century later the Japanese city of Kyoto, which was now the royal capital, permitted no land in its gridlike streets to be set aside for Buddhist temples. Later the temples were permitted. In Korea the creed flourished in the 14th century, but in 1393 the tide turned, and huge landholdings of the monasteries were redistributed. And yet the Buddhists remained tenacious even in adversity, and occasionally they became the favourites again.

Here and there in eastern Asia the Buddhists established huge monasteries, some with as many as 7000 members and nearly all serving as dispensers of charity and resting places for travellers. The Buddha inspired such monumental buildings as the temple built in sombre stone in the early 800s at Borobudur near the south coast of Java, and the temple built at Angkor in Cambodia in the early 1100s. He inspired a religious devotion which he himself would probably have disowned; and his relics became prized possessions. In Burma the capital city is dominated by the gold dome of the temple Shwedagon; and worshippers climb the steps to the top terrace where they are close to the holiest of relics – a cluster of eight hairs from the head of the Buddha.

For centuries Buddhism was like a flock of wild geese that soared out of India and, landing safely in almost every part of eastern Asia, flourished and multiplied. But when its dominance seemed secure, Islam made a successful assault. It moved into the Malay Peninsula and captured most of the Indonesian islands: an early sign of Islam's presence in the Indonesian archipelago is a tombstone found in eastern Java and carved in about the year 1082. Islam swept through the southerly part of the Philippines. The combined success of Buddhism and Islam in eastern Asia, in places so far from home, was a sign of how the world was shrinking appreciably even before the Europeans discovered their own sea lanes to the outside world.

THE TRIUMPHANT THREE

The three crusading universal religions, capable of converting a diversity of lands and peoples, had been born during a special phase of human history. Buddha, Christ and Mohammed arose in a period spanning a little more than 1000 years. The first creed – Buddhism – appeared in about the fifth century before Christ and the last – Islam – emerged in the seventh century after Christ. Since then no new version of a universal religion has achieved wide success.

These world religions reflected a transition from a belief that God was predominantly a symbol of fear to a conviction that love was divine. They embodied a heightened sense of humanity. None of these religions was ever likely to be the monopoly of one race. Admittedly, Judaism was in part a universal religion, being itself the parent of two of the far-spreading religions, but in most periods it did not actively seek converts.

Merchants who traded between cities were initially more likely than the countryside to welcome the new religions. These creeds emphasised trust at a time when the merchants in strange lands needed a climate of trust in which contracts and word-of-mouth agreements could be honoured. The early followers of Buddha were often merchants. Mohammed too was a merchant. Christianity was first disseminated far from its homeland by Jews, many of whom were merchants in strange lands. Though Christ drove the money merchants out of the temple in Jerusalem, it was because they were in the wrong place rather than because they pursued an unworthy occupation. Many of his sympathetic parables about the daily dilemmas of the farmer and shepherd suggest that he was not hostile to business enterprise. As a carpenter or the son of a carpenter, he knew the mercantile world.

The ultimate success of these religions in new lands owed most to the devout and the selfless who were willing to give their lives, or lose their lives, for the sake of the cause. Whether a religion spreads to a new land also depends on whether the ruler is eager to welcome it. The universal religions especially appealed to emperors trying to govern peoples lacking social cohesion. Buddhism and Christianity, which were still struggling after several centuries of faithful preaching, owed much of their subsequent success to the conversion of two mighty emperors, Asoka of India and Constantine of Rome. A king of a large domain was likely to welcome a religion which made his subjects feel content with their simple and sometimes harsh daily life.

By the year 900 the three universal religions had penetrated, between them, most of the known world. Only the American continent, southern Africa, New Guinea, Australia and very remote islands were beyond their reach. Of these three religions, the youngest was perhaps the most vigorous; and with the aid of Arab traders Islam was tapping a vast area of South-East Asia. On the other hand, the oldest of the religions, Buddhism, was influencing the largest number of lives because of its strength in populous China, Korea, Japan and Indochina. Though it had almost exhausted its influence in its Indian homelands, it was still tapping new regions.

Christianity was now the least lively of the three. It held parts of north-eastern Africa and Asia Minor but won few converts in Asia proper. In Europe it was dominant nearly all the way from Ireland to Greece but had lost ground to Islam along the Mediterranean and had failed to penetrate the cold north. It had failed to convert Sweden and Denmark. Other evangelists had made little headway in Russia.

Every major religion relied much on the support of strong secular rulers; but the rulers of Christian Europe were not as powerful as they had been in the era of the Roman Empire. A major religion also relied, for expansion opportunities, on those of its adherents who were merchants and, trading far from home, spread the word or prepared the way for missionaries. In the year 900, however, the Christian merchants of Europe were hemmed in by Islam on one side and by the unknown Atlantic Ocean on another.

If there had been, in the year 900, a few wise observers with wide knowledge of the known world, and if they had been asked which of the major religions seemed to hold the future in its hands, they would not have pointed to Christianity. It was mainly anchored to the stagnating civilisation of Europe; and yet, almost miraculously, its prospects were to be transformed six centuries later.

13

TOWARDS POLYNESIA

The world was still partitioned into hundreds of tiny worlds that were almost self-contained. While Europe and China each formed large worlds, with traffic flowing between them, Africa and the Americas and Australasia consisted of numerous small and isolated worlds: there, a small group typically had little or no direct contact with people living only 1000 kilometres away. In parts of the globe a gap of that width, especially if it was a sea-gap, was really a chasm.

At times the chasm was leaped over, and such leaps had vital consequences for the human race. In the whole of human history there have been only three important leaps across the oceans in order to settle major uninhabited lands. One was the migration, more than 50 000 years ago, from Asia to New Guinea and Australia. Another was the migration from Asia to Alaska more than 20 000 years ago, followed by the slow settling of the whole American continent. The third, in very recent times, was the migration of Polynesian peoples to a long ribbon of uninhabited islands in the Pacific and Indian oceans. It is a mark of how recent this migration was that it took place in the Christian era, though the migrants themselves had not heard the name of Christ.

The Polynesians' voyages across the ocean to new lands were amongst the most remarkable migrations in human history. Some of their voyages were more courageous than that which Christopher Columbus was to make across the Atlantic in 1492. Indeed there is a strange similarity between the procession of Polynesian navigators and the voyages of Columbus. The one left China in search of new lands. The other left Europe in search of China.

The slow migration to the islands began in tropical and wooded southern China. Maybe it was in about 4000 BC that adventurous settlers began to cross the straits to the rugged island of Taiwan. Many seafarers must have died while attempting such a dangerous voyage. Once ashore they established their way of life, presumably as farmers and as fishers. They made their own stone tools; they knew how to make the kind of pottery then commonly used in China; and they probably kept pigs, chickens and dogs. That they were skilled in sailing goes without question. Their chosen vessel, at least by the time they approached the central Pacific many centuries later, was the outrigger canoe. With a hull in the middle, and logs arranged parallel to the hull and roped tightly to it, these outriggers stabilised the vessel in rough seas.

Their succession of voyages went slowly east, in fits and starts, from island to island. In the following thousand years these seafaring peoples reached the islands of the Philippines, patches of which they cleared for gardening. Further voyages carried their descendants to Borneo, Sulawesi and Timor, to Sumatra and Java, all of which were in the process of being settled by the year 2000 BC. Many of these settlements were on new islands but some were in areas which had long been settled. There the existing inhabitants were either defeated in war, reduced by new diseases, driven into the less favourable hills or simply absorbed into the ranks of the invading peoples.

In explaining such a persistent outward movement of peoples it is tempting to offer simple explanations. Perhaps they were reacting to overpopulation, perhaps they were occasionally driven to seek new homes by volcanoes, earthquakes, typhoons or other natural disasters. No single explanation is sufficient. A variety of factors propelled these Chinese-like people, just as many influences drove the first European settlers to North America. Being seafarers, they probably shunned the thought of living in the hills, far from the sea, and instead sought other bays and coastal valleys where they could both fish and grow their crops. In any locality the number of underpopulated bays and beaches was limited, and so the incentive to emigrate to a new island or coastline was frequent.

The voyages of these people crammed in their sailing canoes followed a kind of logic. Venturing in an easterly direction they were likely to discover islands, settled or unsettled, with a tropical climate and a vegetation like that which they had just left behind. In the early phase of migration the winds were also favourable. The monsoons, based on the region's proximity to the big landmass of Asia and its seasonal cooling and warming, enabled the seafarers to travel south or north or east or west, so long as they were content to remain relatively close to the equator. Geography smiled on them. It had arranged islands to the east, thousands of them, like a path of stepping stones. Many could be seen from high hills by the naked eye, while others were found only by a blind voyage.

The slow route of equatorial migration reached the long-inhabited island of New Guinea, occupying a few coastal fringes about 1600 BC, and then entered a region of tropical islands where no human beings lived. By 1200 BC the brown sails of their boats were in harbour-villages of New Caledonia, Tonga, Fiji, the Solomon Islands and Samoa. By AD 500, their boats were seen around Hawaii and Easter Island. In distance travelled along an east–west line – the combined total of voyage after voyage made generation after generation – it was the equivalent of a journey on land from Europe to China, spread over more than 4000 years. Later these navigators doubled back and discovered the remote islands of New Zealand.

Along a line of islands that formed a kind of Milky Way across the Pacific, these sailors left behind eloquent evidence of their origins. Even today, all the way from isolated parts of the mountains of Taiwan to Easter Island and Pitcairn Island in the east, the Austronesian family of languages survives.

For the Polynesians to find volcanic Easter Island was a special triumph. It was merely a dot in the ocean, 1600 kilometres from the nearest inhabited land. Once heavily timbered, it became so deforested by the new settlers that in the end its imposing landmarks were not old trees but stone statues, about 600 in all. One statue – never completed – was 20 metres high. In language and society the Easter Islanders were Polynesian; but their statues and their script suggest an additional ancestry or influence.

The Polynesians ranged from tribes living uneasily one with another to strong monarchies governing many islands. Hawaii, with perhaps 200 000 or more people, was largely a monarchy by the time of the arrival of the first Europeans. Some of these Polynesian monarchs, like their counterparts in western Europe, believed they were of divine descent.

During this long chain of migration other explorers reached the large uninhabited island of Madagascar. To the north-east of Madagascar the unbroken sea stretched to the Indonesian archipelago, some 5000 kilometres away. From Indonesian islands the first settlers of Madagascar almost certainly came.

Even today their language, Malagasy, belongs to the Malayo-Polynesian group. The language spoken today in Madagascar has more affinity with speech in far-away Borneo than with speech in adjacent Africa.

The first voyage to Madagascar took place when the city of Rome was in fast decline, in about AD 400. It was made just when, almost half a world to the east, other Polynesians were first settling on Easter Island. The voyage to Madagascar was aided by the north-east monsoon. To stand on the palm-dotted beach in Madagascar and see the waves of the Indian Ocean lazily breaking on the coral reefs is to envisage the brown matting sails coming slowly into view, a small Indonesian boat or two bobbing on the ocean swell. Everyone on those approaching boats must have eagerly or anxiously viewed the surf frothing just ahead, and the jungle in the hilly background; and they must have wondered if they could reach land before their boats were broken by the surf and reef.

Madagascar and New Zealand were the last two size-able areas of habitable land to be discovered and settled by the human race. Perhaps Madagascar was the more important of the two, for in area it was more than twice as large as New Zealand. Triumphs in the history of human seafaring, both were part of a saga of discovery and migration which was virtually completed by AD 1000.

LAND OF THE MOA

From the sea the fortified villages of the early Maoris must have been easily visible. Some occupied narrow headlands and so were surrounded on three sides by the sea – their first line of defence. The steep and often perpendicular climb from the beach or the sea rocks to the fort was the second line of defence. The third and even higher line of defence was a well-constructed fence with stout posts sunk into the ground at regular intervals and between the posts a line of tall wooden pickets. The picket fence went right around the fortified village or *pa*.

On the upper levels of the village were wooden houses of residence with here and there a storehouse. The storehouses were on platforms so that rats could not steal the food: an occasional pit covered by a low roof also served as a store for vegetables. The houses themselves with their sloping thatched roofs had no walls and let in the sea breeze. In the event of a surprise attack these fortified villages formed a fine defence but they were incapable of withstanding a siege, for as a rule they had no wells, springs or sure supplies of permanent fresh water. Even firewood had to be carried from afar.

On the North Island, the home of the *pa*, the sites of about 5000 forts have been identified. The terraces have eroded and the palisades have tumbled down and rotted away and the bush and creepers and grasses have reclaimed the site, but from a distance the out-line of a fort – like a small open cut with its series of benches or terraces – can sometimes be seen.

A wide radius of countryside was needed to support

each tribe or village with food. Gardens were dug with a long wooden stick rather like a crowbar in shape, the topsoil was heaped into neat rows with a wooden spade and the raised soil was planted with vegetable tubers. Kumara was the most valued of these vegetables. Like a very long yam or sweet potato, slightly nobbly with an outer skin of reddish-pink, the kumara was planted on a day dictated by the phase of the moon.

For the early settlers one prize was waiting. Meat was in unbelievable abundance. On the South and North islands the tall moa bird, able to run swiftly but unable to fly, was easily caught by the hunting Maoris. Growing to a height of about 3 metres, with powerful thighs for running but with a head that could not easily damage human hunters, the moa resembled a genial pack animal. Its back was so straight and long that if it had been tamed it could have carried four or more little children sitting in a row.

The Maoris themselves hunted the moa with such vigour that by AD 1400 or 1500 the species was almost extinct. The long-winged eagles that preyed on the moa chicks were also doomed. They were no longer to be seen soaring in flight when the first European settlers arrived.

Possessing no pottery, the Maoris used the outer shell of the large gourd that in summer grew from vines trailing along the roof of their houses or across the planted gardens. They had no herds and no pigs, their only domesticated animal being the dog. Stone had to serve instead of metal, and was shaped or manufactured with artisan skills that were probably as fine as those required by metalworkers. Sources of toolmaking stone were found, and specimens of stone were quarried and then carried long distances on foot and by canoe to those regions which lacked suitable stone. One of the large Maori grinding-stones, transported from the beach to the floor of the museum in Auckland, today draws clusters of admirers.

Most Europeans who saw the Polynesians, when their way of life was suddenly about to change, were impressed by their courage. Observers also noted the Polynesians' violence: the human sacrifices and the cannibalism. The Maoris' flair in warfare was beyond dispute; so much so that when in the 1780s the British government had to decide whether to plant a settlement in Australia or New Zealand – a decision of profound importance to that part of the world – it selected Australia. The Maoris seemed fearless, and were proven fighters. It was wise to leave them alone.

PART TWO

SIGNPOST

A host of Christians expected Christ to return, or the world to come to a dramatic end, in the year 1000. Instead, life went on, and the new millennium began and proceeded. This would be the most remarkable of all the 1000-year periods that had run their course since the human race first left its African homeland. It would be remarkable not only for the quickening pace of change but for the recovery of the lost worlds.

All the human tribes had been loosely linked before the last powerful rising of the seas. A long chain of human contact, an unbroken chain of nomadic settlements, crossed Asia to Europe and Africa; and it was conceivable that a new idea arising along the Yellow River might eventually reach, 1000 years later, the Niger and the Nile.

Thereafter these human settlements were broken into large fragments. Virtually all contact ceased. Large populations of humans were quarantined by the rising seas. By the year AD 1000, the Americas had experienced more than a dozen millennia in which they were isolated from Asia and Europe. The continent of Australia had experienced long isolation from Asia. In the new millenium all these isolated places, and many more, were one by one to be reunited with the dynamic world-hub situated in Europe, Asia and North Africa.

The most unexpected part of this process of redis-covery was its source. It was initiated by a backward part of the world. The Atlantic shores of Europe were to send out most of the ships which found the lost world. Even more unexpected, one part of the lost world – North America – was to rise to become the new global leader at the end of that millennium.

14

THE MONGOLS

In human history the ocean was sometimes an insuperable obstacle to contact between remote peoples, while at other times the vast stretches of land were more of a barrier. What the sailing ships achieved in transport on the ocean, the horses achieved on at least one landmass. They slowly converted into a rough highway that wide transcontinental corridor of east–west grassland and mountain separating the contrasting civilisations of eastern Asia and the Mediterranean.

Occasionally the people of the steppes burst like a rocket upon the well-armed worlds at each end of the corridor. Several of their victories were remarkable. A westerly group, the Huns, stormed west and made the dying Roman Empire quake with fear. Nearly 1000 years later an easterly group, the Mongols, combining bravery and cruelty and a touch of genius, conquered the largest territory ever held by one ruler up to that time.

The Mongols' early homeland lay well to the north of the silk route. At one time they probably lived near

Lake Baikal, on the borders of eastern Siberia and what is now the Mongolian People's Republic. In about the 10th century they moved from northern Manchuria to eastern Mongolia. Later they gave their name to a dozen other nomadic peoples who joined them in the great conquest. The Mongols and their neighbours and rivals rarely if ever sowed a crop, they knew no irrigation, and they were not even settled peoples.

The families traditionally inhabiting these Mongolian steppes moved their livestock from pasture to pasture according to the changing seasons. They owned the sheep, goats, cattle and horses but the land itself was owned collectively by larger groups. When the time came to move camp to summer or winter quarters, the oxen usually pulled the cart on which the heavy woollen tents were loaded. Possessing no large towns, their population in total was small.

The animals were their capital, their main source of wealth. Reluctant to eat into their capital, the Mongols preferred as much as possible to live off the dividends which came in the stream of milk. From the milk of their cows, sheep and goats they made butter, at least four varieties of cheese, the yoghurt now so popular in the west, a dried cream called *urum*, and a distilled liquor called *airak*. Even the hardy fast-galloping mares yielded their milk, which, fermented, was drunk with relish.

At first sight it was not an environment which would equip a people, few in number, for the task of toppling proud and populous civilisations. But the men used horses with flair, fired iron-tipped arrows with accuracy as they rode, and could cover a vast terrain with speed. The women were competent as managers when the men were away on fighting or raiding expeditions; and indeed the women had a status which surprised many Chinese. In some ways the Mongols could be compared with the Vikings, who flourished a little earlier. What one people did at sea the other did on land. Both came from a harsh climate and thinly peopled territory, which is not necessarily an advantage but becomes one if, next door, lives a rich and populous empire which grows complacent and a little flabby.

THE MONGOLS ARE COMING!

Every shrewd emperor of China saw advantages in enticing the nomads to fight amongst themselves. In the 12th century they were as divided as they were to be united in the following century. In 1206, however, Genghis Khan, the chieftain of the Mongols, miraculously united these riders of the steppes. All clans or groups gave him loyalty: he had already killed or cowed those most likely to be disloyal. A magnetic leader, he was said by some to possess mystical powers. With a mounted army of close to 130 000 men and a network of spies in enemy territory, he began to conquer. Thousands of his cavalrymen rode with a spare horse or two by their side so they could replace a tired horse if a long journey lay ahead.

Genghis Khan moved so quickly that surprise was often his weapon. He occasionally used the new invention of gunpowder if he had to besiege a fortified town. Often he offered a city the chance to surrender. The price of surrender was one in every ten of the city's people and one-tenth of its wealth; and so his slaves and conscripted soldiers and wealth multiplied. Cities that did not surrender were besieged or stormed. Massacre and butchery were the Mongols' trademark. They became so feared that they often found themselves pursuing the backs of the enemy.

Ruthless but intelligent vandalism was another of their weapons. They would destroy the irrigation systems that were the lifeline of many farmlands or lay waste to the land surrounding a besieged city so that its roadsides and fields were strewn with corpses. When advancing towards the walls of a well-defended city the Mongols would sometimes compel their prisoners of war to go ahead of them and form a human shield. And yet the Mongol leaders also enforced a strict discipline among their own people.

The Great Wall of China was merely another hurdle for the Mongols to overcome. They captured Peking in 1215 and eventually made it the capital of China. To the south lay a huge area of country still in Chinese hands, and the Mongols slowly subdued it. To occupy China, the most advanced nation in the world materially, was almost the equivalent of a central African nation today occupying the United States and

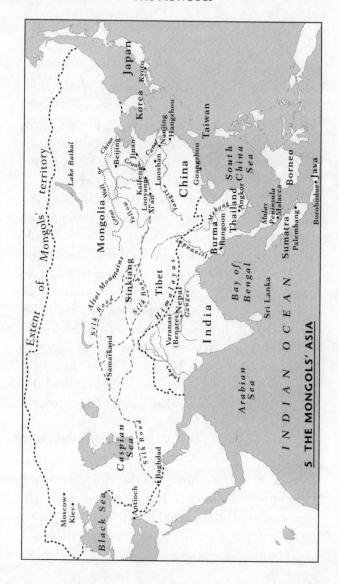

5 THE MONGOLS' ASIA

replacing Washington as capital. In contemplating the Mongols, one conclusion is beyond dispute. There had been no conquest like it in recorded history.

At the other end of Asia the Mongols were almost as remarkable. They captured a succession of Islamic cities that had felt secure behind their high walls. Even Baghdad fell to them. By the end of the 13th century the Mongol Empire stretched from the banks of the Danube to the fishing villages of Hong Kong.

While Genghis Khan achieved in less than 20 years what the Romans as conquerors had taken centuries to achieve, the two conquests cannot easily be compared. The Mongols, when advancing west of China, fought their way across a vast expanse of Asia holding few people. Their main targets were walled cities, crucial river crossings and mountain passes which had to be won at all costs. In effect they had to capture a scatter of small dots or islands in a vast sea. One of their targets was the rich and well-defended city of Hangchow (now Hangzhou), the largest city in the world and the home of close to one million people. The Mongols captured it.

It may well be that the winning of an empire is more easily accomplished on land than on sea. The victories of Genghis Khan and Alexander the Great over a huge area of land, and even the main victories of Napoleon and Hitler, were aided by the fact that they did not primarily have to cope with the temperamental sea. A substantial seafaring city or kingdom was not so easily conquered. The sea was often its ally. When a huge enemy navy appeared in sight, all was not lost. Local knowledge was a vital asset to the defender. An invading fleet, riding the waves or anchoring off a coast which offered no sheltering harbour and winds which were unfamiliar, was highly vulnerable.

The sea tended to favour the defender. Thus if the cities of Samarkand and Peking, Herat and Kiev had been on the coast and not in the interior, and had to face the rampaging Mongols who arrived in fleets, they might have defended themselves with more success. To make such a comment is to place a land invasion in perspective and not to rob the Mongols of their glory.

One of the Mongols' first achievements was to bring law and order to the long silk road: never before had it been under the control of one ruler. They even built new cuttings in high ground and a bridge here or there, with staging camps and simple hostelries along the way where merchants, their servants and pack animals could camp for the night. All kinds of cargoes came through, and it is recorded that between 1366 and 1397 the slave market in the Italian city of Florence sold 257 slaves, mostly young women, who had been brought along that road.

The safety of the road became a legend. It was said that travellers could even journey by night, presumably when the full moon was shining. Ironically the road, busier than ever, was not quite so important to Europe, for its own silkworm farmers were now flourishing in the shade of the mulberry groves. Moreover the sea route to Chinese ports from the Middle East and India was now competing strongly with the overland caravans.

THE WANING OF CHINA'S
SCIENTIFIC STAR

A beehive of inventiveness, China still had much to teach the west. It had probably the most skilled farmers in the world even though some regions were backward. New breeds of rice were found by experiment, including one that resisted drought and an early-maturing rice that enabled an additional crop to be planted each year. The war against agricultural pests was ingenious.

In the art of communicating, the most momentous event since the invention of writing was slowly beginning in China. Paper was being manufactured and the art of printing, using signs cut into wooden blocks, was being improved. Their oldest book dates from 868. The printing of a book instead of writing it out by hand was a wonderful opportunity to spread the message of Buddhism and also the precepts of Confucius, which every candidate for the civil service had to know. In 1273 a handbook for farmers and growers of raw silk was printed, and soon 3000 copies were in circulation at a time when in Italy the same task would have called for a monastery full of monks to give up a whole year in order to write out the copies by hand.

In designing waterways the Chinese were masters. Whereas the Romans had been the masters of the aqueduct or elevated stone canal that conveyed fresh water to the cities, the Chinese were masters of the boat canal that crossed uneven terrain. China's Grand Canal, like its Great Wall, was built over many centuries. A Japanese monk visiting China in AD 838 was astonished to see a convoy of barges slowly sailing along the canal, with some of the barges lashed together so that they sailed three abreast, and the whole convoy being dragged by two water buffalo plodding along the bank. The canal carried grain from the farmlands, especially around the Yangtze River, to feed large cities.

As China possessed in abundance the three ingredients of gunpowder – sulphur, saltpetre and charcoal – it is not surprising that it discovered this explosive. A Chinese work of 1044 contains three different recipes for making military gunpowder, and almost certainly it was used from time to time in the following century.

Several techniques for the building and sailing of ships almost certainly came from China, though some were used more effectively, and improved upon, in western Europe. Suspension bridges made of iron chains were built in China long before England made its famous iron bridge early in the industrial revolution. Five years before the arrival in England of William the Conqueror, a pagoda was made of cast iron in Hubei province: it still stands. In 1400 an observer with the gift of acute foresight might have thought that China was rushing, ahead of England, towards the world's first industrial revolution; but soon the rush was to slow down to a crawl.

In medicine and health the Chinese were vigorous in trying new remedies but also tenacious in clinging to old remedies, especially in herbal medicine, which was probably the main avenue of healing. Many of the Chinese used toothpaste and a cleaning brush – items unknown in Europe. Chinese physicians glimpsed the hazardous diseases which surrounded certain occupations – how the sharp dust raised by the drilling of holes in the underground mines weakened the lungs of the miners, how silversmiths inhaled the mercury they used in their craft, and how the cooks who constantly inspected the fire burning in their pastry ovens slowly impaired their own eyesight. In anatomy, too, Chinese scholars made advances.

Liberty in China, as almost everywhere, was rationed. Even in AD 1200 several million Chinese were slaves. Some had been captured in war and enslaved; many were hereditary slaves presented as gifts to the Buddhist monasteries where they worked for the remainder of their life. Others were children or even adults who had been sold into slavery by a starving family.

The misfortune for the Chinese was that, having led for long in many branches of technology, they were

hot and cold, inventive and lethargic, in that one technique which proved to be the gateway to the future.
They failed at sea. True, they invented the compass,
but they had no persistent desire to sail into the
unknown. They were skilled makers of maps but their
best maps were of their own small-scale farming districts. A map of the globe was of little interest to them,
for they believed that the fertile plains of China were
the centre of the earth, an oriental Garden of Eden,
and that everything far from those plains was of lesser
importance.

Chinese scientists still believed that the earth
was flat with a definite rim long after that comfort-
ing idea had disappeared in Europe. They could see
no point in the tantalising theory – increasingly held
in Europe – that by travelling west rather than east,
a European ship would eventually reach China. For
Chinese navigators in 1492, the corollary of that idea
was that, by sailing east, they would eventually reach
western Europe. If the Chinese had held that idea,
their big ships might have set forth and discovered the
west coast of the Americas long before the east coast
was found by Columbus. But they did not believe the
earth was round.

The Chinese showed high skills in the art of ship-
building. In the years between 1405 and 1430, their
admiral Zheng He supervised major voyages in large
ships to distant lands. His Chinese fleet, when exploring far from home, mostly visited well-known ports

in Asia and the Indian Ocean. Whether it could be called exploration in the Columbus spirit is dubious, and in any case the voyages ceased. Already coastal shipping was curtailed in China; and the widened Grand Canal was used rather than the sea coast for north–south transport. Remarkably, the Chinese shunned the sea, on which they were experts, at the very time when western Europe was embarking on distant oceans with startling results.

15

THE PERILS OF CLIMATE
AND DISEASE

A warm period intervened during the Middle Ages, and the two centuries between the years 1000 and 1200 were perhaps as warm as the 1990s were to be in northern Europe. Harvests were scythed on lands which once had been seen as not worth ploughing, so frail were the summers. Vineyards flourished beyond the present limit of grape-growing. Even the far north of England made drinkable wine.

The island of Iceland was settled during the first hint of a warmer period. Lying on the edge of the Arctic Circle but gaining from the warmth of the Gulf Stream, it was settled by a few holy men from Ireland and then in 874 by Vikings from Norway. The Vikings were shaking northern Europe at the very time that the Islamic Arabs were stirring the Mediterranean and the Maoris were settling New Zealand. While the Vikings' warlike raids are renowned, their peaceful settlements were also effective; and eventually Viking towns and districts extended from the trading towns of Kiev and Novgorod in Russia all the way to coastal France, Scotland and Ireland, the Orkney islands, the Isle of Man and Iceland.

Even icy Greenland, the largest island in the world, seemed to be a prize where, in these warmer years, Vikings might graze their sheep and smoke the fish they caught at sea. In the year 985, tiny ships set sail from Iceland to Greenland with some 400 settlers as well as sheep and goats, cows and horses, and probably bundles of hay. Most were Norwegians, but there was a contingent of Irish too. Landing on the more southerly coast of Greenland, the settlers thrived in the increasingly warm weather. In summer they cut the long grass, let it dry in rows of stooks and stacked it in haysheds, enabling livestock to eat well during the dark winter.

The population of Greenland grew to 4000 or 5000 in less than a century and a half. The small Viking republic eventually possessed a nunnery and a monastery along with 16 churches and a cathedral presided over by the bishop of Greenland. It was the kind of busy settlement of which its founding families were proud: it seemed likely to last for 10 000 years.

Greenland and Iceland were stepping stones across the cold North Atlantic. America was the next stepping stone. The first European landings on the American continent were made by Viking expeditions just when Greenland was settled. Women went with the settlers to Newfoundland, and one expedition and its two ships were said to have been led by the woman Freydis, who used the axe as a personal weapon against her enemies.

Nothing came from these settlements. The American Indians had no reason to welcome the Vikings. The terrain, except for furs, had no commodity that would excite traders. If Christopher Columbus, five centuries later, had discovered that same coast instead of stepping ashore in the balmy West Indies, he would be no more remembered than the Vikings who built huts and grazed livestock on the shores of Newfoundland.

The warm seasons, after only a couple of centuries, began to alter. Even the Mediterranean island of Crete entered a colder phase in about the year 1150. In Germany and England the cold arrived maybe one century later, and most years between 1312 and 1320 were not only cold but also unusually wet. As much of the grain had to be set aside as seed for the next year's sowing, a poor harvest imposed starvation on many people. In 1316 maybe one in 10 of the people of Ypres died of starvation or malnutrition. Here and there, human flesh was eaten.

Religious processions held in western France reflected the poor seasons. Some included numerous emaciated, barefooted people, a few of whom were almost naked. Lean harvests affected the supply of cheap clothes as well as cheap food, for poor people made their linen from the flax plant, which was also affected by poor seasons. Indeed, land which was normally used to grow flax might be desperately needed for the growing of grain.

As the decades passed, the climate of Greenland and the North Atlantic grew chillier. The barns which once were filled with hay now had gaps. Only three bundles of hay were gathered where once were four or five. Ships approaching from Europe or Iceland found packs of ice drifting in places where the sea was usually open. The colonists of Greenland waited in vain for the old-time summers which their ancestors had talked of. Farms and churches were abandoned. The young were few and a wedding became a rarity. In 1410 the surviving settlers went aboard waiting ships and sailed for Iceland and Norway. The European foothold on this cold land had lasted for more than 400 years. It was the equivalent of the Australian port of Sydney being settled in 1576 by Elizabethan England and then abandoned in the year 2000 because of deteriorating climate.

The phase of warmer climate had increased the rate of growth of population in Europe. Between 1000 and 1250 it grew rapidly. Then came cool years, leaner harvests and a slower growth of population. There were more years of famine and more chances of epidemics. Europe was probably ripe for the Black Death.

THE BLACK DEATH

The Black Death of 1348 was not unique. It must have struck centuries earlier in Asia or Africa, but it left behind no detailed record of its casualties. A similar epidemic hit the Roman Empire between AD 165 and

180, and indirectly it promoted Christianity, for many Romans were impressed by the sight of Christians giving bread and water to victims who were too ill to move. About three centuries later another epidemic – a bubonic plague – came from India. It struck Constantinople in 542 and scythed its way across Europe. Most of those who died from this earlier wave of the 'black death' were doomed within six days of showing their first symptoms – a headache, high temperatures, and the emergence on the skin of a lump or bubo about the size of an egg or small orange. Curiously, those victims whose flesh supported a very large lump were more likely to survive. China and Japan also suffered huge casualties from epidemics which perhaps resembled the Black Death. The Chinese city of Kaifeng is said to have lost several hundred thousand inhabitants during an epidemic in 1232. If the city was so stricken, the surrounding countryside must have been similarly devastated by the disease.

A plague is like a compulsive tourist. It takes heart when a new way of travel is opened up. The Mongol invasion, and its unifying presence over a vast area of Asia, revived trade along the old caravan routes and also provided a highway for the bubonic plague to move north-west towards Europe. In European ports, the rats and fleas they harboured were the carriers of the plague. After reaching Europe in 1348 it spread swiftly. Some cities – Paris, Hamburg, Florence, Venice – lost half or more of their population. Villages were more likely than cities to escape the infection. It spread slowly in winter, and rapidly in summer. All in all, perhaps 20 million Europeans died, or one in every three people. A monster of plagues, the Black Death was followed at intervals by lesser plagues.

The scarcity of food of earlier decades was replaced by a scarcity of labour. Farmland was no longer in short supply. In some regions of Germany, more villages were deserted than inhabited, and fields which had once been noisy with harvesters were weed-grown and silent.

The Middle Ages in Europe are often said to have run from AD 500 to 1500. Differing from the previous thousand years, and from the following 500, the Middle Ages were more inward-looking, and less enamoured with individual achievement. That these ages had achieved less, materially, than the Roman Empire was not a source of disappointment. Most Christians probably believed that the Roman citizens in the years of their triumphs were essentially pagans, and that therefore many of their accomplishments were of little worth.

Many of Europe's political and intellectual leaders in the Middle Ages did not feel inferior to the Roman Empire. Rather they disowned it. They believed that they were building their own empire, united by a common religion. They called it the Holy Roman Empire. It was a foretaste of the federal Europe of the latter decades of the 20th century.

16

NEW MESSENGERS

The long Middle Ages or Dark Ages were not entirely suffocated by inertia. For the Vikings in the north of Europe and for Islam in the south of Europe they were not the dark ages but the light ages. Towards their end, in Europe as a whole, the sense of adventure and inventiveness was reviving. In the 12th century emerged the university – an institution which, eight centuries later, would circle the world. In the same century appeared the first windmills and also the first lock, an ingenious device which enabled sailing ships to follow the canal leading to the thriving Belgian port of Bruges. The skills of mining were about to improve, and in northern Europe a mineral that would be crucial for the future, black coal, was mined. At the same time, the deep-sea ship driven solely by the wind, with a magnetic compass to guide her and a sternpost rudder to steer her, was silently pointing to the possibility of exploring the wide Atlantic.

China remained a source of new ideas, including such remarkable innovations as gunpowder, paper and the technique of using ink. Not less remarkable was the way in which Europeans were welcoming these novelties and improving upon them. Nowhere was Europe so important as in the specialised crafts of clockmaking and printing. The clock was a medium which, like a soft metallic drum, subtly preached the message that time was precious.

The mass media were at work even in the Middle Ages. The bell, flag and smoke-and-fire signal were mass media and could send a message simultaneously to thousands of people. The sound of the loud bell, mounted on a high steeple in a medieval city, could be heard several miles away, though those within earshot had to assess whether the message called them to divine service or intimated that somebody of importance had died.

The coloured flag, usually made of wool, sent a clear visual message to generations of people who could not read or count. As late as the 19th century a yellow flag signified infectious disease, and a white flag was a request for peace on the battlefield. Fire and smoke were another medium, when war was in the offing. A succession of bonfires was arranged, each within sight of the other, and each fire could be lit in turn so that a silent signal announcing war could be relayed many kilometres to a capital city or a crucial port. Silent collective prayer was seen as another powerful medium.

Of the traditional media, the human voice was employed the most widely. Most news was passed on by

word of mouth, whether on a Chinese roadside or in a
Javanese temple. Words spoken slowly and deliberately
reached every corner of a large amphitheatre. Christ and
John the Baptist must have possessed voices that carried far. Those now living in the era of the loudspeaker
and microphone do not realise how far an unaided voice
can travel. In 1739 the young English evangelist George
Whitefield was speaking in the open air in the American
city of Philadelphia. Such a crowd gathered around in
the hope of hearing him that Benjamin Franklin, standing on the fringe, wondered how many spectators could
hear his words. He mentally marked those outer spots
where the speaker's voice was on the verge of becoming
inaudible. He computed that more than 30 000 people
were hearing Whitefield that day.

IN SIGHT OF THE CLOCK

In the late Middle Ages, the spoken word was first
challenged as a medium by the printing press, but it
was the clock which preceded the press as a medium
of influence. It could not be foreseen that in Europe a
day would arrive when nearly every adult would own
a clock.

Residents of big Italian towns were the first to hear
the chiming of a clock and to watch its hands move
stiffly around the dial. The clock had to sit high in a
tower so that people in the square and nearby streets
could see its hand: usually there was an hour hand
but no hand to show the minutes. Citizens might

not yet be able to tell the time but at least they could nod approvingly when friends – eager to parade their knowledge – told them what the time was. Probably the first clock in Europe was installed in a large church in Milan in 1335; and the hourly sound of its bells could be heard throughout the night. The public clock must have been a persistent teacher of the art of counting – at least counting to the number 12 – in the centuries before education became compulsory.

A tall public clock on a tower not only told the time: it also proclaimed that time was not to be frittered away. For the day of judgement would suddenly arrive and sternly demand of everyone to affirm that they had used diligently the time granted to them by the Lord.

The western mechanical clock was exported to China, where it was marvelled at. From China, almost as if it were an exchange, came the genesis of an even more influential invention which was set to work in European towns. The invention was the art of printing on sheets of paper.

PAPER AND THE BOOK

Paper and ink had reached Europe long before the technique of printing. Paper was first manufactured in China, Japan and Korea; and as early as the year 751, several Chinese artisans possessing the knowledge of how to make paper were captured and conveyed to Samarkand in central Asia where they revealed their techniques, thus manufacturing the first paper in very thick sheets in what the Chinese might well have called the Near West. This process eventually reached the Arab world and then Europe, where it slowly challenged the use of parchment. As parchment was made only from animal skins, and as a handwritten book of 200 large pages might consume the skins of about 80 lambs, a book consisting of parchment pages was far more expensive than one printed on the new paper.

The early paper was made from remnants such as old rags and ropes, and a waterwheel helped to convert these fibres into paper. In Italy an early paper-making town, Fabriano, still makes paper at the foot of a mountain range though the fast streams no longer turn the waterwheels. Once paper was being manufactured in Europe, the time was ripe for the coming of printing.

The Chinese made their letters and images not from metal but from wood and baked clay. The Koreans made movable type out of bronze as early as 1403 but their innovation did not influence Europe. The distinct printing advances about to be made in Europe involved the casting of individual durable letters of the alphabet out of lead, and the use of a heavy press to apply pressure so that the metal type imprinted the images in ink, firmly and sharply, on the paper.

Johannes Gutenberg, a resident of the German river city of Mainz, was perhaps the first European to print a book, using not only a press but also metallic type.

His technique, when perfected, was like that used later by the typewriter. But whereas the modern typewriter requires merely four neat rows containing each individual capital and lower-case letter of the alphabet, Gutenberg's form of printing called for the making of hundreds of metal replicas of each letter of the alphabet.

Gutenberg and his fellow printers set out, on a bench or shelf in front of them, dozens of the letter *a* and dozens of the letter *b*, and so on through the alphabet. From this assemblage they arranged or composed, with quick movements of the hand, the sequence of individual metal letters that formed a sentence and then a paragraph. A version of the wine press or the bookbinding press was used to press this page-shaped mass of metallic letters onto a fresh sheet of paper. The technique of printing from movable metal type was infinitely more suitable for European languages based on the simple Roman alphabet than for the 50 000 symbols of the Chinese language.

From Gutenberg's printery the new techniques were copied and adapted. By 1480, printers worked in towns as far apart as Cracow, London and Venice. Most of the books they printed were serious and even learned – only the learned could read – and were in Latin.

Hitherto, the cost of producing a book by hand, either on paper or parchment, had been so expensive that most of the smaller churches in Europe could not afford a Bible. They made do with handwritten gospel books, which contained only those passages of the Bible required for saying the mass. These were the medieval foretaste of a *Reader's Digest* version of the scriptures. Thanks to the printing press, a cheap Bible was now possible.

The technique of printing on paper was a social revolution. Europe was ready for it and eager to use and improve it, because the late 1400s were the time of its mental awakening. The printing press quickened that awakening.

Significantly, the urgent desire to spread a religious message, at first for Buddhism in China and then for Christianity in Europe, had been a spur to the inventing and utilising of printing. Islam, however, had no time for the new device and actually shunned the printing press until the 19th century.

THE OTTOMAN CONQUESTS

In this time of quickening change, Europe was becoming more confident intellectually but was far from secure militarily. From the interior of Asia the Mongols had come galloping, and in their shadow came the Turks.

At one time the Turks were living mainly in Turkestan in central Asia. Effective warriors, they came west in stages and, taking advantage of the Mongols' advance, occupied many areas overtaken by confusion. By 1400 the Ottoman Turks held nearly all of the territory of the present Turkey and extended their rule far into Christian Europe. They held both shores of the Dardanelles, including the coastal strip which became the battlefield of Gallipoli in the First World War. They occupied long reaches of the Danube River and large parts of what are now Albania, Serbia, Kosovo, Bosnia, Bulgaria and Romania. In the Balkan lands the invading Turks found supporters as well as opponents. Many Christian peasants, irked by the rich landowners for whom they laboured, silently welcomed the Turks, even accepted their religion, and joined their army as mercenaries.

The Turks surrounded the celebrated city of Constantinople almost completely by land and sea so that it became a tiny besieged island of territory. On 28 May 1453, the day when the last Christian service was performed in the cathedral of St Sophia, the Turks were at the high walls and about to enter Constantinople. After 11 centuries this famous city of Christianity was conquered. In the five years between 1516 and 1521, the Turks captured such diverse cities as Damascus and Cairo and Belgrade. At the very time when the Europeans were forcibly establishing their empires in America and Asia, the Ottoman Turks from Asia were forcing their way into Europe. They were now a European power.

That the Turks could be so tolerated showed a slight lapse of religious intensity in Italy around 1500. This same ebbing of Catholic fervour paved the way, inside Europe, for the rise of protesters or protestants who breathed religious fervour. Their main enemy was not to be the sultan: their enemy was the pope.

17

BIRDCAGE

What happened in the western half of Europe just before 1500 was one of the most remarkable convergences of influential events in the known history of the world to that time. It was like a crossroad where, almost by chance, extraordinary meetings took place between navigators and painters, priests and teachers and scientists.

There emerged a new way of painting and sculpting and a fresh perspective in architecture which, seen as a whole, was called the Renaissance or rebirth. A religious awakening, the Reformation, swept across northern Europe. The technique of printing, a wonderful way of disseminating new and old knowledge, leaped from town to town. An entirely new world emerged with the discovery in quick succession of the American continent and an all-sea route from Europe to eastern Asia. Curiously this momentous cluster of events, each one coming so close to another, has no all-embracing name; and it is almost certainly too late to provide a name that will be accepted.

These events reflected new ways of seeing the world. Many artists and architects saw with new eyes the reality around them, whether the human body or perspective. Many theologians and preachers believed they had rediscovered human nature. Astronomers and navigators saw the map of the world with astonishment. All reflected a wish to bathe tired eyes with salt and see afresh. It would be surprising if these new ways of seeing the world, and the excitement that arose from them, had not been infectious. Printing helped to spread the infection. Along pathways which we cannot necessarily detect – for religion and art and navigation were almost different realms and were presided over by different people – these separate fields influenced each other. Thus Protestantism, one product of this excited time, was aided enormously by the invention of printing.

While these clusters of discoveries were in their way revolutionary, each arose in part from a veneration for the past. Many of the artists were enamoured by the lost world of Greece and Rome and tried to recapture it. Some of the radical theologians were trying to recapture the virtues of religion as practised along the Sea of Galilee by Jesus and his disciples, and also trying to distil the essence of the faded writings of St Augustine and early fathers of the church. Even navigators at first were not searching for the new. They simply wished to find a route by sea instead of land to old China. At the same time, while initially enamoured of the past, the theologians, printers, painters and navigators were all explorers. The times, the air, encouraged a sense of intellectual adventure.

This is not to suggest that the blindfold fastened by the past was removed suddenly. The process of unveiling the eyes took place bit by bit and was probably the most gradual in art and architecture, where it gathered momentum over three centuries.

Around 1500 the new ways of seeing all seemed to flower. Just before Leonardo da Vinci completed his portrait of a young woman, 'Mona Lisa', the Spanish found America and the Portuguese sailed into the Indian Ocean. Soon after, Michelangelo completed his painting of Old Testament themes on the ceiling of the Sistine Chapel in Rome. Martin Luther on the other side of the Alps was protesting against the heretical system of taxation by which Rome financed such displays of scarletry as the Sistine Chapel.

These far-reaching changes in the arts and religion, scholarship, printing and navigation are not often seen as tightly linked because each flowered in a different corner of Europe. Art and architecture flourished mostly in central and northern Italy and in the Netherlands; and religious reformers first blossomed in northern Germany and the Swiss lake-ports. Printing with movable type was invented in Rhineland Germany; and bold navigators set sail from the Atlantic ports of Portugal and Spain. Significantly, this was the first time in European history when the major events were more to the north than south of the Alps and more on the Atlantic coast than the Mediterranean.

One part of Christian Europe did not contribute to the excitement. It had fallen into the hands of expanding Islam. In 1529 the Turks even besieged the city of Vienna. The Protestant Reformation was taking place within 300 kilometres of the advancing Turks.

This awakening taking place on so many fronts had a new patron. In mighty Rome the church was the patron of the arts, but the rich and rising commercial towns nurtured and financed many of these discoverers, whether in art or theology or navigation. The merchant houses of Florence and Genoa, Ghent and Nuremberg, Geneva and Zurich, Lisbon and Seville provided patrons and finance, and often an attitude sympathetic to new ways of seeing. These merchant towns held only a small fraction of the population of Europe, but they were vigorous.

The discoverers were like birds long kept in a large and wintry medieval cage called Europe. The cage door slipped ajar. The birds escaped, in ones and then in fours. In their new freedom they displayed their summer plumage and sang as never before.

OPENING THE BIRDCAGE

The birdcage was never opened with more optimism than in August 1492 when Christopher Columbus and his three small ships set sail from Spain on a hazardous voyage. His sailing might well be classed as the most significant event in the entire millennium.

More than 70 years before Columbus set sail across the Atlantic others had been mapping the route ahead. The island of Madeira was settled by the Portuguese in 1420. Eleven years later the Azores were discovered. Only a blob in the ocean, they were a long way towards the American continent, being about 800 sea miles from Lisbon and 1000 from Newfoundland. Portuguese ships also sailed south, hugging the African coast. In 1487 the brave Dias left Lisbon to follow the Atlantic Ocean further to the south. For weeks, out of sight of land, he sailed right around the most southerly coast of Africa and then turned back. On his return voyage, closer to land, he saw the southern headlands and named one the Cape of Storms. Even then the art of public relations was in the air, and eventually the cape was renamed the Cape of Good Hope.

In essence, Columbus was planning to venture into an ocean of which much was becoming known and much was still a mystery. He had hoped for financial aid from Portugal, but that country was already succeeding with its own straightforward theories of geography. He turned to Spain for help.

In Spain in August 1492, in the full knowledge that the world was round, Columbus set out to sail west in search of the east. He began to cross the Atlantic, believing that he was on his way to China. Such hopes now seem a little far-fetched, but he had reason to believe that he was actually crossing a narrow sea. At

6 AZTEC AND INCA EMPIRES
AND EUROPEAN EXPLORERS, c. 1500

that time it was mistakenly believed that the oceans occupied only one-seventh of the surface of the globe and that therefore a very wide ocean simply did not exist. This was the belief of the ancient geographer Ptolemy, whose name was still revered more than a millennium after his death.

By chance Ptolemy's volumes, long lost to western Europe, had been published in a new printery in the Italian city of Bologna only 15 years before Columbus set sail on his first voyage. Ptolemy gave Columbus the reassuring belief that he did not have to sail far west before he would enter Chinese waters. Simple outlines of the Chinese coastline and ports were actually available; and it is possible that Columbus's destination was the southerly Chinese port of Swatow (Shantou) or Canton (Guangzhou).

With the coast of Spain far behind him, Columbus sailed confidently in a westerly or south-westerly direction even on dark nights. He was actually sailing in the direction of Florida when on 7 October 1492 he saw a wide-spreading flock of birds flying to the south-west. He changed the ship's course in order to follow them, noting hopefully that the sea breezes were balmy and scented 'like April in Seville'.

Eventually a coastline came into sight. He must have felt a sense of triumph as he was rowed ashore. It was an island in the West Indies, but he thought it was India. Henceforth the people of the Americas were to be called Indians, and Columbus himself, on his return to Spain, was to be honoured as the Viceroy of the Indies.

After seeing the islands of Cuba and Haiti, Columbus returned to Spain in March 1493. The news of his discoveries created a level of astonishment perhaps exceeding that created by the first landing on the moon. On his second expedition, with 17 ships under his command, he established on the island of Hispaniola (Haiti) the first European town in the new hemisphere. In August 1498, on his third expedition, he actually reached the American continent and stepped ashore in the present Venezuela. When Columbus died in 1506 the extraordinary empires of the Aztecs and the Incas, far from the coasts which he himself had sailed, had not yet been seen by a European. He had unlocked the great door, but when he died the door was merely ajar.

Four years after Columbus returned from his first successful voyage to what he thought was Asia, the Portuguese planned their own large expedition to Asia by a different route. Vasco da Gama set sail from Lisbon in 1497 with three ships and a crew of 170. In sailing across the equator and around the south of Africa he spent more days out of sight of land than did Columbus on his first voyage. Perhaps no ship had ever been out of sight of land for so long. On the coast of East Africa he entered Islam's sphere of commercial influence and at the port of Mozambique he met Arab ships. Thereafter all was plain sailing. Indian pilots,

Muslim by religion, actually guided him across the Indian Ocean to the west coast of India. Like Columbus he had found, with Muslim help, a new sea route to remote lands.

These voyages of Christopher Columbus and Vasco da Gama were amongst the most important events in the history of the world since the slow invention of farming, thousands of years earlier. The Portuguese voyage joined together two dynamic and rich parts of the world which previously were inaccessible by ship. The Spanish voyage brought together two inhabited worlds that had been far apart and unknown to each other. A comparable event will never happen again, unless advanced life is discovered on another planet.

THE HALLS OF MONTEZUMA

The Vikings, centuries earlier, had landed on a bleak and sparsely peopled part of the same continent as Columbus; and their landing led them nowhere, and was soon forgotten. But Columbus and his Spaniards landed closer to the hub of the Americas, where, unknown to them, were vast gardens, mines of silver and gold, grand cities and even empires.

In the year 1517 the Spanish navigator Grijalva sailed from Cuba to the port-towns on the mainland to the west, and in the course of nine months of leisurely sailing and numerous stays ashore he saw much that impressed him. He also brought back to Cuba the news and rumours of the rich empire of Montezuma II, lying on the highlands further inland. The Aztec emperor was feared and resented by the Maya people on the coast; and any Spaniard venturing into his territory had to be audacious and well prepared. Hernán Cortés, chosen to penetrate the realm of Montezuma, was audacious but in some respects he was ill prepared. Aged 34, he was untested as a leader and fighter. Shortish in build, he stooped slightly when he walked and was also bow-legged. The man who was to achieve one of the most amazing military victories on record did not yet cut a commanding figure.

With a small fleet of small ships, Cortés sailed from Cuba in November 1518. Amongst the 530 Europeans who accompanied him were 30 specialists in firing the crossbow: in fact more of his soldiers were specialists in bow and arrow than in firearms. In his ships were several hundred female and male Cuban Indians, many of whom were personal servants, as well as a few African slaves. On the decks were penned about 16 sturdy horses. They were a weapon of surprise, for no American had ever seen a horse. When they were landed on the shore the onlookers were as frightened by the sight of their big mouths as by their large hooves.

At Easter 1519, Cortés and his party halted their journey into the interior and spent three weeks at the Central American town of Potonchan, where on Palm Sunday they erected a Christian cross in the town square. Before leaving the town, Cortés was presented with a vivacious woman who could speak the local languages he needed, for one language was familiar to the Maya along the coast and another was spoken by Emperor Montezuma in the interior. Cortés soon rejoiced in his gifted interpreter. Baptised into the Christian faith and christened Marina, the interpreter soon learned to speak Spanish. Her value to Cortés was, in the words of one historian, 'certainly equivalent to ten bronze cannon'. Through her words the strange land that he was about to enter became intelligible.

Montezuma's city, called Tenochtitlán, lay on a plateau about halfway between the Atlantic and Pacific oceans. Breathing a rarified air nearly 2500 metres above sea level, it stood on an island set in a long lake with mountains nearby. Mexico City occupies the site today, but the lake has vanished.

To visit the city from afar was one of the most remarkable experiences the entire world could offer. Travellers passed high mountains, one permanently capped with snow and many of them wooded, before at last reaching a plateau from which they looked down and saw the lake and glimpsed in the distance the stone pyramids which were a landmark of this civilisation. Three main causeways led across the lake to the island city and its 200 000 people. It was one of the world's largest cities, and a few of those Spaniards who had travelled widely in Europe before setting out for the New World knew that only the city-ports of Constantinople and Naples were as large, while it was understood that even in China not many cities were larger.

The area of the Aztec empire itself was almost as large as modern Italy and its people numbered six or eight million. They excelled in the crafts of building and architecture, and were goldsmiths and jewellers of the first order, highly competent in mathematics and adept at agriculture, cultivating a variety of plants as well as keeping turkey and muscovy duck. Admittedly they lacked some of the major inventions adopted or contrived by the Europeans, for they were unfamiliar with bronze and iron and screws and nails, they lacked the wheel, and they possessed no mechanical pulley, no gunpowder and no deep-sea ships.

The sacrificing of human lives almost dominated the calendar of the island city. The act of sacrifice was more like systematic butchery than a religious festival. In the previous century, when ritual sacrificing had become more frequent, thousands of chosen victims, most of whom were male, could be killed in the same month. As the afterlife was seen as more important and infinitely longer than this life, a girl and boy who were led to a temple to be ceremonially killed at least had the consolation that their reward would be lasting.

The execution was carried out with high drama, presided over by priests, justified by ideology, and even welcomed by some parents, especially the poor, who came forward with their own children. Prisoners of war torn from their homeland and a very different religion could not be expected to view the sacrificial altar and the stone knife in the same consoling light. To be held down on the altar already stained with blood, and see a priestly hand clutching a blade of sharp flint, was the last conscious sight for tens of thousands of victims. The heart was skilfully cut from the body and then burned ceremonially.

The feeding of such a large city was a feat of skilled organising and hard labour. The city was stocked with food, grain, firewood and building materials by people who served as pack animals. The American continent possessed no wheeled vehicle; and even if there had been a cart, no horses or bullocks were available to draw it. Firewood and foods could be carried in boats a short distance along the lake; but the long-distance items were brought from as far away as the Gulf of Mexico by a procession of human carriers shouldering special packs capable of holding close to 25 kilograms in weight. As parts of the road went up steep slopes, the human carriers had to be strong.

Much of the soil around the lake was fertile. For some 4000 years it had been cultivated with relatively simple implements of wood and in recent centuries it had been sustained in its fertility by manure carried from the city and irrigated by channels of water diverted from the lake or springs. Crops of prolific maize, along with beans, greens, chilli peppers, squashes and other vegetables and fruits, came from the terrain near the lake. Maize more than any other plant was the secret of this successful economy. One square kilometre planted with maize could feed three times the number of people living on the wheat or rye grown on a European area of similar size.

The conquest of Montezuma's city was boldly planned by Cortés. He knew that from the start of the fighting he would be hopelessly outnumbered. Moreover he was fighting far from home, in terrain that the enemy knew intimately. On paper his disadvantages were far larger than his advantages, but he gained vital support from nearby peoples who, hating the Aztecs, were only too eager to serve the Spaniards as advance scouts, carriers, suppliers of food and fighters. He even gained subtle support from the leading Aztecs who thought, when he arrived in November 1519, that he might be the reincarnation of a god whom they had long expected. Cortés's was one of the most astonishing victories of which world history contains a record.

Montezuma II, with his dark features and aquiline nose and courtesy and eloquence, humbly surrendered. Cortés took over the empire and even the emperor's children.

18

THE INCA AND THE ANDES

The empire of the Aztecs had crumpled. Far to the south, in the distant Andes mountains, was a relatively new empire that seemed more formidable. Ruled by an emperor known as the Inca, it was much further away from the new Spanish ports in the Caribbean. Moreover its cities and villages had a protective rampart of mountains and gorges.

The middle and lower slopes of the Andes, and the adjacent Pacific coast, had long been occupied by gatherers and hunters. A backwater of the human world, the area began to stir itself about 3000 BC, when it domesticated three useful breeds of livestock – the llama, alpaca and guinea pig. A thousand years later its people were cultivating maize and the potato, two valuable plants which were unknown in Asia, Africa and Europe. In irrigating their crops they managed to cope with geographical obstacles more difficult than those faced by the valley cities of the Middle East. By the time of Christ the Nazca people were driving tunnels into hillsides in the south of Peru in order to divert the underground streams for the purposes of irrigation. Their building of agricultural terraces and aqueducts became impressive. Their skill in domesticating an increasing variety of useful plants was equally to be admired.

While the Middle Ages for Europe were, by certain materialist definitions, the 'dark ages', the same years in the Andes were the 'light ages'. The towns and villages along the Andes were being altered by new technology, new crops and new instruments. In some ways the small states of the Andes in AD 1400 resembled the rival Italian city-states of the same time, except that the Andes had a multitude of separate states, many of which occupied a single valley and its surrounding slopes. The corrugated landscape made for isolation. At least 20 distinct languages were spoken, and maybe 100 or more ethnic groups each occupied its territory on the middle and lower slopes of the mountains and on the narrow strip of Pacific coast. Then, in a short space of time, one superpower began to fight its way to the fore. It was in command when the Spaniards arrived.

Warfare between these dozens of groups or mini-nations had recently become almost a habit. In the course of the more serious of the wars the enemy's irrigation schemes and gardens – the results of generations of labour and ingenuity – were damaged, women and children were taken prisoner, and livestock and crops were destroyed or plundered. Even 'the stones they had used for grinding' their grain were snatched away from some of the vanquished. In this long bout of fighting the Incas proved themselves superior, and from about the year 1438 their territory began to expand.

Originally from the highlands around Cuzco in the present Peru, the Incas numbered maybe 40 000 people. After a succession of wars and threats of war they won dominance over all other groups and ruled a total of 10 or 12 million people. Their domain, in the month when Columbus first landed in the Americas, made the empires of Spain and Portugal seem small. The Incas ruled all the way from the present Colombia and Ecuador in the north to central Chile in the south. Today five separate republics occupy the territory once ruled by them.

Such was the extent of the Inca empire that soldiers despatched from the centre to a distant outpost might spend 60 or 80 days on the road before they finally reached their destination. It was easy to walk such long distances because the empire was drawn together by a wonderful network of roads. The ancient Roman and Chinese roads and bridges had been the more remarkable, but no other early empire could match the Incas' roads, which their corps of forced labourers constructed. Eventually the Inca roads stretched over 23 000 kilometres – long enough to cross Asia at its largest width. The two main roads ran parallel, one following the Pacific coast and even crossing the desert of northern Chile, and the other following the mountains. The mountain road, the busier of the two arteries, went up and down a thousand hills. In places it was more than 25 metres wide but in steep pinches it was more like a zigzag path. As the Incas owned no wheeled vehicles they did not have to worry if the road was excessively steep or unusually narrow. When a marsh had to be crossed, a narrow embankment was made of earth or stone. When a river had to be crossed, a pontoon bridge – a floating walkway – was built. When a gorge blocked the progress of the road, a suspension bridge of thick rope was constructed to span the gap. Some of these bridges were still in use three centuries later.

Across the bridges, perched high above the rushing streams, ran the official messengers. They were neither barefooted – they wore sandals made of untanned leather and tied by a woollen cord to the feet – nor bareheaded. On the long stretches of level road the messengers moved at an impressive pace. The speed at which their news travelled was expedited by the relay system: every few kilometres along the highway was a hut where another messenger was waiting.

Urgent goods as well as messages were carried by the relays of messengers. Thus a parcel of fresh fish would be carried a long distance for the enjoyment of senior officials in the capital city of Cuzco. Along this road a high official himself could be carried if he so wished, the normal conveyance being two parallel poles carried by four men, with a seat in the middle for the exalted one.

The roads could be useful for an invader, but for a time the Incas were supreme. Fine generals, skilled in tactics, led their armies. While they supplied the senior officers, the subdued peoples supplied the humble foot soldiers, both women and men. And yet it was not entirely an empire of unwilling subjects. The Incas had brought peace to a war-torn region. They had also brought a willingness to cooperate, so long as the minority group surrendered without fighting.

Along the trunk roads might be seen, in certain years, a procession of people walking long distances to a new homeland. The Incas, like the rulers of the future Soviet Union and other empires, knew that the dispersal of alien peoples, and the mixing together of different ethnic groups, lessened the chance of an organised rebellion. On the same roads walked soldiers on their way to distant regions where patrol duty was needed or fighting was likely. Warehouses, spaced along the road and serviced by vanquished peoples, supplied them with food.

People shared the road with that other beast of burden, the llama. When washed down by the rains, many of these woolly pack animals displayed handsome white coats with black or brown spots. A member of the camel family, though lacking the conspicuous hump, a llama could carry a load weighing 40 or 50 kilograms, thereby compensating for the absence of the wheel in Andes civilisation.

SUN, MOON AND THUNDER

The Incas were intensely religious. Important decisions were preceded by pleas to the gods – would they bless this military campaign or this coming harvest? The sun and moon were gods whose help was humbly requested. The sun, as the giver of heat, was seen as friendly and so the afterlife was lived in warmth. In contrast the hell of the Incas was a cold place.

The sun was the male god, and from him the emperor claimed descent; and so he ruled by divine right. The sun regulated the calendar, and in each year that December day when the sun came furthest south of the equator marked the beginning of the Incas' calendar. Thus their year began, in hot weather, almost at the same time as the year began in Europe, in cold weather.

The sun god had his favourite plant and its leaves produced coca, which was spiritual in its qualities. Originally the tropical bush producing coca grew along the eastern foothills of the Andes, but it was domesticated and then transplanted to gardens on the lower slopes of the ocean side of the Andes. It was planted on flat terraces, painfully constructed from steep slopes, and water was conveyed to the terraces in long canals crossing the parched ground. As the coca crop was highly valuable, stone fences or walls were built to protect it from thieves and possibly also to prevent grey foxes from entering the garden and urinating on such a sacred crop.

Coca leaves were carried in baskets and fibre sacks along the highways to the capital city, where they were available only to the high officials of the kingdom and to the custodians of the temples. Mixed with lime, coca was often chewed in such a way as to bring a bulge to the cheek. It also transmitted an excitement to the mind, thus aiding the making of prophecies in those temples devoted to the worship of the sun. From the same plant came in modern days the minor additive which, until 1905, was part of the recipe for the drink Coca-Cola, and also the drug cocaine.

Of all the world's known societies prior to the last 100 years, the Incas should probably be ranked, in their attitude to women, within the highest cluster. Women not only had the right to own property but also possessed their own powerful god. Of the two main deities of the Incas, the moon was the goddess of females, and they served as her priests. The moon presided over the fertility of women: she protected them during the birth of a child. Women's economic role was as honoured as that of men, and burial ceremonies paid tribute to her work and her needs. Whereas in the grave of a man was placed the hoe with which he had gardened, a woman was buried along with the wooden rod or spindle on which she had wound or twisted threads of new cotton.

The sacrificing of animals, especially guinea pigs and the worthy llama, was a vital part of religious rituals. For such grand events as a coronation, or in making the danger-spiced decision to go to war, the sacrifice of a human being was demanded. Children aged from 10 to 15, being considered purer than adults, were usually selected. It was deemed an honour for one's child to be chosen.

In the regions far from the walls and temples of the capital city, a human life might be deliberately sacrificed at an appropriate time of year in the hope that the gods of fertility would bless the growing crops. In the very high mountains, where the growing season was short and a brief and dry summer could be disastrous, the sacrificing of a young girl was an insurance policy.

In the spring of 1995 one such Inca sacrifice was uncovered by the thawing of the snow 6000 metres above sea level. The girl had been sacrificed during the very last decades of Inca rule, and possibly in a year of drought when a human sacrifice seemed the only hope of beckoning down the rain. Frozen and therefore well preserved, she was found to be about 13 years old and apparently in sound health on the eve of her death.

Given the frequency of ritual sacrifice, human blood was so plentiful that it could be used in medical experiments. There is evidence that, long before a blood transfusion was successfully practised elsewhere in the world, the Incas succeeded in transfusing human blood to the body of a sick person. As nearly all native South Americans were of the same blood group, the transfusion of blood from one person to another was safer than in Italy where blood transfusions, involving more than one blood group, were boldly attempted, perhaps for the first time, just one century after the collapse of the Incas' kingdom. Another skill of the Incas was in surgery. They could cut a segment of bone from the skull of a wounded or sick patient, or scrape clean the bone in its set position, without necessarily damaging the brain. A delicate operation, its success rate was probably as high as 60 per cent. This achievement suggests that these pioneering Inca surgeons used antiseptics to ward off infection.

It is possible to understand the economic life of the Incas and of the many mini-nations which preceded them only by grasping the unique geography of the Andes. The terrain and climate were so diverse that as people walked to higher ground they virtually entered one new country and then another and another. Close together in the Andes, as if standing on a sloping ladder, were four distinct climatic and geographical regions, of a kind which normally are separated by thousands of kilometres of ocean or land. The four regions were separated by gaps in altitude rather than gaps in latitude. It was somewhat like Norway sitting on top of Holland which in turn sat on top of Sicily. These distinct regions were linked by zigzag mountain paths and occasionally by roads, rather than by a long ocean voyage.

On the slopes and bottom of the valleys lay a warm and dry region which, with the aid of irrigation, could produce fruit, cactus and even maize. In the middle ground, which was at least 500 metres above sea level, stood the zone best suited to agriculture. Here grew maize and beans, squash and the grain *quinoia*, which was rich in protein.

Much higher was a third rural zone, cooler and moister. Here grew an astonishing diversity of potatoes and tubers – perhaps 250 varieties in all. Even higher than the potato country were the alpine pastures resorted to in summer. On much of this high ground grazed the flocks of llamas. When an animal was slaughtered its meat was cut into long strips and dried in the sun.

The early South Americans had remarkable success in discovering or domesticating plants that are now known in many corners of the world. They tamed the potato, the sweet potato, the tomato, various beans, the cashew and peanut, coca, hot peppers, squash, manioc or cassava – known in Europe as tapioca – and the pineapple. Maize as a garden plant originated independently both in South America and in Mexico. Here too grew rubber trees and a distinctive species of cotton used for making fishing nets and lines.

The mountain peoples, so conservative in religion, were unusually inventive. They invented the crowbar, using it in mining, and also devised a highly effective spade for gardening. They learned how to use rivets and solder metals. This was a civilisation largely of its own creation. What it borrowed from Central America and the Aztecs was probably much less than it devised on its own.

THE FALL OF THE INCAS

The Incas had held their empire of mountain and plateau and desert, of sweaty jungle and everlasting snow, for less than a century when the Spaniards arrived at its fringes. Spain's influence came in the form of diseases, which spread swiftly amongst the native peoples. The emperor of the Incas, having been engaged in frontier wars, was returning south towards Inca territory in about 1525 when he was struck down by a mysterious disease. The onset of his death was swift. The question of who should succeed him was, for the Incas as for many European monarchies, a crucial and divisive question. Suddenly the dominance of the Incas was endangered by civil war even before the real enemy arrived.

On many occasions leaders within the world's most influential centres of power have fought amongst themselves, seeing themselves as immune to outside attack at the very time when they are no longer supreme. The ancient Greeks did this once too often. Even Europe was to slip into that trap of overconfidence in 1914 and again in 1939. Likewise the Incas fought amongst themselves not knowing that a powerful and unknown enemy, the Spaniard, was almost at their door.

The Incas were even more exposed to that other enemy – the new diseases which arrived with the invader. When Christopher Columbus discovered the Americas, smallpox was rife in the Europe he had left behind. A few Spaniards unknowingly carried it in ships crossing the Atlantic. By 1519 the disease had reached the island of Espanola, where it killed perhaps one-third of the population. It was a secret and unintended weapon of the Spanish soldiers who, under Francisco Pizarro, set sail from Panama in an attempt to conquer the Incas. In November 1532 the Spaniards easily captured the Inca emperor Atahualpa. Smallpox, that invisible ally, was already leaping ahead of the Spanish soldiers and killing large numbers of Incas.

The speed with which smallpox killed was itself a cause of despair for those who watched, helpless. Incubated in only 12 days, the disease showed its presence in a quickened pulse, a feeling of dryness in the mouth, a pain in the pit of the stomach, acute aching in the back and often vomiting. Those who survived the disease developed pimples and scabs which began to fall off around the 16th day of the fever, sometimes leaving pitmarks which permanently disfigured the face. The pockmarked face, already a common sight in the streets of Vienna and Madrid, became familiar in the Americas. By the 1530s smallpox was raging – or had done its worst – all the way from Bolivia in the south to the Great Lakes in the north.

Meanwhile in villages and wigwams, on the high slopes of the Andes and on the hills across the Missouri, the nightmare of another disease descended. Measles arrived soon after smallpox. Typhus also arrived: it was relatively new to Spain itself, having been observed first in Spanish soldiers who had just returned from the island of Cyprus. In crept influenza, first noticed in the Americas in 1545, and whooping cough, diphtheria, scarlet fever, chickenpox and even malaria, all of which appear to have been new to the inhabitants and therefore were the more deadly.

How many people died of disease in Mexico alone during the first half-century of the Spanish coming has been the topic of endless calculating and learned guessing. Perhaps eight million Mexicans were alive when Cortés arrived; and half a century later the population was reduced to less than one-third. In the empire of the Incas, far south, the death toll also numbered millions, while in some of the less populous regions maybe eight of every 10 people died.

At first the impact of the Spanish people – as well as their diseases – on the native Americans was disastrous. Civilisations were shattered. Cultural and economic life largely disintegrated in the main towns though it survived for many decades, less altered, in sparsely settled areas. Millions of people died, while others merely exchanged the Inca form of slavery or subjection for the Spanish. For the defeated perhaps the main solace in the long term was Catholicism, which came to dominate Latin America.

The magnitude of these shattering changes can perhaps be grasped by imagining that the invasion had been in the reverse direction and that the Aztecs or Incas had arrived suddenly in Europe, imposed their culture and calendar, outlawed Christianity, set up sacrificial altars for thousands of victims in Madrid and Amsterdam, unwittingly spread disease on a scale that virtually matched the Black Death, melted down the golden images of Christ and the saints, threw stones at the stained-glass windows and converted the cathedral aisles into arms or food warehouses, toppled unfamiliar Greek statues and Roman columns, and carried home to the Mexican and Peruvian highlands their loot in precious metals along with slaves, indentured servants and other human trophies.

19

REFORMATION

In Europe, the all-powerful Catholic church was in peril. It tolerated too many back doors and trapdoors which permitted the rich and the unworthy, on paying a prescribed fee, to hope that they could slip safely into heaven. The saints, it was believed, guarded a storehouse of mercy and indulgence from which they could distribute a portion to those wealthy sinners who at the last moment wished for salvation and could afford to pay for it. Some indulgences and concessions, given in return for money or for services rendered, rested on a sound spiritual basis. Thus in 1095, during the crusades to rescue Jerusalem from the infidels, Pope Urban II promised to forgive the sins of those crusaders who crossed the seas 'out of pure devotion and not for the sake of gaining honour or money'.

Money donated for the building of cathedrals was acknowledged by a holy receipt or passport which could be shown to the eternal gatekeeper. When the grand church at Speyer in Germany was being rebuilt in 1451, at least 50 priests sat 'in their stoles' and, after hearing confessions, granted forgiveness to those pilgrims who donated money. A quarter of a century later the pope allowed indulgences to be sold for the sake of people now dead and residing in purgatory. In short, the rich could pay hush money for sins committed by dead relatives who, at the time of their death, might have felt no need for forgiveness. The poor, because they were poor, were largely denied this concession.

SELLING THE BLOOD OF CHRIST

The church engaged professional collectors, like charity's fundraisers of today, and they sold indulgences. As the medieval church, far more than most Christian groups today, believed in eternal punishment, the selling of exemptions and reprieves was sabotaging a key tenet of its theology. It was almost selling out the church for a few gold coins. The Catholic church still had a host of worthy priests, monks and nuns, utterly dedicated, but the exceptions were many.

Martin Luther, a north German priest, began to question the straying church. The son of a successful miner, he was professor of biblical theology in the small town of Wittenberg. He was aged 33 when he rebelled.

Martin Luther detested the practice of selling indulgences or priced packets of forgiveness. On 31 October 1517, on the eve of All Saints' Day, a notable day in the calendar, he posted his protests in Latin on the door of the castle church in his town. His manifesto contained 95 points or theses, the first of which began: 'Our Lord wished the entire life of believers to be one of penitence.' His point was unmistakable to those who crowded around the door. Why should worshippers be penitent when some hucksters were actually excusing people from the need to repent – in return for a few coins?

Luther can still be seen as in the flesh. The fine German painter Lucas Cranach knew him and captured him on canvas. Here is a strong and slightly coarse peasant face, with small shrewd eyes, hair covering his ears and a little stubble on his face, as if he only shaved himself every few days. The nose is lumpy with strong nostrils, almost as if he is sniffing for the smell of his dinner. The face suggests that he is a hearty eater but it also conveys an ascetic quality. If one saw this strong-looking man walking along the street, or standing in the pulpit on Sunday, the combination of peasant strength and alertness would command attention.

Like most religious reformers, he did not wish to leave the Catholic church, but he was driven further and further towards a point from which he could not turn back. The church understandably dictated the terms on which he could stay. He could not accept them.

In German-speaking cities alone, more than 200 printing presses seemed to be almost waiting for that event which they were so effortlessly to aid: the Protestant Reformation. The Catholic church's monopoly of the Bible was about to be ended by an invention partly borrowed from a land where the name of Christ was almost unknown. The Bible was a precious hand-written book, so scarce that in many churches the only copy was chained to the reading desk. For the first time in Christendom the gospels were to become avail-able at a price which a village church or a moderately wealthy merchant could afford. A pamphlet containing a simple sermon could now reach, through the might of the printing press, more people than one sermon had ever before reached.

Martin Luther saw the printery as God's gift to his work. He wrote religious pamphlets and handed them to the printer along with his latest sermons. He began to translate the Bible into German, completing it in powerful and simple prose in 1534.

Wittenberg, a town with a mere 2000 people, boomed briefly as the heart of the German printing industry. The scent of fresh paper and strong ink must have pervaded some of the town's lanes on the hot days of summer, when the windows and doors of the printer-ies were wide open. Whereas only 150 different books were printed in all Germany in the year of Luther's protest, 990 books were printed in 1524 – just six years later. More than half of those books were printed in Wittenberg. Most were in favour of Luther. To him the printing press was a team of horses 'whereby the Gospel is driven forward'.

Luther was a protester, or a protestant in the vocabulary of the times. While his protests were somewhat political and social, they were primarily religious. Partly through his influence, hundreds of towns in Europe were shaken by a remarkable religious awakening. Millions of people felt that God was by their side. They could not express adequately the joy and sense of release and relief they felt. Luther came to think that salvation lay not in doing good but in a simple, self-forgetting faith in God. Tens of thousands who heard him preach were profoundly moved by his arguments and his passion.

The lightning with which Luther lit the skies might have slowly faded but for the efforts of the French-speaking preacher John Calvin. Born in the north of France and educated in Paris, he lacked the magnetism of Luther. When he preached, he showed little sense of theatre. It was his original mind, arresting message and nervous sincerity that impressed those who, eager to hear him, stood shoulder to shoulder in the big church by the lake at Geneva. Ruled by Calvin, those clergymen known as the Company of Pastors, and the city-state authorities, Geneva became the religious and moral showplace of Europe.

Every reformation and revolution carries a tension between those who insist that everything must be reformed and those who say, after the first bout of reforming, 'We have gone far enough!' Calvin aroused animosity even amongst his own supporters by denouncing as papist many of the old Christian names so popular in the city. In 1546 the Company of Pastors, without formally announcing its policy, resolved that babies brought before them for the ceremony of infant baptism should be given sound biblical names and not the names of local Catholic saints. A barber of the town brought his baby son to the crowded church to be christened Claude – one of the three most popular names in Geneva – but the pastor solemnly christened him as Abraham. The barber snatched the child away and carried him home. There was uproar in the congregation and in all those places where gossip was exchanged.

A centrepiece of his doctrine was a belief which now is highly controversial but seemed reasonable and even congenial to people living in a more religious era. He believed in predestination. He believed that God in his all-seeing wisdom knew in advance how each human life would unravel. In essence, some people from the day of their birth were predestined to win a place in heaven. Others were destined to fall by the spiritual wayside, and nothing they could do would alter their ultimate fate. Mainstream Catholic doctrine said a person might be saved by good deeds, and Luther said that people could be saved only by their deep faith in God's mercy, but Calvin dismissed these views. God was all-powerful and only his decision could save a person's soul. To us the doctrine seems preposterously unfair. Calvin would have argued that our concept of fairness was irrelevant. In his own opinion, and in God's view,

all people were in one sense worthless. The fact that so
many were ultimately saved was a sign of God's over-
flowing generosity to those who had no innate right to
generosity. Calvin was not unlike Mohammed, who
believed that God ordained far in advance what each
single human being would do, whether good or evil.

Pastor Calvin's stand on predestination was both
reassuring and electrifying to his flock. In a typical
Calvinist congregation some listeners were probably
terrified by this creed which Calvin expounded in long
sermons constructed on the stepping stones of biblical
texts. Most of his listeners, however, joyfully assumed

7 WESTERN EUROPE, c.1500

Bergen
Stockholm
North Sea
Baltic Sea
ATLANTIC
OCEAN
Copenhagen
Skanor
(Scania)
Gdansk
(Danzig)
Dublin
Norwich
London
Amsterdam
Bruges
Ghent
Wittenberg
Leipzig
Jena
Zwickau
Cracow
MORAVIA
Paris
Strasbourg
(Strassburg)
Mainz
Speyer
Basle
Nuremberg
Augsburg
Vienna
Bay of Biscay
Geneva
Lyons
Zurich
Alps
Padua
Venice
Genoa
Florence
Ancona
Camerino
Pyrenees
Lisbon
Rome *Adriatic Sea*
Seville
Cádiz
Mediterranean Sea

that they were already amongst the chosen ones.

In these emotion-charged years, a host of ordinary people showed courage in clinging to their old faith or in embracing the new. Of course most, when threatened with death or prison or the loss of property, fell in with the view of those who governed their land. But hundreds of thousands took risks in flirting with the new faith or clinging to the old.

WOE, WOE, WOE!

A far-reaching revolt against the Catholic church came from the sects called Anabaptists. Named after the Greek word for 'rebaptised', they were the militants of the Reformation. They first appeared in Zwickau, to the east of Wittenberg, and then surfaced in Zurich and hundreds of other towns in northern Europe. When driven from towns they were willing to worship in the fields in the warmer months and baptise adult converts by immersing them in running streams. They came in many varieties and nursed many beliefs. Most opposed the idea of infant baptism, believing that it was too precious a gift to be bestowed on day-old infants who were unable to make a conscious decision to live and die for Christ. More than any other protesting group, the Anabaptists were powerful amongst the poor. The sects' leaders, at risk to their life, were disposed to poke out their tongues at those who ruled.

The Anabaptists were denounced as mad or evil by Luther, Calvin, Zwingli and the preacher-heroes of the early Reformation. They were seen by many rulers as the scum of the Reformation. 'Anabaptist' became a term of abuse. Notorious were the five female and seven male 'strippers' who in Amsterdam in 1535, to emphasise that they preached only the naked truth, took off their clothes and ran along a street calling out 'Woe! Woe! Woe! – the wrath of God.' The 12 Anabaptists were executed. Feared as opponents of the religious and social order, Anabaptists almost everywhere were persecuted. In Holland and Friesland alone, some 30 000 were killed in the 10 years after 1535; and yet it was in this region that they survived.

Calvinism, which began to flower in the decade of Luther's death, gave the Reformation new energy. For 40 years the reform message took wing, landing in districts far from its birthplace. For a time it seemed that most of western and central and southern Europe might be converted to one of the competing new creeds. Most of northern Germany fell to the Lutherans. From Finland to Denmark and Iceland they took over the cathedrals. In Poland and Hungary the Calvinist creed swept through towns, making its mark especially with wealthier families. Holland and the island of Britain – except for the Scottish Highlands – were won by the reformers. Into France walked or rode a long procession of young pastors from Geneva and they won wide support in the seaports, especially along the Atlantic coast. Even Italy was penetrated. The Anabaptists worshipped in Vicenza and other sects took root in nearby Venice.

The Protestants turned against many of the hallmarks of Catholicism. The Catholics believed in grand religious ceremonies and rich processions and jewels in the mitre of the archbishop. In contrast, many of the reformers insisted on simplicity, and even when rich they preferred a church without stained glass in the windows. Catholics believed in a holy circle of saints whose help could be invoked; but many of the reformers dismissed the saints as needless intermediaries standing between the humble Christian and Christ himself. Catholics often decorated the walls of their church with statues of Christ; but the reformers cast out the statues, along with the Virgin Mary.

Catholics believed in the guiding power of the priest, but many reformers believed in the priesthood of all believers. In their eyes the humblest Christians who faithfully read the Bible and waited humbly for God's inspiration conveyed as much spiritual authority as the Catholic parish priest. Catholics had long abandoned the idea that priests could marry but now Protestants revised the idea. Luther himself married a nun.

The new Protestantism fostered dark and light shades of revolt against the Catholic church. Most Calvinists, believing that there should be no majestic music and no lofty choirs, emphasised the singing of the whole congregation, with their voices unaccompanied by instruments. The word was all-important: music was simply a servant which carried the word. In treating music both as an aid to worship and also a seductive snare, the early Calvinists echoed that plea for simplicity which had been made in the Middle Ages by Cistercian monks.

On the other hand, the Lutherans maintained the rich musical tradition of northern Germany, which, with their aid, flowered astonishingly just two centuries after Luther first made his protests. In northern Germany two young musicians, Handel and Bach, had each made a pilgrimage on foot to the port of Lübeck to hear the special religious services for which the Lutheran organist Buxtehude provided the music. George Frederick Handel was himself the grandson of a Lutheran clergyman. Johann Sebastian Bach wrote nearly all of his magical output of music while working as a Lutheran organist, cantor or director of church music. Most of his oratorios and cantatas were written for the Lutheran congregations at two large Gothic churches in Leipzig, which, in the three-hour service that began every Sunday at 7 a.m., allocated half an hour for a cantata that Bach usually composed and conducted for 30 or 40 singers and instrumentalists. A church service of long duration was a characteristic of the first three centuries of Protestant ardour.

SHARP SWORD AND CUTTING WORD

The Catholic church examined itself critically after Luther and Calvin had held up their Bibles in protest. It prohibited the main abuses, some of which were far from as frequent as Luther had argued. The selling of indulgences by a professional collector of revenue was curbed by the Council of Trent in 1562. A bishop could no longer be absent from his own diocese for long periods. The music and the liturgy – almost as diverse as that of Protestantism – were taken in hand. The new baroque architecture, which especially flourished in Spain and the Spanish Indies, became a new affirmation of faith within a rejuvenated and chastened Catholicism. Seminaries were opened in order to train young clergy. New religious orders brought purpose to the church; and the Jesuits and Capuchins joined the old Catholic orders in sending missionaries to new lands.

After 40 years the tide turned against the protesting Protestants. In central Europe most of the rulers, determined that all people should belong to one religion, their chosen religion, began to harry the protesters. To practise a dissenting faith was to practise treason. The strongholds of the Protestants were now confined to north-western Europe: to Scandinavia where their victory was complete, to England and Scotland, to most of the principalities of northern Germany, to Holland and to certain cities and cantons of Switzerland. In all these lands the Catholic faith was banned. Likewise in Catholic lands – and they held most of the population of Europe – the worship of any other faith was banned.

The early decades of the Reformation resembled the early years of Islam. The reformers depended on the sword as well as the word. Luther's message could not have won a huge territory on both shores of the Baltic without the support of princes and regiments. Calvin succeeded only because he was backed by the rulers of the Swiss republic of Geneva. In France his doctrine, failing to win over the monarch, began to lose its strong footholds in the south and west of the land. In Paris on St Bartholomew's Day in 1572, some 20 000 Protestants were slaughtered.

While the Protestants tended to centralise power in most of the lands where they were victorious – or where they were allowed by the ruler to be victorious – they also initiated a democratic stream. Calvinism set up a system of governing the church in which the senior members of the congregation were influential. Like Lutheranism it preached that the Bible and not the church was the ultimate court of appeal, and to the Bible every devout and intelligent Christian could appeal. In Calvinism ordinary people had more influence than in any Catholic congregation.

In the end the Protestants made no headway south of the Alps or south of the Pyrenees. Their triumph was on the far shores of the Atlantic. Whereas Spain refused to allow Jews, Muslims and Protestants to emigrate to its new colonies, Britain and Holland allowed Protestant dissenters to sail away to the new American colonies. In Boston and other New England towns the Calvinist Reformation burned with a fierce flame. The rise of the United States, its distinctive culture, its early fostering of intense debate and its ultimate democracy probably owed as much to the Protestant reformers as to any other single fact.

At first the Reformation seemed to be a blow to women. Probably the only institutions in the western world in which women held power in their own right were the convent and the monarchy. Women governed the female convents; and when a convent held valuable properties in a city, the woman in charge held additional power. Thus in Zurich the abbess of the Benedictine convent helped to administer the town. The closing of the powerful convents in most of the states that were now Protestant indirectly reduced the power of women. There was one compensation. Most Protestant churches believed that as many people as possible, whether women or men, should read the Bible; and that led to the opening of more schools which taught reading and writing.

Steadily the rate of female literacy began to grow. Prussia, a Lutheran stronghold, made education compulsory for boys and girls in 1717. In the Dutch city of Amsterdam in 1780, a remarkable 64 per cent of brides signed the register when they married, while the others clumsily drew a cross in the place where their signature of consent was called for. In England, about 1 per cent of women could read in the year 1500, but this had risen to 40 per cent by 1750. Belatedly, Catholic countries followed this revolutionary trend.

The Russian church, in contrast, turned its back on literacy. No Christian church in any other nation had as many adherents as the Orthodox church had in Russia; but its priests were poorly educated, and many were far more skilled in chanting from memory – or from forgetfulness – than in reading the scriptures. The authority of the priest was cemented because few of his congregation could read the Bible. The full Bible, with testaments old and new, was not freely available in modern Russian until 1876.

WATCH OUT FOR THE WITCH

The surging interest in religion took unusual forms. More evil was detected as well as more saintliness. In many parts of Europe witches were multiplying, or so it was said.

In an era of religious fervour, belief in mercy and goodness went hand in hand with belief in the power of evil to ruin people's lives. Evil was personified in the witch. When tragedy appeared it was increasingly attributed to the plotting of a witch. When an economic blow struck a village or family, a search was made for the offending witch. Most accusations of witchcraft arose out of the quarrels, tensions and hardships of daily life. The encountering of witches was like the sighting of flying saucers in the second half of the 20th century. Once the idea caught hold of a region, it spread with speed.

In Europe during the three centuries between 1450 and 1750, most of the 100 000 or more 'proven' witches were concentrated in a small number of regions. In the south-east of Scotland and in eastern France, witches were said to be especially active. In Europe over a long period, close to one in three of detected witches lived in Germany.

There were patterns in the spread of witchcraft. Thus in England and Hungary nine of every 10 convicted witches were women, though in Iceland and Estonia most of those accused and convicted were men. Of the tens of thousands of people sentenced to death for witchcraft in Europe, three of every four were women. Many were old and disfigured but some were young and pretty, and a few were children. In Britain a typical female witch was either a spinster or a widow, was old and poor, and tended to quarrel with her neighbours.

Religious tensions sharpened the search for witches, and they were often found in towns or regions where rival sects were face to face. A land with religious unity was much less likely to produce accusations of witchcraft. Russia was almost devoid of witches. In Ireland, Poland, southern Italy and several other Catholic lands and regions the arresting of witches was rare.

In an ultra-religious era, nearly everyone believed in the power of organised evil. It was assumed that the devil was at large in the world, with a million pairs of evil eyes and a million pairs of hands, and that he was choosing witches as his personal servants. It was believed, and even more so in Africa than Europe, that witches did immense harm to human lives. This emphasis on the might of evil – and it is no longer prominent as a belief in western civilisation – was the essence of the crusade against witchcraft and the justi- fication for the cruelty inflicted on witches.

The tragedy was that western civilisation, when at last it ceased to believe in witches, was also ceasing to believe in humankind's immense capacity for evil as well as good. In the first half of the 20th century, millions of educated and cultivated people were not prepared for the ruthless way in which Evil, by what- ever respectable name it adopted, would so devastate Europe that the era of the witches seemed a mere mishap.

20

VOYAGE TO INDIA

Portugal to India became a regular sea route. It was the most arduous that the world had so far known; and the voyage to the Americas had no counterpart. Four or five ships set out each year from Portugal to India, and their captains planned the voyage carefully so that they could make best use of the winds and curb the prospect of encountering dangerous storms or hazardous coasts. The favoured time to sail from Lisbon was in the first half of March, for this would allow them some six months to sail beyond the Cape of Good Hope and some way into the Indian Ocean where the winds were likely to turn in their favour. There, if they were too late, they might encounter difficult winds that would persuade them to turn back to a place of shelter. A voyage to India could last a year or more if it was commenced at the adverse time of year.

Some Portuguese ships called at Brazil on the voyage out, but most ships called at no port. Indeed in the early years the captains knew no African port where, on calling, they could feel welcome or even safe from surprise attack. Once a well-loaded Portuguese ship had passed the most southerly coast of Africa and turned north, she usually sailed through the wide Mozambique Channel which separated Africa from Madagascar. Following the coast almost to the Red Sea, the ships then turned east, following the Arabian coast and so making their way towards their Indian destinations. The soldiers and merchants who came aboard at Lisbon were not mentally prepared for such a long and tempestuous ordeal.

After a few weeks the fresh water, which was usually stored in wooden casks, began to taste foul. It also became scarce as the voyage went on, and so the washing of the face let alone the rest of the body was not a frequent event. With so many people crammed together, and with the ship spending much time in the tropics, and with no fresh fruit or vegetables, disease spread with ease. In the years from 1629 to 1634 more than 5000 Portuguese soldiers set sail from Lisbon but fewer than half reached India alive. Most ships carried a surgeon whose favoured remedy was simply to bleed three or four litres of blood from a sick patient. The cure rarely worked miracles.

Goa became the chief Indian harbour for the Portuguese; and indeed it remained a province of Portugal until the 20th century. From Goa would set out, once a year, a large ship loaded with trading cargoes for Malacca (Melaka) on the Malay Peninsula and for Macao in China and so to Japan. Again the captain would try to adjust his time of sailing to gain the benefit of the monsoons of the western Pacific. The start of the new monsoon was like a traffic light, proclaiming the green or 'go' signal to ships coming from one direction and the red or 'stop' signal to ships coming from another.

The cargoes exchanged between Asia and Europe were mostly high-priced luxury goods that could afford the high costs of transport. In China and Japan would arrive scarlet cloth, woollen apparel, crystal and glass, Indian chintzes and Flemish clocks. In the hold of the ship returning to India and eventually to Europe were Chinese silk and silken goods in large quantities as well as exotic medicinal ingredients. Another item of 'cargo' might consist of Chinese slaves or servants.

In Goa at certain times of the year the Portuguese ships prepared for their homeward voyage. In addition to Chinese goods they took on loads of pepper – western India was the home of pepper – and cinnamon and other spices. There also was carried aboard containers of nitrate of potash, which was the crucial ingredient of gunpowder; indigo dye; cotton piece goods; and eventually Indian diamonds that came from the mines of Golconda. Such cargoes made India seem magically rich. About the year 1600, in the eyes of most Europeans, the name India was a synonym for dazzling wealth. Several of William Shakespeare's plays display that dazzle. In the play *Twelfth Night* Maria is addressed as the golden girl, 'my metal of India'. To resemble shining metal from India was to be doubly precious.

In addition to the cargoes which were literally crammed into the Portuguese homeward-bound ships there were personal cargoes which were placed or roped together on the open deck, where they would be exposed to spray and salt wind. Every member of the crew had a right to load cargo and sell it in Lisbon. Even the ship's boy had the right to fill one-third of a wooden chest with cinnamon – if he could afford to buy the spice in the Indian street market. The officers and crew indeed held the sole right to use the open decks as a storage place for their personal cargoes. The decks were packed high with bundles, packages, wooden chests and crates to the point of making the ship unstable in certain winds. A walk along the deck was like an obstacle race.

This roundabout sea route past the Cape replaced in economic importance the long caravan trails and silk roads that for centuries had traversed the centre of Asia from the Black Sea to the walled cities of China. One century or so after the sea route was established, the Dutch language could be heard in the riverside alleyways of Canton, and Portuguese was becoming the pidgin language of the Asian trade and the precursor to pidgin English, while a few pots of Japanese or Chinese tea – bought at astronomical prices – were being brewed in western Europe.

Priests had rounded the Cape in early Portuguese ships. One of the first was Francis Xavier, an early Jesuit who vowed to lead a life of poverty and dedication.

Arriving in India in 1542 he made the Portuguese port of Goa the base for missionary voyages. He was not the first Christian in India – several congregations of Syrian-speaking Christians existed on the Malabar Coast by AD 600 – but he was dynamic. He travelled as far away as Japan, where he won converts.

The Catholics far more than the Protestants were the early missionaries in the New World, and their courage in venturing there was to have far-reaching effects. They were to the fore partly because in both the Americas and Asia the two pioneering European colonisers were Catholic nations. Indeed Protestantism was not born until a quarter of a century after Columbus sailed.

Perhaps nothing did more to restrain Lutherans, Calvinists and Anglicans from organising missions to the heathens than the fact that most of their clergy, as part of the revolt against the papacy, were married. To encourage a wife and young family to accompany a clergyman to an unhealthy tropical port in America, Africa or Asia in 1600 was an invitation to an early death. Furthermore the Catholic church had relative unity – a powerful aid to the spreading of its message.

Long after Protestant nations had become the dominant traders and governors in India and most of coastal Asia, they were slow to foster the work of missionaries. It was not until 1704, more than a century and a half after the death of Francis Xavier, that a Protestant king, Frederik IV of Denmark, founded a missionary outpost in India.

SPIKED BY DISTANCE

In southern Asia these Portuguese, Dutch, British and French empires – and the extension of the Spanish empire in the Philippines – at first occupied only a necklace of steamy Asian ports and a few inland trading depots. They could be called empires only with hesitation. Their power, away from the coast, was usually weak. Compared to the Roman Empire their cultural impact was weak because so few Europeans settled in the ports and trading posts, being deterred by the hot climate, the fear of tropical diseases and the distance from home.

Europe was too divided to be able to dominate vast tracts of overseas land. Moreover Europe could apply in Asia only a fraction of its military might: Asia was simply too far away. Distance in effect still spiked Europe's guns and retarded its fighting ships.

In eastern Asia the advance of the Europeans, so confident in the first century, was halted. Japan, which at first was friendly to alien merchants and missionaries, had sent a deputation of four youths all the way to Europe, where in the 1580s they were handsomely treated by the mighty of Madrid, Lisbon and Rome. Early in the following century the Japanese had second thoughts. They expelled nearly all Europeans and killed many Jesuit and other priests who did not wish to be expelled. Only Dutch traders were permitted to make occasional visits.

China, dominant in its own part of the world,

extended its long land borders in the 18th century. It occupied Tibet and eastern Turkestan, areas which it had long regarded as within its sphere of influence. Rarely before had China commanded so much of the silk road. At the same time, some of the Indian rulers took a lesson from the Chinese and defied the Europeans. In June 1757, one of the blackest months in Britain's colonial history, more than 100 of its soldiers died while imprisoned in the Black Hole of Calcutta.

While western Europe was revelling in a phase of global conquest, central Europeans still lived in fear of the Ottoman Empire. Turkish armies camped outside the gates of Vienna in the summer of 1683, and once again they laid siege to one of the mightiest cities of Christendom. Now it was the Turks' turn to retreat. In the late 1680s they were driven from Buda, being one half of the present city of Budapest, which they had ruled for more than a century. They lost the city of Belgrade and even, for a few years, Athens. For lovers of art the defeat of the Turks in Athens was to prove a calamity, because, in the course of the fighting, part of the Parthenon was toppled. Soon the Turks regained Athens and they ruled it until 1829. There was no starker sign of the limits of influence of Christian Europe than that the city of Jerusalem, century after century, remained in Islam's grip.

In 1600 the rise of Europe to dominate much of the world was not preordained. So far its victories were more in coastal America than in Asia and Africa. It had made little impact on Japan, China and the Ottoman Turks. And yet its confidence and commercial drive, its new technology, and its prowess in war – even when hopelessly outnumbered – were portents of the coming era when it would shape a diversity of cultures far more extensive than Rome had ruled.

21

THE NEW WORLD BEARS GIFTS

Spain and Portugal had won the first phase of colonisation and conquest partly because they were strong in seafaring and partly because they were also the two European countries which were closest to Central and southern America. After 1600, however, they began to lose impetus.

The new phase in colonising the Americas belonged to France, Holland and Britain, seafaring nations which also had a geographical advantage over the Mediterranean states. By 1650 their little ports, wooden fortresses and fur-trading posts in North America dotted the Atlantic coast and the near interior. France was busy in Canada and on two of the West Indian islands, Martinique and Guadeloupe. Britain held colonies extending along the Atlantic coast from the island of Newfoundland – which it shared with the French – to New England, Virginia and the West Indies. Even the Danes were soon to set up plantations in the Virgin Islands. Of the states in western Europe only the Germans were missing.

On the Atlantic coast of North America the Dutch and the Swedes each held colonies that broke the continuity of the chain of British coastal colonies. New York was founded by the Dutch, and the island of Curaçao in the Caribbean was Dutch too, while Delaware was Swedish. In total, six western European nations held colonies in the Americas, but the Spanish and Portuguese territories were still paramount and together they probably produced the most wealth.

A SUPERMARKET CROSSES THE ATLANTIC

The Europeans were beginning to dominate the Americas, but the stream of influence ran in both directions. Never before in the history of the world had so many valuable plants been transferred from one continent to another.

Maize was the most remarkable of the new plants, and Christopher Columbus himself carried seeds back in his ship. Maize, or Indian corn, had the amazing ability at harvest time to produce, for each grain planted, far more grains than wheat or rye could. Maize did not spread with miraculous speed, but it eventually reached farms in the warmer parts of Europe. By 1700 the tall green stalks of maize could be seen waving in the breeze in much of rural Spain, Portugal and Italy.

The American potato was to northern Europe what maize was to the south. The Irish welcomed the potato, for on their tiny plots of land it grew more calories than any other known crop. It was growing in County Down by 1605, and by the end of that century the hot potato was the chief food of Ireland's poor. From Ireland, curiously, seed potatoes were taken to North America, where this South American food was still unknown. Germans also rejoiced in it, knowing that a crop of potatoes – unlike a crop of ripe corn – was not easily damaged or destroyed by a rampaging army.

In European gardens could also be found other American novelties: the sweet potato, the tomato – which was astonishingly slow to please European palates (it was still a novelty in Britain four centuries after Columbus returned) – and the artichoke, which gained in France an early popularity far exceeding that of the tomato. Mystifyingly a new kind of artichoke, also introduced by the French from Canada, was called the Jerusalem artichoke.

Turkey, the only meat to be introduced from the Americas, was equally disguised by its European name. In fact, the names 'turkey cock' and 'turkey hen' were first given to the exotic guineafowl seen by European explorers off the west coast of Africa and then were transferred to the tall Mexican birds which eventually reached European farmyards. The turkeys, which strictly speaking should have been called *mexicos*, were popular on Spanish and English dinner tables as early as the Christmas of 1573.

That lands as far apart as Turkey and America should be viewed as the same by cooks in the kitchen was a sign of how much mystery centred on the whereabouts of East and West. Even American maize was called turkey corn or turkey wheat by European peasants who rightly marvelled at these prolific plants unknown to their grandparents.

From the Americas came such delicacies as the pineapple – to be eaten only at the tables of the very rich – and the capsicum pepper, as well as such luxuries as cocoa and tobacco. Like nearly all the transatlantic novelties, tobacco spread slowly across Europe; and two centuries after Columbus's first voyage a typical rural worker in Poland and Sicily probably had not yet sniffed for the first time the sweet aroma of burning tobacco.

The monarchies of Europe were not sure how to handle this new fashion for smoking tobacco in a pipe or sniffing it in the form of snuff. Some kings tried to ban it. In Russia a smoker could be punished by the amputating of his nose. Other countries which held tropical colonies tried to ban the growing of tobacco on their home soil so that it could be grown in their colonies and then imported through a port where a tax could be collected on each lot of tobacco carried ashore. England set up colonies in Virginia and Maryland mainly for the growing of tobacco. Distant Turkey was to become one of the most enthusiastic growers of American tobacco which – to increase the confusion – became known as Turkish tobacco!

The traffic in minerals, in the short term, was the most dramatic of all the Atlantic trades. The first prize for the Spaniards in Central and South America was gold and silver. Once they gained full control of their American territories and sent forced labour to work the mines, they would ship home, in heavily armed convoys, so much silver and gold each year that monetary inflation began to convulse Spain and then Europe. There will always be debate about the role of precious metals in igniting Europe's inflation of the 16th century, but one fact seems clear. The dramatic bouts of inflation across the western world have coincided with the fighting of large wars or, even more significantly, a major change in the supply of just two crucial commodities: precious metals in earlier centuries and oil in the inflationary 1970s.

In the early ships which carried precious metals and precious plants and seeds across the Atlantic came another tourist. The disease syphilis almost certainly came from the Americas. Syphilis became common in the 1500s; and a gnawed or nibbled appearance of the nose was often a symptom.

A PEACOCKS' PARADE

The European voyages also tapped Asia. For centuries a stream of Asian wares and plants had crossed the width of Asia by land but now it flowed along the sea lanes. Chinese tea found its way to Europe, as did the secret of porcelain and many other manufactures.

Kaolin, the raw material for porcelain, was a word which originally seemed strange to most European ears. The word was actually the name of the hill in China where the soft white clay was mined. An enterprising French priest sent samples of kaolin to Europe around 1700 and pointed out that it was vital for the manufacture of porcelain. Soon prospectors found similar deposits of kaolin in Germany, France and England. In Europe the first true porcelain was made at the Meissen factory in Saxony in 1707.

From China came garden flowers new to Europe. The chrysanthemum was a favourite. Solely a yellow flower until the eighth century, it was honoured in China as the floral aristocrat, and praised by poets in verse. It adorned the street markets in parts of China after the summer flowers had passed their prime. By the year 1600 the Chinese had bred some 500 varieties, of which a few reached Europe in the new wave of floral imports.

The New World also gave to eager Europeans a delight which was not common. It gave them bright colours. As late as the year 1500, most cities and villages had been drab in their colours. A cottage might be whitewashed but rarely was it painted. Timber houses looked drab, though in Holland the bricks then in favour emitted a cosy red glow. Admittedly stone houses could be enhanced by the colour of the stone, but the building stone was usually chosen not for colour but convenience. In many cities the stone was naturally dark, and over the years even pale stone was slowly discoloured by wood smoke – a foretaste of what coal smoke would do more thoroughly. Admittedly in some medieval cathedrals the stained glass was beautiful when the sun was shining, but the colour was heightened because so much in the city streets was dull.

Europeans' clothes were usually drab, except those worn by the rich. Goods were not packed in bright colours because any form of wrapping was expensive, and wrapping paper was a sheer extravagance and never coloured. Banners and flags were attractive because they were far richer in colour than the clothes worn by most citizens.

One of the miracles from the new-found Americas was new colours. Mexicans, long before the coming of the Spaniards, had observed how a wingless insect, feeding on the cactus plant, contained when pregnant a vivid scarlet colour. The dried bodies of 70 000 insects were required to produce just half a kilogram of cochineal powder, which could then be used to create the most vivid of dyes. Scarlet had long been the name of a colour used for banners and clothes, but the scarlet freshly made in England from cochineal dazzled the eye. The new scarlet became a buzz word, and was even conferred on scarlet fever, which in the 1670s was first diagnosed as a disease in its own right rather than a form of measles or smallpox.

The sea route around Africa opened up a cheap source of the colour blue. Indigo, the plant from which the best blue was extracted, was farmed in Bengal. Cut in the fields and carted in bundles to the drying yards and water tanks, the indigo plant released its indoxyl by a process of fermentation. For many centuries small and expensive consignments of Indian indigo dye had occasionally reached the Mediterranean by the overland route, but now it began to arrive in thousands of wooden chests stowed in Dutch and Portuguese ships. Indigo produced such a brilliant blue that the blue colour traditionally extracted from the European woad plant seemed dull. Soon, in the more fashionable precincts of Amsterdam and Venice, men and women wearing coats and hats, capes and tunics of bright indigo blue paraded themselves like peacocks. Even the French army abandoned its russet uniforms and dressed in blue.

Colours may seem to be a mirror of the vanities, but they were central to the rise of Brazil, now one of the most populous nations. The Portuguese were the first to assess the coast of Brazil. Thirteen of their ships, sailing towards the southern tip of Africa and so on to India, were deflected by the tropical winds to the coast of Brazil, where they spent a week in April 1500. Thereafter Portuguese ships occasionally used Brazilian harbours as a halfway house on the long Indian route. They carried away Brazilian people, monkeys and parrots in small numbers – as captives and curiosities – but their main prize was the logwood tree. It was so valued in Europe that it led directly to the opening of the port of Pernambuco where, protected by a coral reef, Portuguese ships could safely anchor.

A lesser variety of the tree grew in the East Indies, and was already known as brazilwood. So the land of Brazil received its new name. The brazilwood tree, stripped of its thick bark and soaked in a tub of water, produced a red colour known sometimes as the juice of Brazil, and prized by dyers in Europe.

NEW DOSES OF EXCITEMENT

Many tiny packages, boxes and casks came in the new cargoes to European warehouses and were deemed as precious as gold. From China came caddies containing small quantities of that precious ingredient of medicine, perfume and the art of embalming – musk. Dry and light, dark in colour, it sometimes resembled dried blood in appearance. Cut from a sac in the abdomen of a small male deer that flourished in the mountains of central Asia, it was sewn up in a small skin by Canton operators. In the era of few pain-killers, musk induced drowsiness. The first edition of a celebrated encyclopaedia vowed that it was better than opium, for it did not leave an aftermath of 'stupor or languidness'. By the 17th century the Chinese were importing from the west opium itself, which they smoked in pipes or consumed as a pain-stifling medicine. China tried to ban the smoking of opium, a ban which failed to halt the inflow of opium extracted from poppies specially grown in British India for the illicit Canton market.

Everywhere the market for new medicines was large. Europe then suffered much from malaria, and in the marshes of Italy it was virulent. A cure was offered by the bark of a Peruvian bush, the *cinchona*. Mainly imported to Europe by Catholic priests, it was at first known as Jesuit's bark. That the crucial ingredient in the bark was quinine was discovered by the French during the time of the Napoleonic Wars.

In Europe cloves from the Indonesian archipelago were prized as a medicine, especially for toothache, as well as a spicer of food and drink. In the eyes of most merchants, pepper was the prize in South-East Asia. A creeper that clung to the branches of trees, its berries were picked when bright red and then spread on mats under the hot sun, where they were allowed to shrivel and become black. It was so costly that in many European kitchens it was sprinkled on special meats as meticulously as if it were gold dust. Like many items of food that were once expensive, pepper lost some of its glamour as it became cheaper.

Not only the meal table of the wealthier Europeans but also the face of agriculture itself was being altered. The voyages of Columbus, Vasco da Gama and other European sailors across the Atlantic, Indian and Pacific oceans promoted a revolution in the world's agriculture. Alongside the cargoes stowed on deck or locked below were small consignments of seeds and seedlings which eventually were carried, by a series of deliberate and chance happenings, to every continent. Coffee, cotton, sugar and indigo plants went to the Americas to be grown on a large scale, with their harvests being exported to Europe. To Argentina went cattle and, eventually, to Australia went sheep, and ultimately the one land held more cattle and the other held more sheep than had been pastured on any land in Europe.

A similar transfer of plants and animals had happened again and again in the distant past, whether 10 000 years ago in Asia Minor, 5000 years ago in northern Europe or in the early Christian era in central Asia. But this latest exchange spanned much of the surface of the earth and was conducted with unprecedented speed.

Here was an early version of the information revolution, with the erratic sailing ships serving as a lifeline along which was carried an incredibly small number of new seeds, seedlings and breeding animals. Their effects were only slowly appreciated. The same unpredictability was to be true of the steam revolution, and is probably true of the information revolution in which satellites and computers, fibre optics, microchips and the fax and Internet are driving forces. A remarkable journey had been commenced but nobody knew where it would end.

During this international interchange of plants and raw materials, casualties arose. Many birds, animals and plants were endangered by the arrival of new people, new animals and new guns and snares.

On the volcanic islands of Mauritius and Réunion had lived for countless years a flightless bird, the dodo. A member of the pigeon family, big and docile, with thick horny legs and white feathers and an unusual head, the bird lived safely, assailed by no predators. Its body was so large that, when plucked, it would not have fitted into a domestic cooking oven. Then the European explorers arrived, bringing pigs and rats. The eggs laid by the dodo in nests on the ground were vulnerable.

The last-known dodo, caught on the island of Réunion, is said to have died in a French ship sometime before 1746. The phrase 'dead as a dodo' became a synonym for extinction. In every region of the New World a variety of species, whether the passenger pigeon of North America or the marsupial striped 'tiger' of Tasmania, went the way of the dodo.

22

THE GLASS EYE OF SCIENCE

Science was stirring itself in Europe. Ceasing to crawl, it began to walk and even to run. It was running for some time before it passed China in most fields, but by the 1520s there were strong signs of its gathering speed. The same printing presses which were expounding Luther were explaining the latest discoveries of science. The printed page travelled with ease, whereas the typical European scholar did not. Most of Europe's famous scientists of 1550 had never met most of their foreign contemporaries face to face, even when they lived only a few hundred kilometres apart.

New advances came from studying the sun and earth and stars. In this field the mighty discoverer was Nicolaus Copernicus, a Polish scholar, who used all his powers of measuring and observing as well as that uncommon activity known as 'thinking' to prove that the sun was at the centre of the universe. He dethroned the planet earth, a victory so momentous that it seemed at first to challenge the Bible and the very essence of Christianity, which saw the earth as the centre of the universe.

Copernicus began to dethrone the earth in about 1510, soon after Columbus and his voyages of discovery had enlarged it. The victory of Copernicus, however, was not assured even after he died in 1543. In a sense his insight is only half-grasped even today. Common speech and poetic imagery still imply that the earth is the centre of the universe. Each morning, in the mind's eye, it is the sun that rises and not the earth that sets.

An emphasis on measurement and observation, indeed a whole new scientific method, drove these advances. Anatomy gained from the new eagerness of Italian medical schools to dissect the human body rather than rely on what old Greek scholars had written. The Christian embargo on dissecting a body was eased. An autopsy had even been sanctioned on the body of Pope Alexander V after his mysterious death in 1410. The brilliant young Flemish doctor Vesalius frequently dissected bodies, and at the University of Padua he taught his bold findings in the 1540s. He rewrote the old anatomy books.

The wave of discoveries, made on many scientific fronts, were the work of hundreds of hobby scientists, stargazers, medical men, and clergymen with an hour to spare. Many were all-rounders who were intent on solving a cluster of intellectual riddles. Thus Isaac Newton, who was acclaimed in his lifetime as the greatest of all physicists, investigated theology, chemistry, astrology, astronomy and the making of telescopes as well as the laws of motion and gravity. Rarely in the 16th and 17th centuries were famous scientists full-time investigators, and rarely did they live long lives. Isaac Newton was unusual in that he lived into his eighties, at which time he possessed all but one of his teeth and an eyesight so keen that he needed no spectacles. Such was his versatility that he could have made his own spectacles.

A breakthrough in science is said by some observers to be no more than the application of common sense, but several of these theories seemed to defy the common sense of their time, both the spiritual and the secular versions of common sense, and so were not readily accepted. Many discoverers wisely hesitated to publicise what they had found, whereas today's discoverers are tempted to leap into print without a day's delay. Copernicus spent one-third of a century nursing his central idea before he was persuaded to entrust it to a book. Newton is said to have glimpsed his major discovery in physics while watching an apple fall from a tree in an English garden in 1666, but 21 years passed before he expounded his theory in print. William Harvey, the English physician who discovered that the blood perpetually circulated, lectured about his discovery for a dozen or more years before he put it on paper in 1628, publishing it not in London but in a German city.

While the printer disseminated many of the discoveries, the priest and parson were tempted to impede them. Religious leaders opposed or were highly suspicious of several revolutionary ideas in science. The very idea that natural laws, hitherto unknown, operated in the universe, and that similar laws might be found to be operating in the human as well as the physical realm, was a potential danger to a religion which preached that God, all-wise and all-knowing, presided over every corner of the world and could suspend natural laws and work miracles. Even China, which was sympathetic in most eras to most sciences, set up religious obstacles to the investigating of the stars, for the stars gave rise to predictions, which were a prerogative of the emperor.

GLASS AND THE TRANSPLANTED EYE

The scientific revolution was a marvellous advance in the way the world was *seen*. Whereas, before 1550, the skilled worker in metals was responsible for such advances as the mechanical clock and the printing press, it was the skilled worker in glass who facilitated such later discoveries as the microscope and telescope. Glass became the scientist's transplanted eye for seeing the invisible.

The ancient Egyptians had produced the first vessels of hollow glass. The Syrians invented the blowpipe for blowing glass into round thin-walled vessels in about 200 BC, and the Romans manufactured a rough glass which was usually a little muddy but at its best was clear. It was Venice, the Silicon Valley of its era, which improved on the old Roman methods of making glass. The glassmakers of Venice had become so numerous, and the fires burning in their workshops posed such a danger of setting fire to the whole city, that in 1291 the government moved them to the adjacent island of Murano. The first mirrors or looking glasses of any clarity were made in Venice about 1500, and the Venetians kept secret their novel process of manufacture for more than 150 years. Mirrors did more than anything to enhance Venice's reputation as the home of luxurious, vain and maybe immoral feminine wares: a reputation already created by Venetian gloves, fans and those embroidered Venetian breeches which tightly fitted the legs.

A revolution in science was also in the hands of the glassmakers. The power of curved glass to magnify an object under examination had been known even before the rise of Greek civilisation; but specific glass lenses for use in spectacles and reading glasses were not invented until about 1300. Spectacles preserved in the Deutsches Museum in Munich date from 50 years later; and it was possible for a physician doing his painful duty during the Black Death to put on his spectacles in order to examine more closely the skin and tongue of victims. When printed books came into vogue the demand for spectacles increased, especially amongst men and women who wished to read in the poor light of a northern European winter.

The illuminating power of glass was dramatically revealed in the seafaring town of Middelburg in the Netherlands. In 1608 Hans Lippershey, a maker of spectacles, began to construct useful telescopes. To the astonishment of those who employed his telescope, they could clearly see a person standing 3 kilometres away. The idea but not the telescope reached Galileo Galilei, who was teaching mathematics at Padua in northern Italy. Making his own version of what he called a 'spy glass', he was delighted to find that it could magnify by a ratio of three. Grinding his own glass lenses he increased the ratio of magnification to eight and then 32. In the nearby city of Venice, merchants and shipowners carried the exciting telescope to the top of towers and, looking out to sea, saw ships which were invisible to the naked eye.

Galileo's improved telescope was achieving in the skies what Columbus and Magellan had done by sailing the seas: it was mapping new worlds. Through his telescopes, mostly made from Venetian glass, Galileo inspected the moon, which he described as a 'most beautiful and delightful sight'. He also detected what nobody else had seen – the moon's craters and unpolished surface. He was the first to see the spots on the sun, and found that the Milky Way consisted of stars.

He also came to the same conclusion as Copernicus: that the earth was not the centre of the universe to which every other heavenly body paid court. This insight carried profound implications for certain sentences in the Old Testament which Galileo denounced as written by the ignorant for the ignorant. The church raised a heavy hand against him in 1616 and an even heavier hand after he persisted with his theories. He spent the last eight years of his life under house arrest on his little farm near Florence.

To the telescope, the Dutch and Italian glassworkers added the microscope. Anton van Leeuwenhoek, who sold dress materials and clothes in the Dutch town of Delft, became a master maker of microscopes. With a magnification of at least 270, his microscopes saw far more than had ever been seen by human eyes. In 1677 he described for the first time the spermatozoon. He described with accuracy the red blood cell. His microscope enabled him to puncture various widely held myths: that the flea was born out of sand and that the eel was hatched out of dew. Meanwhile in England, Robert Hooke, while looking at plant tissues under the microscope, coined the crucial word 'cell'. It was not yet realised that all plants and animals consisted of cells.

The microscope was an eye-opener for botany and zoology. At the very time when the exploring of new lands multiplied known plants and animals, the Swedish botanist and physician Carolus Linnaeus perfected his method – soon to be the whole world's method – of classifying all living things by giving them two Latin names, the one specifying the broad genus and the other the particular species.

What Linnaeus did for the classifying of plants, other scientists, south of the Alps, achieved in the classifying of time. The reform of the calendar was a snail-like process. In the heyday of Rome, Julius Caesar and his advisers had reformed the calendar by abandoning the cycle of the moon and turning to the solar year. The solar year extends over 365 days, five hours, and 48 and three-quarter minutes; but those overhanging hours created a difficulty for the new calendar. Julius Caesar adopted a sensible compromise. His calendar, later named Julian in his honour, assumed for the sake of simplicity that the sun ran its annual course in 365 and a quarter days. Accordingly it counted 365 days for every first and second and third year, and 366 days for every fourth or leap year.

Caesar died long before the inherent difficulty of his calendar became prominent. The awkward fact was that his calendar in each succeeding century fell a little further behind. Indeed in each year the calendar lost just over 11 minutes and in its initial 1000 years it lost about seven days. It also interfered with the fixing of Easter Sunday, an event unknown in Julius Caesar's time, but later of profound importance.

At last, in 1582, Pope Gregory XIII acted decisively. Using the computations of the Naples astronomer and medical man Luigi Ghiraldi, the pope announced his solution. In that very year he would eliminate the 10 days running from 5 to 14 October. In short, the calendar would be brought up to date with one stroke of a quill pen. The future would also be handled with the same decisiveness. As a long-term corrective the new Gregorian calendar would embrace a leap year in 1600 and 2000, though not in the intervening years of 1700, 1800 and 1900.

Those living in Spain, Portugal and Italy would long discuss the memorable October of 1582. Ten days, to their puzzlement, simply vanished from their life. A few months later France and the various Catholic states of Germany lost their 10 days. Protestant countries, however, were not sure whether they should follow a reform initiated by a pope. England continued to follow a different calendar to that which prevailed in Catholic France and Spain. When it was Christmas Day in England it was already January on the other side of the English Channel. In Germany two towns only a few kilometres apart followed a different calendar, depending on whether they lived within a Lutheran or a Catholic state.

When Britain at last adopted this new calendar, 11 unlived days had to be deleted. Thus in 1752 its calendar jumped overnight from 2 September to 14 September, a change that made for dislocation in many quarters and consternation in others. In London a mob in an understandable state of confusion was heard to chant: 'Give us back our eleven days.' Russia and several other nations within the Eastern or Orthodox church continued to follow the old calendar. Russia was to wait until the year of its communist revolution,

1917, to adopt what the pope and Italy had initiated more than three centuries earlier.

The search for new ways of counting and measuring was hastened by the variations and confusion in the existing ways of measurement. The measuring of a mile was a subject of argument and doubt whenever a border of European lands was crossed by a traveller. An English mile was 1760 yards, an Italian mile was 2029 yards, an Irish mile was 3038, a German mile was 8116, and the Swedish mile exceeded 10 000 yards.

At least hot and cold were now measured with more precision, though not with total agreement. In 1714 Gabriel Fahrenheit, a Baltic inhabitant who became a maker of instruments in Holland, invented the mercury thermometer. On his scale the boiling point was pegged at 212 degrees, but a few decades later a new scale was invented by the Swedish astronomer Anders Celsius, who set his boiling point at 100 degrees. These disagreements were aggravated in 1799 when revolutionary France introduced the metric system of weights and measures, with its simple logic and its verbose names.

IN SEARCH OF VENUS

James Cook's first voyage of exploration in the Indian and Pacific oceans was driven by the demands of science. It was confidently predicted that on 3 June 1769 the planet Venus would briefly cross the face of the sun.

Here was a rare chance to learn the exact distance of the sun from the earth – a calculation which, if accurate, would provide vital information for astronomers as well as for ships trying to learn their exact position at sea. On this day of the transit, however, it was possible that the sky might be clouded in Europe, and so the chance to observe would be lost. The decision to seize this opportunity to observe Venus was intensified by the knowledge that the transit would not happen again until 1874.

Britain decided that the most promising place to observe the transit of Venus was on the new-found island of Tahiti, where it was assumed with cheerful optimism that the sky was always clear. The voyage to Tahiti in the far Pacific was meticulously planned. Perhaps the boldest scientific expedition the world had known, a minor foretaste of the moon probes of the 1960s, it was staffed by a tiny team of scientists more talented probably than any previous team which had been assembled for a long expedition. In his ship *Endeavour* went the finest glass telescopes and the finest mechanical clock. Science was the first-class passenger in Cook's wooden ship.

In due course the ship reached Tahiti. A portable observatory was erected, the instruments of science were cleaned and assembled, and the observations were made on the day of days. A haze around the sun, however, made them of little use.

Cook then proceeded to carry out his instructions to search for the great south land which, it was believed, must surely lie somewhere in the vastness of the Pacific Ocean. It had long been an article of faith that to maintain the sheer balance of the ever-spinning globe there must be an equal amount of land in the Southern as in the Northern Hemisphere. Somewhere a continent must lie, hidden. The theory was incorrect, but the conclusion culled from it turned out, by accident, to be correct. Australia was the missing continent, and Cook first saw it at daylight on 20 April 1770.

In fact, various Portuguese, Dutch and British sailors had already seen – or been wrecked upon – parts of the shores of Australia. It was Cook who found the more attractive eastern coast where most Australians live today. In company with his botanist Joseph Banks he so praised its grasslands, soil, fish, natural vegetation and harbours that it was later seen by Britain as a promising site for a colony.

After returning to England, Cook sailed again to southern seas. At high risk to his two wooden ships he sailed south to the wild seas and winds beyond the Antarctic Circle. In three successive summers, he sailed closer than any previous navigator to that frozen continent. Again and again he found bays of ice, actually sailing into them in the hope that he might find land at the far end.

Without knowing it, Cook sailed right around Antarctica. Indeed, the sea of floating ice was so hazardous that he thought no other ships would ever venture further south. The actual land of the Antarctic, beyond the ramparts of ice, was not sighted until 1820, and decades passed before the jigsaw of the long coastline of icy cliffs was pieced together. Here was an area of land larger than the United States, covered with thick ice and topped by mountains rising even higher than the European Alps. Slowly it would be realised that this vast refrigerator of a continent had profound effects on the level of the world's seas and on the winds and climates of a vast area of the Southern Hemisphere.

Cook was a true child of the new age of measurement. On this second voyage he carried the novel chronometer, an accurate and delicate watch invented by James Harrison. Cook was the first navigator and explorer to be able to calculate accurately, in fair weather, the position of his ship on an east–west line: in short, he could determine his longitude. When mapping new lands and reefs, he made charts of unprecedented accuracy.

Cook's three voyages into the Pacific and Indian oceans were in effect like switching on a time machine. Many Pacific islands, settled by the sea-skilled Polynesians in the course of several thousand years, had remained in isolation until Cook arrived. At such strange meetings between such different peoples and cultures there was bound to be some puzzlement and suspicion, even with goodwill on both sides. Captain Cook, normally tactful in his contacts with native peoples, was the victim of a misunderstanding. In 1779 in Hawaii he was clubbed to death.

23

DETHRONING THE HARVEST

In Europe and Asia, the typical family lived close to the breadline. Whether in 1500 or 1800, in France or in China, most families either owned no land or such a small holding that it could barely feed them even in a prolific year. Countless males and unmarried females left their tiny farm or their rural village to work on other farms or at other trades. Often they received free meals while on the job, and those meals represented a considerable part of their earnings.

Much of the rural work fell to women or young children: the weeding of gardens and crops, the shepherding of geese, the carrying of water from the well to the house, the spinning of fibres and making of cloth, the brewing of homemade beer, the foraging for the herbs that served as medicines, and the gathering of firewood for the stove and manure for the garden.

Scavenging and foraging were almost a way of life. A peasant owning one cow and a tiny pocket of land might send his children out each day in summer to cut grass on the roadside, some of which was preserved as hay to feed the cow in the winter. In forests mushrooms and wild berries were sought, and birds' eggs were collected. In many parts of China the population of birds declined, so intensive was the use of land and so eager were the hunters of birds and the collectors of eggs. Daily life, in every part of the world, centred on the production of food.

In 1800, in the whole world, a few millions were still nomadic hunters and gatherers but most were farmers. Their daily life was ruled by the sun and the rain. From the shores of the South China Sea to the shores of the lakes of inland America the triumphant event of the economic calendar was the bringing home of the harvest, a task performed by women and children and men because, once the grain was ripe, all hands were needed to reap it and bind it and carry it to a place of storage. In most parts of the world, though not in the fertile tropical valleys of Asia, the harvest was a once-a-year event.

Grain dominated the meal table to a degree which is now unimaginable in a prosperous country. Much of the grain was eaten as bread or damper but some found its way into mouths in the form of porridge and soup. Gruel, served piping hot, was eagerly devoured in winter. In hungry times, water was plentifully added to a small amount of flour in order to give temporary relief from hunger. One homespun recipe for gruel was 'nine grits and a gallon of water'. In Russia and Poland the *kasha*, a gruel made from rye, was thin and watery after the leaner harvests.

In many European lands the grain, especially barley, was also used for brewing beer. In England home-brewed beer, drunk at nearly every meal, was almost as essential as bread in the daily diet. Children drank it each day. At a well-known boarding school in London in 1704 breakfast for the boys consisted of bread and beer, while the poor people living at the workhouse received beer at nearly every meal. Tea, widely drunk in China, was a drink only for the well-off in Europe. Coffee was also a luxury, except in such coffee-growing lands as Arabia and Brazil.

In Europe and Asia the various grains must have provided more than 80 per cent of the diet of a typical household. In Europe the bakehouse in the village street was in effect a simple supermarket with two kinds of bread for sale. Dearest was a loaf of wheaten bread, baked from almost-pure flour, while the cheaper loaves consisted of bran and second-rate grain. The price of bread was often the barometer of social stability. A rise in the price of bread often denoted the likelihood of unrest.

The failure or half-failure of a harvest was frequent all the way from Sudan to China. In Finland in the early 1690s a long famine killed one-third of the people. France, which in a lush year could almost overflow with cream and honey, suffered a nationwide famine in 16 of the 100 years after 1700. That century which ended in revolution was probably the worst for harvests since the 11th century.

The coming harvest was often mentioned in the prayers of young unmarried women. If the harvest was plentiful, their long-planned marriage was likely to take place. If the harvest was lean, the marriage was postponed. Women in western Europe did not usually marry until they were aged 24 or 26. Late marriage was the main reason why a typical woman gave birth to only four or five children. The big family of eight or 10 children was to be more common in the late 19th century.

A fine harvest was not enough. Sometimes it was at risk when the granaries were invaded by mice. Cats were kept in houses, granaries and barns less because they were pets than because they were mouse-hunters. When in 1755 Dr Samuel Johnson produced his dictionary of the English language, he bluntly defined a cat as a 'domestick animal that catches mice'. But surely a cat was entitled to be stroked and petted for its own sake? Johnson disagreed, labelling the cat as 'the lowest order of the leonine species'.

Traditionally each grain of wheat that was planted in the ground yielded only a few grains at harvest time. In the Netherlands and France between, say, 1500 and 1700 the average yield was perhaps seven to one. In northern Russia the yield was often only three to one. After such a harvest, about one in every three grains had to be stored as seed for next year's harvest. This posed a dilemma if famine set in. With the children crying for food, the temptation was to eat some of the grain that had been set aside as seed for the next harvest.

In Europe the main cereals harvested by the regiments of scythe-carrying reapers were wheat and rye. Crops of millet also occupied a vast expanse in northern China and Africa as well as in Europe. Though the grains of millet were coarse, they lasted up to 20 years; and in the 16th century millet was kept in the granaries of the fortified ports of the Venetian empire as an insurance policy against famine or siege. Oats, another widely used grain, were fed to working horses that pulled large wagons in peacetime and heavy guns in wartime. In the age of the horse, oats served as the equivalent of cheap diesel fuel; but in poor northern countries such as Scotland the same oats were also the food of the poor. Rice was the main crop in the warmer parts of China and could also be seen in Italy. Maize, the wonder crop from the Americas, was increasingly grown on river flats in southern Europe but the price of its wonderful yields was often an exhausted soil.

Of the food consumed in a typical European or Chinese rural household, all but a fraction was produced locally. Salt was the one common food to be carried long distances. In 1500, the salt traffic earned fortunes for carters and shippers. The city of Venice had a virtual monopoly of the salt collected along the Adriatic, and the shipping of salt helped to maintain its economic ascendancy. The warmer part of the Atlantic coastline of France produced salt – by evaporation of sea water in summer – and this salt supplied England and the rich Baltic ports. Between 1427 and 1433 a count was made of the ships which entered the Baltic port of Tallinn. Of the 314 ships, an astonishing 105 came with cargo from the saltworks in the Bay of Bourgneuf in France. The Baltic was the home of the herring trade, and the salting of fresh herrings called for a little mountain of salt each year

Upper Austria held rich deposits of salt that were excavated by underground miners. Mozart was born in a salt town – 'Salzburg' virtually means 'salt town' – and from the nearby mountains each week set forth a procession of small carts carrying nothing but rock salt. Usually the raw salt mined underground required treatment. To purify it called for iron boilers or vats filled with brine, with a fire roaring underneath day and night.

Small villages might run out of salt while waiting for the winter snow to melt. Housewives rejoiced when the wagon – or in China the salt barge – at last arrived with bags of salt. Most villagers bought little salt and used it frugally – a mere 'pinch of salt' was sufficient. The frugality with salt points clearly to the people's precarious standard of living in the era before steam transport dramatically transformed the distribution of salt and grain.

Sea salt or kelp produced soda, which in turn was an ingredient of soap. In much of Europe the other ingredient of soap was tallow – the fat of animals – or a mix of olive oil and rapeseed oil. To make soap was therefore to use raw materials which would otherwise be eaten. In times of starvation the making of soap, and even the act of washing with soap, was like taking food from the mouths of the hungry.

Indians and Turks were more interested in soap and personal hygiene than Europeans. Indeed western Europe was more regular in washing its face and hands back in 1300 than in 1800. The Black Death probably made people suspicious of baths as places where infections might be caught. Baths were seen too as hothouses of moral laxity. In Germany, Frankfurt held 39 public baths in 1387, but a century and a half later – with a new self-consciousness towards nakedness – it held only nine.

Health suffered as the inland cities became larger. No large city had a system for disposing of sewage. The river was the favourite outlet, and someone's sewage, after floating 200 metres downstream, became someone else's washing water or drinking water. In eastern Asia, on the other hand, the sewage from villages and towns was often carted to the surrounding fields and put on the soil as fertiliser. The defect of this method was that many people, in consuming food grown on manured soil, infected their digestive tracts. In Thailand as late as 1970, perhaps two of every three rural people suffered from these infections.

While the population of Europe was usually rising, it was cut back by occasional disasters. Thus, during the Thirty Years War which raged in the years 1618 to 1648, Germany lost perhaps one-third of its population.

While the war was raging, Italy was hit by plague. In 1630 about one million people died on the plains of Lombardy, with Bologna and Parma and Verona losing half of their population in a year. During the two major wars of the 20th century, only Leningrad (St Petersburg) and a few other Russian cities suffered losses of similar magnitude.

For the typical labouring family in some regions of Europe and China, lean years were punctuated by an occasional year of abundance. From about 1570 luxuriant harvests became less frequent in the north of Europe. The climate was colder, and Baltic ports such as Riga were closed by ice more often. Near the Mediterranean the olive groves and their young fruit were hit more often by frost. Called in retrospect the Little Ice Age, this new era of climate continued for about 300 years.

The prolonging of winter and the spread of the glaciers tended to cut off Europe's south from its north. Between Italy and Germany the mountain passes, accessible in the time of Luther, could be dangerous even in the early summer. Not every part of Europe, however, suffered from the changing pattern of weather. Dozens of farming regions still received more than enough sunlight to ripen crops in a typical year. Germany had highly favourable years for wine between 1603 and 1622. Moreover, during these three centuries of a colder climate, wiser farming methods could compensate.

As for China, it suffered from its own run of natural disasters in every century: its epidemics, droughts, floods and fires as well as that pervasive self-inflicted disaster, a long war. In northern China in 1557 one earthquake killed 830 000 people. A long drought would have killed many more by way of starvation and the diseases that were aided by malnutrition. China was more vulnerable than Europe to natural disaster.

Increasing population in Europe and China called for more crops. Between 1500 and 1800 the number of small landowners grew by millions. They cultivated areas previously covered by forest and marshes. Chinese peasants went to the far south and west and took up poor lands. Many Europeans moved as tenant farmers into the hills of central France and Tuscany, where they eventually built simple two-storey stone houses which today, after renovation, are the charming holiday homes of Dutch bankers and English politicians. Where peasants stirred the poor soil with a hoe and planted beans and maize and vines, holiday-makers now bask in the sun, drinking chilled wine on terraces which, decade after decade, were built up with soil carried in a never-ending procession of baskets from a valley far below.

A vast area of land had to be set aside to grow natural fibres for blankets and clothing. Whereas today much clothing is made from synthetics, as late as the year 1800 all the raw materials of clothing came from farms. Land which might have been set aside to grow food had to grow the flax or hemp from which linen sheets and shirts were made or, to a lesser degree, the mulberry leaves with which silkworms were fed. Likewise, land was needed to feed the sheep which supplied wool and the various animals which, in death, supplied hides for the making of leather. In Japan it was common to wear a leather garment when outside the house, and in Europe most boots and shoes were made of leather or wood. Likewise, additional land was needed to grow crops such as woad and indigo, from which were extracted the colours for clothing.

Linen was one of the major products of northern Europe. An ancient textile woven from flax, it provided mummy-cloth for the Egyptians and clothes for millions of ancient Greeks and Romans. In early modern times, linen was widely used for sails for ships, white cloths for tables and sheets for beds (for those who could afford such a fine wrapping) as well as for making trousers, overalls, heavy pinafores and even underwear.

The Dutch painter Rembrandt, around 1651, sketched with pen, ink and brush a 'view of Haarlem'. The Dutch town and its tower-like churches stand in the distance, while on the outskirts rise the big arms of the windmills. But in the foreground are neat rows of what at first sight seem to be small hothouses covering an extensive area of pasture. In fact they are a patchwork of linen cloth, spread out to dry in the fresh air and sun. Wherever linen was woven, these spacious 'bleaching fields' were needed in order that the fresh but dirty linen could be whitened. Nearly every village from Bavaria to East Prussia worked its linen looms.

Cotton, a foreign crop, was a special help to Europe. Grown in India or on slave plantations on the far side of the Atlantic, calico and other Indian goods helped Europe's population to expand by allowing more of its own land to be cultivated for food. Manufactured cotton, especially Indian calico, was shipped in large quantities to Britain before that nation became a great manufacturer of clothes from imported cotton. After 1820, wool also arrived in increasing amounts from Australia and New Zealand. Without the wool and cotton increasingly imported from the New World, Europe would have had to divert huge areas of its own soil to the growing of linen, flax and other raw materials.

In China, cotton was far more important than wool as a material for clothing. Increasingly replacing hemp as a fibre, cotton was using up vast expanses of farmland by 1400, and at picking time bales of cotton filled the thousands of little boats that sailed along Chinese rivers and canals to the towns. Many farmers alternated crops of cotton with rice.

In the year 1800 most people in Europe did not buy even one item of new clothing from shops or fairs. They made clothes at home, inherited them from the dead, or bought them second-hand from the female dealers who dominated this branch of clothing. Within each family there was a busy unpaid trade in clothes.

Garments normally passed from sister to younger sister, brother to younger brother, and were patched and restitched and mended and darned as they changed hands. One of the perks of being a servant was to receive second-hand clothes handed down by the master or mistress. The clothes might be a little frayed, but were received with outstretched arms.

It was an enormous effort for Europe and Asia and Africa to produce enough food and clothing to keep their people alive and well. Sometimes the effort failed, and millions of people had empty bellies and threadbare clothes. If one village was hungry it could not expect outside help, partly because the next village was also likely to be hungry.

Houses in Asia and Europe and Africa were of the simplest: most would now be called slums. In Europe and China the shared bed was normal, and three or four children crowded into it. Sometimes the whole family slept together on a homemade mattress filled with straw collected on the farmlands and renewed each harvest time. Rushes cut on the edge of a nearby swamp might form the covering of the wooden or earthen floor. In winter the house was usually cold – the bed was warmer. The Chinese sensibly tended to warm the family's shared bed rather than the whole room, and millions of Chinese families slept on a brick rectangular box heated by a brazier.

In large towns, many people living together in the one room generated heat. Even if a fire was burning in that room in the depths of winter it radiated scant heat, partly because firewood had to be used frugally. The fuel had to be gathered in the forest and carried in the arms or on the shoulders to the home; and that required hours from the small stock of leisure time. Sometimes there was no forest nearby, and so fuel was very scarce for poor people. Cheap firewood in the year 1500 was more vital to the average home than cheap oil was to be in the year 2000.

A house chimney was a small hole in the roof. The smoke hovered inside the house and provided heat as well as smarting the eyes. Even in daytime a house was usually lacking in light, and window-openings consisted not of glass but of wooden shutters which, on being flung open, let in cold as well as light. In Europe in the 1400s the house window, though small in area, became more common. The glazed window was almost normal in Vienna in 1484. Two hundred years later the Royal Hall of Mirrors at Versailles was perhaps the most astonishing interior of a building to be seen in the world up to that time and a dazzling display of what glass could achieve. Many peasants who heard about it could only marvel, for in their village not a glass window was to be seen.

In China and India and Europe, wherever the population was large, the pressure on forests was intense. The salt-mining and metalworking industries were devourers of whole forests; and one large iron-works might use 2000 hectares of forest in a year.

The scarcity of wood explains some events which are easily misinterpreted. Thus when the acclaimed film *Amadeus* depicted the burial of the composer Mozart in Vienna in 1791 without even a coffin to contain his remains, the audience was quick to surmise that Mozart must have been a pauper. In fact, three years previously Emperor Joseph II had banned burial in coffins, partly to encourage simplicity in the place of extravagance and to encourage the body to return to the soil. But an important motive was to economise on the use of wood.

When firewood became scarce, ingenious substitutes were tried. The straw of the sugar cane was burned in Egypt, dry cow dung was burned in India, and the skins of crushed olives were burned in some Greek islands. Coal as an alternative to wood was slow to compete. In the north of China, where the forests almost vanished in some regions, coal was even used for house-cooking. In the north of England and France in the 1200s coal was being mined, and English coal was carried in sailing ships across the channel to the Low Countries city of Bruges. In the following six centuries more and more coal was shipped to London, making it perhaps the first big town in the world to use coal on a large scale, whether in the kitchen stove or the factory.

There were limits almost everywhere on cities growing beyond a certain size. A city could not grow too large simply because it could not secure in its neighbourhood the food and firewood it needed. A town of, say, 30 000 people needed firewood on such a scale that 600 or 1000 horsedrawn carts would arrive each week with loads of firewood. The town needed another 200 cartloads of grain in an average week. As horses or oxen pulled the carts, a large area of land had to be set aside to provide grass or hay for them. A freakishly large city like ancient Rome or modern London could be sustained only by bringing food and fuel long distances by sea and river.

The need to spend much time and devote much land to growing fuel for heating and lighting, and the raw materials for warm clothing, was a perpetual curb on the standard of living of much of Europe. In contrast, tropical peoples, in their standard of living, easily kept pace with Europe until the 18th century partly because they needed little clothing and warming fuel. They needed fewer calories, for they did not have to ward off the winter cold. In fact, several fortunate parts of the tropics even possessed a supply of cheap lamp oil. Burma produced oil for some generations before the liquid was dramatically discovered by drilling a hole in Pennsylvania in 1859.

THE BREAKING OF AN OLD DEADLOCK

For maybe 4000 years the standard of living of the average person in Europe, Africa and Asia had risen little, if at all. There had been abundant years and terrible years, minor rises and falls in people's material wellbeing and an increase in the luxuries available to the rich; but for the two-thirds of the population living on the lower rungs of the economic ladder, daily life was a struggle. Between 1750 and 1850, however, came hints of a dramatic change. Britain especially showed signs of a leap forward. Its population grew rapidly but the standard of living of most families was also rising above its humble base. Prosperity was increasing not because of a fortunate sequence of fine summers and lush crops, but because of the application of ingenuity to daily work in all its forms, on sea and land, on farms and in factories.

When farmers became more skilled in breeding livestock and plants, and in maintaining the fertility of the soil, then one small farm could produce more food than ever before. And if transport was improved by canals and stronger roads and later by railways and steamships, then each district or each country could specialise in the kind of economic activity for which it was best suited, and exchange its products in return for others. In essence, if ingenuity was applied to all kinds of daily work, and not least to transport, the output of food and other products would multiply faster than the population increased. And more food, fuel and shelter and clothes and leisure would potentially be available for each family, at least in the more efficient nations.

This interplay of events and trends was to shape the following two centuries. It was to disrupt all traditional ways of life, but its rewards would be large. In the favoured countries the standard of living of the people standing on the lower rungs of the income ladder would become almost as high as the standard had traditionally been for those standing on the upper rungs.

PART THREE

24

THE FALL OF A PACK OF CARDS

Unpredictable events, or the coincidence of vital events happening side by side, play their part in history. In the emerging of the United States of America, the South American nations, South Africa, Canada and Australia the unforeseen mixture of events was especially powerful in the final decades of the 18th century. Many of those events pirouetted around the fortunes of France, whose influence was as decisive when it was losing as when it was winning wars. The French language, of all the European languages, held the strongest claim to be the international language when these events began to unfold, but when they had finally unfolded the foundations were laid for English to become the global language of the 20th century.

In 1750 the continent of America had been split into two or three overlapping worlds. Dozens of native tribes and mini-nations were still self-governing, especially in the cold extremes of the north and south and in the prairies of North America, but their influence on the wider world was faint. In contrast, many parts of the continent under European influence – and they were mostly near the coast – were brimming with vitality and a sense that the future would be overflowingly in their favour. The population of these colonies was growing, their wealth was soaring and their influence on western Europe and western Africa was pervasive. And yet they were governed from Paris and London, Lisbon and Madrid – an arrangement that had persisted for generations but might not last forever. By 1750 the combined economic strength of the European colonies in the Americas was probably greater than that of most individual nations in Europe.

The intriguing question was not whether America would become independent but on which European nation it would remain dependent. In 1763, at the conclusion of the Seven Years War between France and Britain, control of Canada and Nova Scotia passed from France to the victors. In the eastern or more European half of North America, Britain now held a dominance that seemed likely to grow. Nearly all the way from Hudson Bay in Canada to the Gulf of Mexico, Britain was in control. Moreover most of the colonists of North America favoured continuing British control. Strongly supportive were the colonists of Boston, New York and Philadelphia, many of whom had fought in the recent war. They had no wish to be governed by Catholic France or its commercial regime.

Once the war ended, relations between Britain and her colonies in North America lost a layer of the old warmth. The cost of fighting the Seven Years War had doubled the national debt of Britain, but the American colonists contributed little towards meeting that debt. A vital source of government revenue was the duties collected on imports, but many American importers tended to evade duty, preferring to smuggle into their home ports such items as West Indian molasses, which they then distilled into rum. Rum was only one of the American channels of tax evasion. As a result, the average North American colonist in the early 1760s paid one shilling in taxes whereas the average Briton paid 26 shillings. The attempts to correct this distortion were to cause resentment and anger.

THE UNPREDICTED UNITED STATES

Many of the American colonies already had parliaments through which they could vent their grievances. The parliaments by their very nature provided an emphatic hint that these colonies, if necessary, could govern themselves, completely free from British control. The 13 British colonies at one end of the terrain now called the United States each operated their own parliament. Rhode Island and Connecticut even had the right to elect their governor, in sharp contrast to most of the colonies, which accepted a governor sent from Britain. Already the Americans had a framework for independence. They did not agree, however, whether they should seek independence, for the loyalists were dominant in Canada. Even in the 13 colonies to the south those loyal to Britain were initially more numerous than those who believed ultimately in rebellion. These colonists were predominantly of British descent or birth, the main exceptions being the Germans in Pennsylvania and that one-sixth of the population consisting of black slaves, who had no political voice.

Britain and the 13 colonies drifted apart. In 1775 armed colonists began to fight the British garrisons. The rebel leader was George Washington, an American-born plantation owner who had fought against the French as a militiaman. In the first 12 months his forces gained spotted success. Capturing Montreal they were weakened by an outbreak of smallpox and failed dismally to drive British troops from Canada. But Washington drove the British from the port of Boston and thereby showed such a prospect of military success that he began to win substantial and secret support from France and Spain, who were Britain's old enemies and eager to retaliate by stealth. Without that aid the American rebellion would ultimately have been defeated.

If the war was to be won, sea power was all-important. The European navy that controlled the Atlantic could send its own reinforcements to North America or prevent its opponent from sending for help. Britain was the main naval power but after 1778 its superiority was diminished by the interference of the French navy and by the open enmity of Holland and Spain. The war dragged on, becoming another seven-year war.

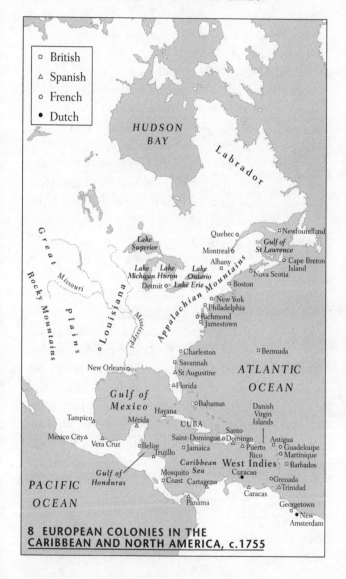

Key

- □ British
- △ Spanish
- ○ French
- ● Dutch

HUDSON BAY

Labrador

Lake Superior

Quebec ○ □ Newfoundland

Montreal ○ *Gulf of St Lawrence*

Albany □ ○ Cape Breton Island

Lake Michigan *Lake Huron* *Lake Ontario* □ Nova Scotia

Detroit ○ *Lake Erie* □ Boston

○ New York
□ Philadelphia

Richmond □
□ Jamestown

Great Plains

Rocky Mountains

Missouri

○ Louisiana

Mississippi

Appalachian Mountains

□ Charleston ● Bermuda

□ Savannah

New Orleans ○ △ St Augustine

Gulf of Mexico △ Florida

ATLANTIC OCEAN

△ Bahamas

Tampico △ Havana △

Mérida △ CUBA

Danish Virgin Islands

Mexico City △ Santo Domingo
Saint-Domingue ○ ○ ○ Antigua
Vera Cruz △ □ Belize △ Jamaica △ Puerto Rico ○ Guadeloupe

△ Trujillo *Caribbean Sea* ○ Martinique

□ Barbados

Gulf of Honduras Mosquito Coast ○ West Indies

PACIFIC OCEAN

□ Coast Cartagena △ Curaçao ● △ Grenada

△ Caracas △ Trinidad

△ Panama Georgetown

● New Amsterdam

8 EUROPEAN COLONIES IN THE CARIBBEAN AND NORTH AMERICA, c.1755

In November 1782, Britain accepted peace rather than continue such an expensive war.

Most of the territory within the present United States was still in the hands of colonial powers. If those boundaries had endured, the United States, with its vast resource bowl and its ability to attract immigrants, might some day have become an important power in the world but it would have had no hope of becoming one of the supreme powers. Confined to the eastern side of the Mississippi River, its population would for long have remained inadequate.

Sometimes events in retrospect seem neat and predictable but at the time, looking forward, they are peppered with the unpredictable. The victory of the rebel American colonies, with French help, had strong repercussions in France. Much debt had been incurred and the king had to increase taxes in order to fight the war. But the events on the far side of the Atlantic had shown that even the most powerful monarch was vulnerable if people, in demanding more freedom, stood up to him. The outbreak in 1789 of a popular revolution in France, the outcome of a whirlpool of major and minor causes, was strongly propelled by the revolt in the United States and the principles enunciated in that revolt.

Erupting in Versailles and Paris in May 1789, the French Revolution at first seemed to be a declaration of hope rather than a prelude to turmoil. By July, however, a mob was running loose in Paris. In the next month the

French assembly issued a declaration of 'the rights of man'. Such declarations, to be almost a monthly event in some years of the late 20th century, were a rarity as well as an act of treason in the 18th century. Three months after the declaration, the extensive properties of the Catholic church in France were nationalised, and many priests as well as royalists were wisely fleeing the kingdom. By 1791 the King of France was a captive in his own land. And yet the collapse of the old regime in France initially pleased or delighted many liberals. In London in February 1790, where the democratic tradition had long been more vigorous than in France, the House of Commons could still debate whether the tumultuous events in France were to be welcomed or feared.

Meanwhile France was at war with the main European monarchies. Fervently it proclaimed that it had a duty to impose its own popular secular revolution on all the lands it conquered. Originally for the French people, the revolution was now marked 'for export'. But the command of the revolution, and therefore its message, was slowly passing from the hands of radical politicians into the hands of a young soldier. Napoleon had enjoyed his first celebrated victory at Toulon in 1793, when he was in his mid-twenties. He proved to be a brilliant general who thought that almost nothing was impossible, and for nearly two decades his faith was fulfilled. In 1799 he became the head of government or first consul of France. In 1804 he became emperor, and in Paris he was formally crowned by Pope Pius VII.

The new United States stayed out of the French revolutionary wars, thus refusing to continue an alliance with the nation which had probably saved it from military defeat in the late 1770s. Thereby it launched that long tradition of self-imposed isolation from events in Europe. As before, the quarrels in Europe provided an opportunity for the United States to expand. Napoleon had taken back Louisiana and the western side of the Mississippi from Spain, which was too weak to say no. In 1803 he was desperate for revenue and decided to sell to the United States all the land on the western side of the Mississippi River. Known simply as the Louisiana Purchase, this secured for the United States, at three cents an acre, ownership of North America's longest river system and a vast expanse of land running all the way from Canada down to the Gulf of Mexico. This transaction embraced the territory now occupied by one-quarter of all the states in the USA.

If this tract, far larger than any European nation except Russia, had remained in French hands, or if it had passed into the hands of a group of French-led colonists, there might in the end have been two rival but independent Americas, with one displaying the stars and stripes on the eastern seaboard and the other displaying a version of the French tricolour in the far interior. Would the United States later have been able to annex Texas and California if a French land barrier had continued to intervene? It is likely that the USA would have remained a middle-sized nation with its only ports facing the Atlantic Ocean.

What Napoleon sold in 1803 was land belonging to many native American tribes or nations. Originally it was the intention of the British and perhaps the French rulers that these tribes or nations should be able to retain most of their western lands. In 1763 the British, still in control of much of North America, tried to draw on the map a Proclamation Line across which white settlers must not trespass. The native Americans were permitted to retain the western lands or in effect the vast interior, but not for long.

Soon the line reappeared further to the west, like a vanishing trick. After the United States became an infant nation, the official dividing line between native Americans and Europeans chased the sunset. The rights of the native peoples were pushed westwards or ignored. If they had been a united people they might have succeeded in halting the expansion. But they had never been united; and indeed the European colonisers had long discouraged unity. Much of the history of the world has been shaped by disunity.

The United States, in winning independence, set a precedent that was more infectious than could have been predicted. One of the sugar colonies in the West Indies was the first to follow the path of the new United States. Santo Domingo, a long and mountainous island, was held by the Spanish in the east and the French in the west, where the colony was called Saint-Domingue. The French Revolution temporarily weakened France's control of its colony. Likewise the message of the revolutionists that all people were equal was seized upon in 1791 by those inhabitants of the French colony who decidedly were not equal: the African slaves on the sugar plantations owned by the French and the mulattos who were neither slaves nor citizens. In a sudden uprising they took control. In 1803 a black man proclaimed himself the emperor of this new nation of Haiti. Now the Americas had two independent nations: the USA and Haiti.

The turbulent events in Europe paved the way for more independent nations. When in 1808 Napoleon invaded Spain, the Spanish colonies on the far side of the Atlantic were given their chance to take the side of Spain or seize their liberty. By 1810, all the way from Spanish Mexico to the Spanish colonial ports near the Andes, there were civil wars or wars of liberation, battles on sea and land, executions of mutineers and innumerable reprisals.

By 1821 the present map of Central and South America had largely taken shape, with a free Mexico, a new cluster of Central American republics, a free Peru, a free Chile and a free Paraguay, along with a free Republic of the River Plate which later was divided into Argentina and Uruguay. One year later, Brazil completely broke away from Portugal and became a monarchy. Three years later Bolivia was formed, taking its name from Simón Bolívar, its liberator. In North America too the Spaniards withdrew, having ceded Florida to the United States.

Whereas in 1775 the seafaring nations of western Europe had laid claim to the Americas all the way from the icy tundra of the north to the rocky tip of South America, they largely retreated in the next half-century. Their quarrels and rifts undermined their empires. Most of their colonies became independent.

By 1830 the Americas largely consisted of independent countries. In the north the main exceptions were British Canada and Russian Alaska where the Russians traded in furs and Russian Orthodox missionaries conducted their missions and the occasional Russian ship arrived bearing stale news from St Petersburg. Alaska was to be purchased by the United States in 1867.

South of the Gulf of Mexico, in 1830, the movement towards independence was almost complete. Hardly a European flag was to be seen, except on the masts of visiting ships. Only in the Caribbean did the European powers remain supreme. Britain still held Jamaica and much of the West Indies, France held Martinique and other islands, the Danes held part of the Virgin Islands, and Spain clung to Cuba, the richest of all the islands. Never perhaps in the history of nations had such a huge area been rearranged so quickly; and yet the languages and religion and many of the social and political institutions of the conquerors largely remained in place. Even slavery remained in place.

In this sequence of events – falling into place like a pack of cards, in retrospect, but really so unforeseeable – the Americas was not the only continent affected. The connecting sequence of events in the Americas had repercussions on Australia, South Africa and other lands.

BEYOND THE CAPE OF GOOD HOPE

The loss of many of its American colonies served to turn British attention away from the Atlantic Ocean to the Indian and Pacific oceans. The war against France, beginning in 1792 and continuing on and off for nearly a quarter of a century, provided Britain with opportunities to seize French colonies and some Dutch possessions, for Holland had become a satellite of France. In that huge arc of sea stretching from the Cape of Good Hope to Cape Horn, Britain had not been the dominant power. Whereas Britain's main possession in those seas in 1780 was a foothold in various parts of India, it became far and away the dominant colonial power in that extensive part of the globe in the following half-century. It controlled the key port of Cape Town and the coast of South Africa, the strategic islands of Mauritius and Ceylon (Sri Lanka), most of India, parts of the Malay Peninsula and all of Australia, along with potential or real control of New Zealand, many other islands in the Pacific and much of the Pacific coast of what is now Canada.

Britain was now stronger in the Indian and Pacific oceans than it had ever been in America. It now governed a population dwarfing that which it had governed in America. Largely defeated in one continent, it had turned to new oceans and quickly built up the largest empire the world had seen.

One change set in motion by these events was the rise of English to become, in the second half of the 20th century, the first language that could be called global. In 1763, outside the British Isles, only about three million people spoke English as a first or second language, and nearly all of them lived in North America. Nothing did more to give English an opportunity in the long term to become a global language than the consolidation of a huge territory into the hands of the United States, and Britain's acquiring of so many scattered colonies in the Indian and Pacific oceans. If the United States had remained small in area, clinging only to the Atlantic seaboard, and if most of India had never come under British control, the prospect of English becoming a global language would have remained small.

The collapse of one card sometimes brought down another card. Britain did not plan to place a settlement on the eastern part of the Australian continent which Captain Cook had discovered. The plan was forced upon it by the rebellion in the American colonies. Britain had been sending many of its convicts to its southern ports, where in effect their services had been auctioned to slave-owners and they had been used as overseers. The final breaking-away of the Americans forced Britain to look elsewhere for a place to which convicts could be usefully sent. 'Usefully' was the key word, for Britain ran a mercantile empire and tried to use labour in the interests of its own shipowners and merchants.

Finally, on the strength of reports brought home by Cook's *Endeavour*, the British government selected Botany Bay, the sandy shores of which now hold the runways of Sydney's airport. It was hoped that in Botany Bay the convicts would soon grow all the food they needed. Nearby lay a bonus. On the uninhabited Norfolk Island, north-east of Sydney, grew a unique and tall pine which seemed likely to provide first-class masts for British fleets, and a superior species of the flax plant which, it was hoped, would produce fine sail-cloth and rope for the British navy.

A British fleet carrying convicts and marines sailed into Botany Bay in January 1788. They soon discovered in that hot month that the landscape was not the green utopia which had been seen in cool April some 18 years previously by Cook and Banks. Abandoning Botany Bay and resuming their voyage for a few hours along the coast, the 11 ships straggled through the gap in the perpendicular cliffs and entered sunlit Sydney Harbour in which, the commander observed, space existed for 1000 ships to gather in safety.

At Sydney Harbour the new colony struggled to

grow enough food. Only when the colonists crossed the narrow coastal spine called the Blue Mountains and began to disperse huge flocks of sheep on the vast warm inland plains did Australia emerge as a place of importance in the eyes of the world. A generation later, tens of millions of people facing the cold winters of the far Northern Hemisphere were clad in clothes or sleeping beneath blankets made from Australian wool.

The Aborigines who quietly peeped at the British ships roped to shoreline trees, and watched the building of huts and stores, the boiling of water in pots, the noisy firing of guns, the quick lighting of fires and the felling of trees with axes made of iron – all metals being unknown to them – could only wonder at these activities. It was possibly the strangest set of encounters in the recorded history of the world, for the ways of life of these new and old peoples were much further apart than when the Spaniards confronted the Aztecs, the Dutch first settled themselves at the harbours at Cape Town and Jakarta, and even when French and British navigators came face to face with the Polynesians who had long lived on the islands of Tahiti and New Zealand.

In contrast, the peoples of Australia were still quarantined from nearly every radical change that had happened in most other parts of the world during the last 10 000 years. The gap between the newcomers and the natives was almost a chasm. The Aborigines' talents, so different to those of Europeans, could rarely be comprehended or appreciated by the newcomers. There was no way in which they could initially understand that most Aborigines had a knowledge of several languages and several dialects, an extensive knowledge of the botany and zoology of each region, subtle as well as simple skills in hunting and fishing, and a diet offering more variety than that available to most people of Europe. They could not possibly understand that the Aborigines, in their marriages, diet, rituals and concepts of ownership and land, obeyed a set of long-held rules that, though difficult to fathom, in some senses were as sophisticated as the rituals guiding the aristocracies of Stockholm and Warsaw.

Nor could the Aborigines understand the British way of life, laws and institutions, religion, manners and dress, modes of farming and manufacturing, the acts of reading and writing, the hoarding of food in barrels and bags and storehouses. They could not glimpse the depth of scientific knowledge in the civilisation which the newcomers – so many of them uncivilised – had left behind. The technology of the strangers, whether large ships or firearms or ticking clocks, was baffling. Domesticated animals were entirely new to the Aborigines, who sometimes assumed that the sheep and cattle must be the wives travelling with the white men.

The Aborigines of Australia did not defend their territory effectively. Compared to the New Zealanders they lived in less populous groups, were not so well organised, did not build forts, and did not easily unite with neighbouring groups in order to resist an attacker. Decade after decade, this unaccountable procession of white faces and new animals was moving further into the sparsely peopled continent. In a thousand isolated places there were occasional shootings and spearings. Even worse, smallpox, measles, influenza and other new diseases swept from one Aboriginal camp to another, just as they had raced through the Americas when the first Spaniards arrived there nearly three centuries previously. The main conqueror of Aborigines was to be disease and its ally, demoralisation. To this tragedy scientists, in this first age of science, had no answer.

25

BEYOND THE SAHARA

For centuries, most of Africa was virtually beyond the reach of the peoples and empires of Europe. Maybe it was more accessible in Roman times than later. Indeed the Romans colonised Africa with more success than possibly any other European power before 1900, though they colonised only the northerly fringes.

How far was the Sahara a barrier that blocked the movements of peoples and how far was it a mirage? A lot of evidence suggests that the desert was such a formidable barrier that, until modern times, it prevented European and Asian empires from entering most of Africa. Indeed the heart of Africa proved to be less accessible to scores of generations of Europeans than did the heart of Asia, which was much further away from Europe. Moreover it was too large for any of the surrounding countries to control completely.

THE PUZZLE OF THE DESERT

This largest desert in the world covered one-quarter of all the land of Africa. Consisting of expanses of rock as well as sand, it was vast enough to cover continental USA. Perhaps it should be likened more to sea than to land – a dry sea into which people ventured, sometimes losing their life while journeying between the distant desert-ports. Like a sea it concealed pirates who swooped on traders. Like the sea it was swept by storms, and sensibly the Tuareg people wore cloth veils across the mouth as a guard against the biting, flying sand.

Here and there, rising from the desert, were rocky mountains which caught the rain. Much of it pattered down in a few cloudbursts and was quickly evaporated by the sun and burning earth. The desert shifted, and over the millennia it shrank or expanded as climate changed a little or as goats and cattle fostered erosion in the outlying zone of thorny bushes and prickly grass.

The desert was far from a complete barrier. Caravans of camels crisscrossed it. Century after century Islamic traders crossed it and won a host of converts. Potentates from western Africa crossed it, and in 1324 the Emperor of Mali arrived in Cairo where he was long remembered for the gold he sprinkled – almost as if it were confetti – on those he favoured. European merchants crossed the desert more than is realised. In 1470, at the time of the Renaissance, merchants of Florence were observed trading in Timbuktu, on the far side of the desert. But a white skin was rarely seen in the wealthy, walled, irrigated towns on the edge of the Sahara.

With its waving date palms visible to the approaching traveller, the tropical African town of Timbuktu for long conveyed an aura of mystery to the ears of Europeans who heard its name. The town was an inland depot for the northern third of Africa – a depot for caravans crossing the Sahara and for loads carried on the heads of porters or on the backs of asses and oxen from Sudan, and a terminus for the occasional cargo from southern Europe. It was approached less frequently from the closer coast of western Africa than from the Mediterranean coast and the inland Moroccan town of Marrakesh. In the late 1500s, Marrakesh welcomed mules and camels laden with Timbuktu gold along with the occasional cargo of slaves. One consignment of 15 virgins was especially noted. Significantly the commodities which crossed the desert and its expensive trade route were those which, like gold and ivory and pretty women, commanded a high value per kilogram.

Just as Africa's desert was one bulwark against outsiders, so too were its rivers. Most were interrupted by waterfalls, rapids and cataracts. No ship could pass up or down the turbulent, frothy stretches to be found in nearly every major river. The Zaire and the Congo had their rapids. The flow of the majestic Zambezi was interrupted by the Victoria Falls. The history of Europe would have been different if the Danube, Rhine, Rhône and Elbe had also been interrupted by waterfalls.

Navigable rivers promote trade and the exchange of ideas; but Africa had only one long and navigable river, the Nile. It may be that Egypt's success as a creator of civilisation owed much to the role of the river valley as a highway and source of food and to the fact that the river entered the sea not far from the centre of other early civilisations. If the Nile had flowed into the ocean in western Africa, its influence would have been less.

South of the Sahara, in the vastness of tropical Africa, there was no river to match the Nile. Moreover Africa as a whole was weak in those gulfs and deep bays, those tongues of sea which enabled a sailing ship or galley to penetrate a considerable way towards the interior. Whereas more than 33 per cent of the land-mass of Europe was peninsula and island, only 2 per cent of Africa was so shaped. These were considerable disadvantages for Africa, to which must be added the vast area of jungle.

In the moist woodlands of tropical Africa the bloodsucking tsetse fly, no larger than a housefly, was a danger to all beasts of burden, infecting their blood and weakening them with sleeping sick-ness. In about one-quarter of the area of Africa the infection killed all domesticated animals except poultry. Malaria, sleeping sickness and other tropi-cal diseases helped to build a wall around tropical Africa, dispelling or killing outsiders as well as Afri-cans. The sleeping sickness especially obstructed economic development. The lack of farm animals in such a big area not only deprived Africans of protein in their diet but also robbed them of beasts of burden, and so they themselves had to become the beasts of burden, the carriers and packhorses. The absence of domesticated animals meant that manure was scarce, and so crops lacked the fertiliser available in other parts of Africa where, the tsetse fly being unknown, herds of cattle flourished.

Other obstacles limited useful outside contact with the African heartland during the last five millennia. Perhaps Africa lacked the botanical diversity of Asia. If central and southern Africa had produced the world's first tea and coffee, pepper and nutmeg, silks and dye-stuffs and a variety of other products that tingled the palates and aroused the acquisitiveness of the peoples along the shores of the Mediterranean, the geographical barriers inside Africa would have been less significant. Barriers are not a deterrent if something valuable lies on the other side.

For many centuries it was Asia, as much as Europe, which influenced Africa. The Indian Ocean was the main gateway to eastern Africa, and the ships or dhows sailing from Persia, India, Arabia and even the Indonesian archipelago often entered the fine harbours of East Africa. They were busy at a time when no Europeans were to be seen there. On the island of Zanzibar the Persians were settled for maybe 500 or more years before the first Portuguese sailed past.

The places standing near the crossways of the world have advantages. They are stimulated by new ideas – as well as crushed by new armies. Africa, apart from its Mediterranean coast and strips of its east and west coasts, was too remote to be stimulated.

THE TRAFFIC IN SLAVES

Africa for long exported a controversial commodity which was in high demand almost everywhere. That commodity was the slave.

It must be said at once that slavery was nearly as important in the history of a variety of other countries and tribes. Ancient China possessed slaves by the millions, and the practice of selling people into slavery in China was not banned until 1908. Indians owned slaves before and after the time of Christ. Many tribes and some states in America, long before the coming of Columbus, owned slaves and half-slaves. Europe's serfdom, which survived in Russia until the very decade when slavery ended in the United States, was a version of slavery.

A slave was a familiar sight in the Greek city-states. In lands ruled by Rome slaves were to be seen on thousands of rural estates. Each slave was in effect an extra pick or axe or shovel, an extra hand at harvest time, an additional pair of hands in the building and road-mending gangs or the household kitchen. So long as these slaves produced more than they ate, they were an asset.

In many parts of the world it was almost a rule of warfare that prisoners were either killed or enslaved. As wars were frequent, the count of new slaves in each century was high. To be a slave was preferable to the alternative – to be a corpse.

Early Christianity, like early Judaism and Islam, understood that slavery was an ancient and useful institution, and not to be meddled with. Learned and compassionate opinion in the 21st century cannot understand how slavery for so long could have been accepted without question, but then this new century is the heir to ideas of human equality and dignity which were uncommon in earlier centuries. Moreover today the prosperous countries have no economic need for slavery. Thanks to technology, they have a glut, not a scarcity, of unskilled muscle power. Moreover they have a new and tireless slave known as fossil fuel, which was not known to early civilisations.

Long before European ships began to carry slaves from Africa, the Africans themselves were busy traders in slaves. Since 1500, more African slaves have probably been sold to Islamic lands than to Christian lands, and Muslims have been the main slave-traders in Africa. Presumably there was an active slave trade in Africa long before Islam arrived.

Inside Africa many people were enslaved by their own kinsfolk. Fathers sometimes sold their own children into slavery, and brothers sold brothers. Maybe half of the slaves who ended their days in foreign lands or regions had been enslaved by the African group or society of which they were a member. Slaves were usually debtors, criminals, misfits or rebels and they were especially prisoners taken in war.

In the 16th century most slaves exported from

western Africa were women and were sold to Islamic lands. A century later most slaves were men and were shipped in European-owned ships to Christian colonies in America. The Portuguese pioneered the slave trade to the Americas – they already used African slaves in their own sugar plantations in the Cape Verde Islands and in Madeira – and the British and other seafaring nations soon joined in the highly profitable but callous trade. A long strip of coastal western Africa, stretching from the Senegal River to Cameroon, supplied most of the slaves; and in the busiest years of the 1700s they were shipped across the Atlantic at the rate of 100 000 a year. Working in sugar, tobacco and cotton plantations scattered all the way from the mouth of the Amazon to Jamaica and Virginia, they did not see their homeland again. Most of the sugar eaten in Europe was grown by African slaves working in exile.

The voyage in little sailing ships across equatorial waters from western Africa must have been an ordeal. Most slaves were crowded below in the hot darkness, often in chains. Their supply of drinking water was meagre, and they had not previously been at sea. For the European crew the voyage was often as hazardous, and many died of tropical diseases.

Generations of African-Americans were born into slavery but few escape routes were open to them. A baby born to a black mother and a white father – the father was usually the owner or overseer – was virtually free. Another path of escape was simply to run away.

Many slaves ran in fear of a coming whipping, or as a result of a whipping. Sometimes dogs pursued them. Many of those who did escape to a nearby forest or swamp voluntarily returned to slavery with its secure supply of food and shelter and the consoling religious faith of their fellow slaves.

Slavery was a lottery in its tempo of work, its punishments and its rewards. Much depended on the personality of the owner and his wife and his overseer – who was often black – and on the attitudes of the government under whose laws the slave worked. Almost certainly the United States was superior to Brazil and other lands in its treatment of slaves, and some observers of American slavery agreed that on a typical cotton or rice plantation, the cabins of the slaves were at least as comfortable as those of poorer people in Scotland and Sicily. But outside the cabins there was no freedom.

The ports of the United States received in total, by the year 1820, slightly more African slaves than free European immigrants; but the Europeans – with the benefit of a lower death rate and higher birth rate – formed the great majority of the American population. After the 1820s African immigration was to decline, for the very concept and legitimacy of slavery was under assault.

It almost seemed that Africa now was jinxed. It seemed cut off from the throbbing parts of the world. Its geographical selling point by the 16th century was that it could supply millions of slaves, acclimatised to working in tropical heat and living only a short sailing distance from the rising plantations in the Americas. But now that slave trade was in jeopardy.

26

NOBLE STEAM

In 1801, the *Annual Register*, a popular book which chronicled the year's events, declared that the outgoing century had been remarkable. Science and technology, more than in any previous century, had leaped ahead. While Europe was often at war with itself, it was busy spreading science, religion and civilisation into the remotest forests and gorges. Never had there been such exploring 'of the most remote and unknown regions of the globe'. The thirst for knowledge, claimed the *Annual Register*, had supplanted the thirst for gold and conquest. Never had long-distance trade so increased. On the familiar sea lanes the sailing ships were much faster than before; and even the long voyage from Europe to India was no longer feared as an ordeal.

The world had shrunk but even rich people did not travel far in search of knowledge or pleasure. A queen rarely travelled outside her realm. Only a few European missionaries crossed the seas to work in strange lands. In eastern Asia a few pilgrims sometimes travelled far to visit the great Buddhist shrines, but few Islamic pilgrims travelled far to worship in Mecca. Scholars – and in every nation they were few – stayed at home and learned of the world through books. When the young London poet John Keats wrote the words 'Much have I travell'd in the realms of gold, and many goodly states and kingdoms seen', he signified that he travelled by reading. At that time he had never moved far from his birthplace.

The most travelled people in the world were not scholars and priests but ordinary European and Arab sailors, who, in their mobility, were the air crew of their day. Between 1700 and 1800 the largest category of long-distance travellers in the world consisted of those who had no wish to travel: the millions of African slaves led as captives across their own continent or shipped across the tropical sea to the Americas.

The world was composed of tens of thousands of small, self-contained localities. Even to sleep one night away from home was an uncommon experience. This was true of China, Java, India, France or Mexico though not of Australia and its Aborigines. People spent their whole life in one place, and from it came nearly all the food they ate, and the materials they used for clothing and footwear. Here originated the news and gossip that excited or frightened them. Here they found their wife or husband.

A holiday by the beach or in the mountains belonged to the future. Spa towns, where people drank the mineralised waters for the sake of their health, were the only specialised tourist towns in Europe. In these 'watering places', tourists drank the waters according to a strict formula that prescribed so many jugs or glasses a day. In the early 1800s perhaps the most international of the spa resorts was Carlsbad, a pretty town hemmed in by steep granite hills and pine forests a few days' ride from Prague and Leipzig. In 1828 an average of no more than 10 visitors arrived each day in order to partake of the medicinal water. Its main spring still rises in a hot perpetual stream, and the water still has an excruciating taste which improves with amnesia.

The industrial town, not the spa and holiday resort, symbolised the new era. In the north of England, especially from the 1780s, arose factory towns full of ingenious machines which spun and wove wool or cotton. Visitors from abroad marvelled at the vigour of Manchester, Leeds, Birmingham and the new industrial cities, but they threw up their hands when they toured the factories and mines and counted how many little children were employed. An American describing a Yorkshire woollen mill in 1815 noted that about 50 girls and boys were at work, arriving at six in the morning and leaving at seven in the evening. In winter they arrived in the dark and left in the dark. The eldest child was not over 10 years of age. All were smeared with the dirt and grease of the raw wool they handled. The new factory – unlike such rural jobs as the minding of geese and the milking of cows – was a tireless tyrant which demanded the day-long attention of the children, even when they were on the verge of falling asleep through exhaustion.

THE STEAM HORSE

The mechanical and human energy expended inside the new factory was an eye-opener. Often a waterwheel on a fast stream supplied the motive power for the factory's machines. Increasingly the latest factories used coal and steam power, but for a time the noisy steam engine gave little sign that it would transform the world.

Steam as a driving power was first used effectively in the mines of England. In 1698 Thomas Savery applied steam, produced by coal, to work the pumps in a Cornish mine. Eleven years later a Devon blacksmith, Thomas Newcomen, built a reciprocating steam engine which eventually could do what an army of men or horses had done. To this kind of engine James Watt, a Scot, brought vital improvements. His wonderful device of 1769, the distinct condenser, eventually produced about three times as much steam or energy from the same tonne of coal. Nearly every big step in the evolution of the steam engine was made by resourceful Britons trying to solve practical problems arising from the daily work in new and expanding industries.

But the steam engine had little effect on the world of commerce until its power was applied to transport.

The shriek of a steam locomotive was first heard in the north of England, the heart of the infant industrial revolution. The puffs and whistle-cries of the locomotive at first startled many people and frightened the horses working on the roads and grazing in the pastures nearby. The speed and power of the locomotive astonished the first passengers. They were almost blinded by the steam and coal smoke.

In land transport this was probably the most important invention since the Roman road. Even when a railway train was pulled by horses on a track of iron rails – and the first railway wagons in Hungary and the USA were harnessed to strong horses – the cost of carrying goods was dramatically reduced.

The first steam train ran between Stockton and Darlington in England in 1825; and its main cargoes were coal and other minerals. France opened its first steam railway in 1828, Austria in 1832, Germany and Belgium in 1835, by which time the first train was about to reach the city of London. Into the countryside in Europe and the United States went an army of railway builders, defacing strips of peaceful landscape with their railway cuttings and their impressive clay and earth embankments. By the early 1850s remote provinces of the New World were building their first railways – Egypt, Mexico, Peru, Brazil and eastern Australia. Even backward Russia decided that a railway should link its capital St Petersburg with the inland city of Moscow.

Before the age of steam it was difficult to imagine

a sailing ship or a wheeled vehicle arriving on time. Admittedly a horsedrawn coach might arrive punctually in a distant city, but on many wintry days it was delayed by floods and snow and fogs, and even on fine days it could be retarded by heavy traffic on the busier stretches of the road, or an accident to a horse. In contrast the train usually arrived at each station at the exact minute specified. The brand-new word 'timetable', a symbol of the modern breathless world, was coined in England in 1838.

Not everyone welcomed the new railway. Many rural folk, assuming that they would never possess enough money to buy a ticket for a train, could see no purpose in it. The shattering noise of the passing trains, they thought, would frighten the cows into giving premature birth to their calves. George Eliot in her novel *Middlemarch* recorded other fears: 'Women both old and young regarded travelling by train as presumptuous and dangerous.'

Those who lived through the first 30 years of the railway age realised that the world had changed forever. The novelist William Thackeray, writing in the early 1860s when England became the first country to be crisscrossed by railway lines, spelled out the magnitude of the change. He thought that the train had so changed daily life that the railway embankment was like a wall that divided past and present. Climb the embankment, he wrote, and stand on the railway line 'and look to the other side – it is gone!' An old way of life, in which few people travelled far from their native village, had vanished.

The black steam locomotive butted its way into nearly every facet of life. Fresh eggs and meat reached the city from far away. City fashions quickly reached the draper in the remote valley. In most countries a national daily newspaper was feasible for the first time because a fast mail train could convey bundles of news-papers to most towns on the very day of publication. The newspaper was also cheaper, for it was printed by a steam printing press devised in Germany.

Almost everything, from postage and holidays to war, was transformed by the iron rails. The quick war between France and Prussia in 1870–71 was heavily influenced by the organising skill of Prussian generals in using trains to bring their huge army together and disembark it at crucial parts of the French border. The Prussians poured into France while many French sol-diers, still in their home towns, were buttoning on their tunic or saying goodbye to their girlfriend.

Steam was slower to transform transport on sea than on land. The early steamships were wooden paddle-steamers, unable to make long voyages unless they used their sails as well as their coal-burning engines. By 1840 fast steamships were regularly crossing the North Atlantic, at the very time when European immi-grants were crowding into America. Charles Dickens, the famous novelist, decided to visit the United States with his wife Kate and they boarded the steamship in Liverpool in January 1842. Encountering wild seas – both were seasick for at least five days – they observed with dismay that at night the flames danced above the top of the tall red funnel. On steamships the fear of accidental fire was high.

A crucial advantage of a steamship was that it could sail in windless weather, even reverse in narrow spaces and voyage along a narrow canal – tasks impossible for a large sailing ship. The steamship made it feasible to build the narrow Suez Canal. It joined the Mediterranean and the Indian Ocean in 1869, and obviated the long slow voyage around Africa. India was suddenly tugged closer to Europe. For a voyage between Bombay and southern France the Suez Canal shortened the sea distance by 56 per cent. As a result of this initiative by French financiers, the Middle East – once the hub of the known world but now a backwater – became important again. The discovery of oil in Iran four decades later was to increase its importance.

Steam engines were not the end of the fast changes in transport. Operators of the first railway trains decided that they needed a courier to run ahead of the trains. They adopted what was christened the telegraph – a word which stemmed from the coupling of two ancient Greek words meaning 'from afar' and 'to write'. A telegraph was a single line of iron or copper wire, resting on a succession of tall posts and running alongside the railway line. With the aid of an electric battery, the wire carried signals from one station to the next. One signal might warn an approaching locomotive that the railway line was already occupied. Another signal might announce that a train had broken down and an emergency locomotive was needed. Probably the first public telegraph line in the world ran, in 1843, alongside the English railway linking Paddington station in London with the town of Slough.

Inventors were quick to improve the telegraph system first used on English railways. Dr Samuel Morse, an American, devised an early version of his morse code for the Washington to Baltimore railway in 1844. Many telegraph lines were built between towns which possessed no railway. By 1849 a web of telegraph lines spanned 15 000 kilometres in the United States.

To send the telegraph wire under oceans and straits was the next ambition. The favoured solution was to enclose the wires or cable in a padding of gutta-percha, a kind of indiarubber collected from the sap of a tree in the Indonesian archipelago. In 1850 a telegraph line crossed the seabed of the channel between England and France. To cross the North Atlantic was a more testing task. A cable laid painstakingly on the seabed by a deep-sea ship was completed in 1858, amidst jubilation. Alas, it conveyed messages only for a fortnight. A permanent cable across the Atlantic was finally laid in 1866. Within a decade a combination of overland and undersea telegraph lines reached nearly all the main cities of Asia, Africa and South America.

The telegraph wires and cables had almost reached

the most remote of the Australian colonies by the mid-1870s. They strode on long legs across Asia and then, on land and on the bed of the sea, across the Indonesian archipelago. Reaching the north coast of Australia at Darwin Harbour, the wire ran south on a procession of poles across the arid wastes to Adelaide, on the southern coast. Another telegraphic cable crossed beneath the Tasman Sea to New Zealand. It was now possible to send a telegram to London from nearly every remote port of Australia and New Zealand.

With good fortune a message could cross the world in 24 hours. A magical, record-breaking night was 16 February 1871. From Karachi, then in British India but now in Pakistan, a telegram was cabled to London. Passing through the repeating stations it reached London in 50 minutes. In contrast the sun next day would take four and a half hours to traverse that distance of almost 9000 kilometres, thus prompting an English journalist to report this swiftest of telegrams with the headline 'The Sun Outdone'. The same message would have taken weeks to reach London by mail steamer.

It has become almost normal to view far-reaching inventions as the work of one or two lonely individuals, standing far above the ruck. But invention is the outcome of a team game as well as a contest between individuals. The struggle to devise and improve steam engines, railways, telegraphs, ironworks and textile machines took place in many nations and hundreds of go-ahead workshops. Some of the major changes stemmed from a multitude of contributions by now-forgotten people. Only a few of the inventor-heroes are remembered.

Nothing so far in the history of the world had done as much to unite all lands as this slender thread of wire crossing steppes and plains, jungles and icy valleys, factory suburbs and mountain villages, and the very bed of the sea. In 1876, just when the international telegraph was reaching the remote parts of the world, the telephone was born in North America. Business houses living nearby could talk to each other. They could not dial directly to a nearby phone but depended on a long line of women, working in a central exchange and commanding a row of plugs and switches which, manipulated by hand, linked one phone to another. When the women went home for the night, the telephone lines became silent.

A conversation on the long-distance telephone remained difficult, the voices being distorted and not easily heard. The ocean was even more of a hindrance to the telephone cable. England and France were linked by underwater phone in 1891 but the wider oceans remained impassable for wires. For decades the long-distance call on the telephone was only for those with a large business or a high income.

THE RUSH TO THE SMOKY CITIES

The family farm was still the focus of millions of dreams and hopes, especially in the New World where land was cheap and abundant. During the numerous centuries before governments provided social security, a farm – if it was large enough – was itself the main form of social security. Providing food and shelter and the raw materials of clothing, it also kept the family together, for most sons and daughters could live and work there before their marriage, and the parents could live there in old age – if they lived to old age. In a range of countries from Chile to the Transvaal, struggling new farmers were defeated by drought and pests, debts and poor prices, but the dream of being a farmer remained alive.

A vivid snapshot of the farmlands of Massachusetts survives from about the year 1820. Winter has set in, and in the weak light of the afternoon the small farm of the Whittiers is full of bustle. Women are at work in the kitchen. In the barn the old horse is 'whinnying for his corn'. In the stalls the cattle are being fed with the hay that was made in the summer. The rooster is crowing, an east wind is blowing and heavy snow is expected. The logs and sticks of sawn firewood are being piled in readiness for the lighting of the fire in the room where the family gather after the day's work is almost over. These simple scenes are described in John Greenleaf Whittier's poem 'Snowbound', first printed nearly half a century later.

There were similar scenes in farms stretching from Ohio to Sweden and Siberia, but it is Whittier's poem that caught the feeling of snug security which so many farming families felt when their own ceaseless work had provided them with all they needed for the long winter. So they sat, the uncle smoking his pipe, the mother spinning wool on her hand-turned wheel, and a story being read aloud, until they saw the time was close to 9 p.m., their time to go to bed.

Even as the Whittiers sat at their fireside, there were signs in Europe of one of the extraordinary changes in human history, a change which is still embracing country after country. In a few nations, most people were no longer tilling the soil. England and Belgium were perhaps the first nations in Europe, probably in the world, where the majority of the workforce was no longer needed for the producing of food. Only 30 per cent of the English workforce was needed for rural pursuits. In Australia, Chile and Argentina a similarly small part of the workforce was needed in rural industries. Those lands were now producing far more food – and also wool and cattle hides – than they themselves could use. A way of life which had slowly emerged some 10 000 years ago and spread across virtually the whole globe was about to be supplanted as the main provider of daily work. Most farms were producing more than in the past, and needing the labour of fewer people.

A simple measure of the increased supply of food is that serious famines, so common in France in the 18th century, become rare after 1800. The scarcity of food in Ireland and the lower Rhine in the 1840s was the last death-dealing famine in western Europe.

Another trend was visible in Europe: the population was increasing more rapidly than at any time since the years of warm climate between 1000 and 1250. Plagues were fewer, and the knowledge of how to combat disease was increasing. Furthermore, in much of Europe each hectare of farmland produced more food for the multiplying population. Between 1750 and 1850, Europe's population jumped by more than 80 per cent, a rate of increase which was viewed as astonishing – until the population of nations of the Third World began to grow at a more astonishing pace after the Second World War.

Across Europe most of the cities grew, and several became as large as China's largest. By 1800 the population of London had passed one million. By 1860 it was three million – by far the largest city the world had known. Early in the new century, by some reckonings, London was to hold close to 10 million people, and they consumed wheat and butter and jam, bacon and mutton and apples which came not only from English farms but in ships from distant lands. Most of the increase in population in western Europe took place in cities. In 1600 Europe had held a mere 13 cities possessing more than 100 000 people. In 1900 there were to be 143 such cities.

The rising cities themselves were dirty, and most houses were small. Even in 1850 most houses in some of the finest cities did not have access to clean running water. Large cities usually lay beside a river, and water for cooking and washing was fetched from the polluted river or from nearby wells. Most people carried the water along the street to their house in a wooden pail or bucket. As water was scarce the washing of clothes was infrequent. In any case the washing of the naked body was believed to drain away essential oils and so allow disease to gain a bridgehead in the body.

Sewage found its way to the rivers and, flowing downstream, polluted the water used by the next city. Death-carrying infections were spread by poor sanitation. Asiatic cholera had first appeared in eastern Russia in 1823, and nine years later a fierce strain of it reached New York, filling the streets with apprehension. It came again and again to Europe, filling the corners of many cemeteries about once in each decade. Russia, one of the less sanitary countries, lost a quarter of a million people through cholera in 1892.

Increasingly engineers built reservoirs for supplying fresh water to cities and laid underground pipes and dug tunnels to carry away the city's daily sewage. The death rate of the cities also fell because of advances in medicine. It was in the mid-1870s that the German bacteriologist Robert Koch made the momentous discovery that bacteria – so tiny that millions could inhabit a drop of spit – caused disease. In 1882 in Berlin he announced that he had located the bacterial cause of tuberculosis – a disease first identified by the ancient Greek Hippocrates and long known as 'the captain of the men of death'.

The ease of travel in the age of steam expedited this lightning run of medical discoveries. Koch hurried to Egypt, hoping to study the latest epidemic of cholera, but he arrived just in time to learn that it was over. Later he sailed in a mail steamer through the new Suez Canal on his way to the home of cholera, India, and there in 1883, with the aid of his powerful microscope, he made his discovery of the bacillus that carried the disease. Fifteen years later, Ronald Ross, a medical officer working in India, discovered that malaria did not emanate, as had traditionally been believed, from marsh air or from stagnant water. Instead it was distributed by the bite of what he called 'the dapple-winged mosquito'. Thus he located the cause of this most catastrophic of all tropical illnesses.

It was a mirror of this inventive, confident earth-shaping century that, in many European circles, death was no longer seen as an act of God which could occur at any time. In many circles the human race was over-optimistically seen as the architect and inventor of its own future. God was being challenged in his own heaven by engineers, shipbuilders, bacteriologists, surgeons and all the other heroes of the new technology, and by political leaders who let it be known that they were now tackling many of the world's longstanding ills, including poverty and slavery.

27

WILL ALL BE EQUAL?

The crusade to abolish slavery was in part an equalitarian crusade, led by people of compassion. Victory against the slave-owners, however, depended on more than compassion. The crusade on both sides of the Atlantic was led by increasingly wealthy nations which no longer depended on slavery for a significant part of their wealth. Thus in the 1790s, Denmark abolished the slave trade in its West Indian islands and revolutionary France abolished slavery in its colonies. It was easier for these European nations to liberate slaves still at work in their tropical colonies: their whole economic life was far less dependent than was the USA on the work of slaves.

The United States was late in throwing its weight against slavery. The spearhead against slavery was in the wealthy states of the north, which depended not on slaves but on ironworks, factories, free farms and shipyards. In their hands the United States was becoming a great industrial power; and by 1860 its output of iron and steel – now the barometer of industrial success – was ranked third in the world, with only Britain and France ahead of it. The Americans could now afford to abolish slavery, but the political and economic cost was still high. The crusaders, most of whom were devout members of churches, were willing to pay the price, though the real cost was likely to be carried by the slave-owners themselves and the states whose economy depended on slavery.

In the United States the importing of new slaves was already banned, thus forcing the plantations to rely on the sons and daughters of slaves. The labour of slaves was still considered vital to daily life in the subtropical southern states; and in 1861 eleven of these southern states rebelled. They seceded from the United States and created their own nation, the Confederate States. Amidst this tension Abraham Lincoln was inaugurated as president of the old United States. A month later, in April 1861, the Civil War began, with a Confederate victory at Fort Sumter in South Carolina.

Lincoln did not bring his nation into the war primarily to abolish slavery. He fought initially to preserve his country and its unity in the face of the secession of some of its oldest and most important states. Lincoln was trying to find a compromise. If necessary he would allow slavery to continue, so long as the nation remained one. He simply wished to save his nation from a harsh amputation.

It now seems slightly strange that this most famous of the world's democrats should be proclaiming the brand of political equality known as democracy while tolerating, reluctantly, the harsh inequality of slavery. But democracy in its modern version was still in its infancy, while slavery in stark contrast was an old institution. Moreover the United States had been built on the federal principle – that a variety of states could gain strength from their unity but cling to their political and economic differences. The essence of federalism was that enemies and opponents could coexist, and Lincoln had to cement that coexistence. In 1861, in his eyes, the sin of the slave-owning south lay less in its support of slavery than in the unpalatable fact that it opposed federalism and the very existence of the United States.

The hero of the war against slavery came from humble stock. In 1816 his parents had moved from warm Kentucky to the more northerly state of Indiana where they were small farmers. Abraham Lincoln, who was then aged eight, learned how to handle an axe and became adept at the strenuous work of chopping down trees and splitting them into the rails from which, at that time, tens of thousands of simple farming fences were being constructed across the North American plains. When as a young lawyer he entered politics, his supporters called him 'The Rail Splitter', but Lincoln by then was more proud of the education he had won for himself than of his earlier life as a son of toil.

His mother and father worshipped at the Separate Baptist Church, one of the many splinters of Protestantism that flourished in North America, and like most believers in that sect they opposed horseracing, dancing, the drinking of alcohol and the keeping of slaves. Their opposition to slavery was based not only on religion but also on their own financial interests. In such slave states as Kentucky, the Lincolns and other small white farmers had trouble in competing with the big farmers who employed the cheap and unfair labour of slaves.

Like most politicians in a democracy, Lincoln had to swim with the stream if he was to summon the popular support required for big tasks. He swam with the stream, even on the topic of slavery. While he held definite views about slavery, he was not an advocate for the equality of black and white people.

In 1862 he supported the idea of creating a separate nation in Africa for blacks, 'for the good of mankind'. When black leaders said no he accepted their no. A year passed before he finally conferred freedom – still a theoretical freedom – on the slaves living in the northern states. He did not then abolish slavery in the southern states: indeed the constitution of the country had to be amended before slavery could be abolished.

Soon after the victorious battle at Gettysburg the Union's dead were reburied in a neat war cemetery, to be dedicated on 19 November 1863. For the ceremony in the cemetery Lincoln dressed himself in a new black suit and a stovepipe hat that made him seem even taller than he was. The hat was circled by a black band of mourning, so placed not to commemorate those killed in battle but his own young son, Willie, who had recently died after a short illness. Lincoln listened to a long speech and then stood up and delivered his own speech in the space of about three minutes.

He himself would have been astonished to learn that the words of his speech would endure. After all, it consisted of only a few sentences. Yet it had an eternal sound. It concluded with a sentence that would remain alive: 'we here highly resolve that these dead shall not have died in vain – that this nation, under God, shall have a new birth of freedom – and that government of the people, by the people, for the people, shall not perish from the earth'.

Lincoln's stand for the unity of his nation was to be, in the history of the enlargement of human freedom, even more influential than his campaign against slavery. If the United States, from the 1860s, had been divided into two nations, with little in common, then the influence of North America on world affairs would have been much weaker, and the outcome of the Second World War might well have been different.

Just before the victorious end of the four-year war in 1865, Lincoln was at ease, watching a play in a Washington theatre, when he was assassinated. Slavery was already doomed in the Americas. It was abolished in the United States in that year, and was increasingly challenged in Cuba and Brazil. No new slaves were arriving there from Africa, and the babies born into slave families were declared to be free. At last, in 1886, slavery was abolished in Cuba and two years later the last slave was liberated in Brazil. In many parts of Africa and a few scattered parts of Asia, slavery continued. It was not officially abolished on the sand-swept plains of the African state of Mauritania until 1980. Nations continue to condemn it, even in the 1990s, but here and there it persists.

REBELLION IN CHINA

The two most deadly wars in the long period of peace between 1815 and 1914 were fought inside nations rather than between nations. Moreover they were fought inside important nations and so the final outcomes had strong potential effects on the weights and balances of world power. While the American Civil War is still widely known – television and films have revived the memory of it – the other war, the Taiping Rebellion, is little known outside China. The dead in the American Civil War exceeded 600 000 but in the Chinese war the dead perhaps exceeded 20 000 000, making it more deadly than the First World War.

This uprising of simple peasants was a clamour for equality at a time when population was soaring and farmland was scarce. The nutrition and housing of most Chinese peasants were poorer than those of most slaves in the United States. But poverty and hardship do not automatically lead to an uprising: if poverty actually led to rebellion, the history of the world would be nothing but a chain of rebellions. A spark was needed and was provided by Hung Hsui-chüan.

Hung had the ambitions of a bright Chinese youth, but between 1828 and 1843 he failed four times in his exam for the civil service. He was compelled to be a village teacher instead of an honoured bureaucrat – until he fell under the spell of an American missionary, a Southern Baptist who, without realising it, rekindled the ambition in the frustrated teacher. Receiving Christian visions, Hung wrapped them in Chinese patriotism and set about leading the people towards 'the Heavenly Kingdom of Great Peace'. In Chinese the phrase for 'great peace' is *taiping*, and that name was given to the rebellion he led.

Marching through the welcoming countryside, Hung's troops were bound to win early victories while the government, in disarray, was assembling its forces. Surprise was on Hung's side. Town after town, city after city, perhaps 600 in all fell to his armed forces, which eventually numbered close to one million.

This amateur theologian and general preached his own blend of Confucius and Christ. There was also an equalitarian strand, and if he had controlled the countryside rather than the cities he might have redistributed the land on a large scale and set up communes. But in 1856, a turning point, the senior ranks of the rebels were split by personal disputes and thinned by a purge. Thereafter the troops had less success.

On 1 June 1864, after nearly 14 years in the field, Hung stared at the certainty of defeat. On that day he committed suicide. But the Taipings had shaken what seemed unshakeable. Thereafter the prospect of rebellion was enhanced in the minds of a host of Chinese intellectuals and dissidents. The fighting example of Hung deeply influenced the nationalist Dr Sun Yat-sen, who, half a century later, was to overthrow the Emperor of China. Even the communists, who later overthrew the nationalist republic, were helped by the gale which Hung had unleashed.

AN AGE OF SOCIAL EXPERIMENT

The seeds of the plant Equality had lain in the earth for thousands of years. Those Greek philosophers known as the Stoics emphasised that all human beings, whether slaves or free, shared the power of reason and a capacity to show goodwill, and that these qualities distinguished them from other creatures. The Roman Empire and the concept of natural law emphasised common rights; and in the year 212, most freeborn men of the empire became equal before the law.

These ideas of equality, though of small influence in the Middle Ages, were revived by the Renaissance with its stress on individuality and by the Reformation with its insistence that all who humbly read the Bible were entitled to be their own interpreters of God's word, and even entitled to be their own priests and pastors. An emphasis on equality led to an emphasis on education for all. Those Protestant lands which built schools assumed that every child had potential, and that reading and writing were the keys to unlocking it. Democracy in the United States owed much to the hundreds of thousands of literate people who, governing their own congregations, believed that they should also be entitled to sit in local parliaments.

In Europe in the second half of the 19th century the demand for economic equality became loud in certain years. It was louder in the cities because it was easier to organise unofficial protest movements in cities than in a village. The call for equality was also spurred by the sharp extremes of wealth. Whereas the monarchy, the nobility and large landowners and merchants had often been conspicuously wealthy, the rise of factory owners who earned vast sums in their own lifetime heightened the sense that their wealth had been created largely by the sweat of their present employees. Demands for economic reforms were spurred by the increase in unemployment in bad years, and the fact that to be unemployed in a big city was to be more helpless than in the countryside where at least firewood could be gathered and where relatives might be called on for food and shelter.

Most of the strong protest movements were in the cities; and in 1848, the year of revolutions, they were on the brink of success. Whereas many of the early protests wanted nothing more than cheap bread in a year of dear bread, the new reform movements were often comprehensive and sophisticated. Karl Marx and Friedrich Engels, the young German architects of what became communism, displayed an insight into some of the directions being taken by the fast-changing European economy. Marx predicted with acute foresight that in the industrial nations the new machines and skills would produce enormous wealth and a wide gulf between rich and poor. By 1875 he was dramatically emphasising equality: 'From each according to his abilities, to each according to his needs.'

Economic reformers did not have to point to the need for action. In Italy a host of little children walked barefoot in the middle of winter. In big German cities a host of families each lived in an apartment of just one room. In Russia countless families shivered in the cold in winter because they could not find enough fuel to keep the fire alight. In industrial cities, unemployment in some years of the 1880s exceeded 10 per cent; and most of the unemployed were people who were eager to work and had a lifetime's experience of hard work. The slow swing between economic boom and depression was now a feature of economic life in industrialised Europe, and levels of unemployment rose and fell like a yo-yo.

Initially the demand for equality was heard less in economic than in political life. To ask for the right to vote was less revolutionary than to demand that all land be redistributed equally amongst poor and rich. The right to vote, however, was a rarity even in Europe. In 1800 only a tiny proportion of the world's nations possessed a parliament exercising even a modicum of power, and only a limited number of citizens were allowed to vote in elections or sit in those few parliaments that did exist. The English-speaking world was to the fore in parliamentary government, but the so-called mother of parliaments on the banks of the Thames was far less democratic than the United States during the early decades of the 19th century.

In the late 1850s three of the five Australian colonies served as a political laboratory, and there nearly every man gained the right to vote, including the right to vote by secret ballot and the right to stand for the lower house of parliament. At that time the five major European nations – Britain, France, Germany, Austria and Russia – were far behind Australia, Canada and the United States in their pursuit and practice of democracy.

At the end of the century, New Zealand and Australia were still pioneers in extending democracy. Indeed the wide extension of voting rights and the practice of paying members of parliament led to the election of the world's first Labour government in Queensland in December 1899. It was a foretaste of an era when most of Europe would be governed intermittently by social democratic governments.

Women gained from the new interest in equality, though voting rights came to them in slow steps. The American territory of Wyoming was the first to give women the right to vote. It made this radical change in 1869, in the hope of attracting more women to settle in its gun-carrying, masculine territory and so give a softer tone to a frontier society. A year later the nearby state of Utah gave women the vote. As Utah was largely a Mormon society, and many of the householders lived with several wives, it could not be easily classified as a haven of feminism. The effect of the new law was simply to give long-resident Mormon families more votes, at the expense of newcomers to Utah.

To admit women to a medical school was also an audacious step. In the United States, Miss Elizabeth Blackwell, obsessed with the desire to study medicine, had to engage various private tutors before at last, in November 1847 at the age of 26, she was admitted to the medical school at tiny Geneva College in a small town in New York State. Her victory was premature; and at first she was not allowed to attend practical classes and view the human body in company with men. Eventually she opened an infirmary in New York for poor women.

Even in Europe one generation later a woman working in the professions was a rarity, except in teaching. The first female scientist to win world esteem was probably Marie Curie, the Polish-born physicist who in France in 1898 coined the word 'radioactive' to describe one of her findings. At that time a woman in a parliament was still unknown in the entire world, though Queen Victoria, the formal head of the largest empire, had already reigned for 63 years – a 'term of office' longer than a female prime minister in any democratic country will ever experience. Not until

1924 did the world's first female cabinet minister, Nina Bang, take office in Denmark.

The stirrings of a welfare state in western Europe were another sign of the vogue for equality. If all peoples in a nation were worthy, should they not be cared for by the government when they were ill, old, permanently deprived of work or absolutely destitute? In Germany in the 1880s, Bismarck set up a scheme of national insurance, while in Denmark, New Zealand and parts of Australia the old-age pension was in place by 1900. Under pressure from trade unions, Australia introduced the bold idea of a basic wage for factory employees. In a variety of nations the tax system was altered to reduce the tax on small incomes and to increase it on large incomes. Somebody had to pay for the welfare. The rich were the popular choice.

Even in prosperous cities many families with a regular income lived precariously by today's standards. In the English city of York, a family of five who sat towards the bottom of the income ladder could not afford the luxury of beer or tobacco, a halfpenny newspaper, or the postage for a letter. They did not have enough weekly income to place a small coin in the collection plate of their church, and they could not afford a Christmas present for their children unless they themselves made the present. Sometimes they would take their Sunday clothes to the pawnbroker on Monday morning in order to have enough money to buy food until payday arrived. For the family of a breadwinner

369

who suffered an accident at work or a bout of sickness, the loss of income was shattering. If the husband died, the widow had to take in boarders – if there was room to spare – or washing. With luck she might remarry.

There was one consolation. These families usually enjoyed a higher standard of living than their grandparents had known in their rural village. Furthermore they lived longer, and in more comfort, and were the beneficiaries of more education.

The rising call for equality expressed itself in the goal of primary education for all children and in the principle that every young man should be ready to serve in the armed forces. It also burst onto the religious arena. Hitherto most governments had given strong preference to adherents of the official religion. In Britain as late as the year 1820, the law emphasised the inequality of religions. Thus Catholics and Jews could not vote or sit in parliament, and Baptists and most Methodists could not teach in universities. Members of the nonconformist religions could not be married in their own church by a pastor of their own religion. Long before the end of the century, however, adherents of all religions became equal in most respects within the British Isles, though not in every European nation.

The European surge towards equality expressed itself in a growing suspicion of hereditary rights and a preference for some form of republicanism. Venice for centuries had been a powerful aristocratic republic, but the rise of a powerful United States and the new chain of South American republics was the herald of a more republican era in the entire world. France, after abolishing and then restoring the monarchy, became a committed republic in 1870. China, perhaps the oldest continuous monarchy in the world, became a republic in 1912. In most European nations the monarchy, reduced much in power, seemed likely to survive; but the turmoil late in the First World War removed three of the powerful monarchies of Europe, and they were not restored. Most of the new nations founded in Europe after the war chose to be republics.

THE BOTTLES OF EQUALITY

This thirst for equality was a hallmark of the era, but the equality was labelled and sold in bottles of different shapes and sizes. In some bottles so labelled lay a sparkling brew of inequality. Nationalism was in one of those bottles. While every citizen of a nation might feel a sense of togetherness and equality in the presence of kinsfolk, the equality did not so easily extend to people of other nations. While a keener appreciation of equality was in the air, it might not always extend to people belonging to other social classes, and it might not be extended to new immigrants.

The interest in equality sometimes clashed with the interest in race felt by many Europeans. A characteristic of the second half of the 19th century, the fascination with race stemmed from an unusual mix of factors. This was a century when the search for general laws about human nature – and the confidence that such generalisations could be found – was intense. At the same time the dramatic increase in contact between people who had long been apart, geographically and culturally, drew attention to the sharp differences that did exist – differences which were wider than probably exist today. Much of this comment on race was neutral but some was aggressive.

Western European peoples were enamoured by their own progress in this age of steam and compulsory schooling. From the lofty platform on which they stood, it was easy to think that they were inherently superior, mentally and physically, and would remain so. That their civilisation was far ahead of central Africa's and even China's they had no doubt; and certainly it was far ahead in a material sense.

Many who did believe that there was something special about their own branch of European civilisation were romantics and often generous in spirit. Many were eager to spread their culture amongst coloured peoples in their own colonies. That this surging tide of racial and nationalist ideas could carry such grave dangers was appreciated almost nowhere in Europe.

The Jews were ultimately to be the tragic victims of this tide of ideas, but in 1900 the signs were few, outside the Russian Empire, that this tide was necessarily malevolent. The Jews, for the first time, were permitted to rise to the fore in public life in many European nations. They seemed to be one of the special beneficiaries of the equalitarian tides of the time. Indeed Germany was seen as relatively friendly, and thousands of Jews emigrated to German cities where they graced professional and intellectual life, were prominent in music, painting and writing, and built handsome synagogues.

The main home of the Jews was in central and eastern Europe. In a wide band of country running from the Baltic Sea to the Black Sea, a distance of more than 1200 kilometres, the Jews averaged more than 10 per cent of the total population in every major district. Russia governed most of this area and, unlike most other European nations, tightly restricted the rights of Jews. They had to live in specific areas, the so-called 'Pale of Settlement', and could not enter certain professions.

As a people Jews were easily identified, for they worshipped on Saturday. For religious purposes they spoke and wrote their own language, Hebrew, and in everyday discourse they mainly spoke Yiddish, a dialect of medieval German. In a few European circles they were the target of Christian bias, being seen as the descendants of those who allegedly had crucified Christ. Some European theologians and intellectuals even argued that Christ was not a Jew.

As bankers and moneylenders the Jews were often prominent. Some of the anti-Semitism, particularly in years of serious unemployment, had an economic edge. It was directed against those rich Jews who formed a tiny minority or against the Jewish moneylenders operating in small towns in eastern Europe.

Late in the 19th century, whether in the arts or sciences or medicine or the law, Jews were prominent out of all proportion to their numbers in western Europe. In England, where they were few, they were able to attain high office. The conservative prime minister presiding over England from 1874 to 1880, the eloquent Benjamin Disraeli, was descended from Italian and Portuguese Jews; and his own father when young had frequented the synagogue.

From this slow enthroning of equality, several hundred million people living in Africa and Asia did not gain. The demand for equality and freedom in much of Europe coincided with some loss of freedom in parts of other continents. With so many Asian and African peoples now ruled by distant European monarchs or parliaments, it was not easy to talk convincingly of equality in Cairo, Tashkent, Shanghai or Calcutta. For perhaps the first time in human history, equality was widely lauded as a virtue, but ironically hundreds of millions of people lived under the colonial rule of those European nations which were foremost in preaching equality.

28

A GLOBE UNWRAPPED

In Burma in 1900 the typical shopkeepers near the Rangoon River knew about happenings in Europe. Schoolteachers in African villages knew something about China, a land which their grandmothers might not even have heard of. A skeleton of knowledge about remote lands was now in the curriculum of a thousand schools. Coloured maps of the world became commonplace. It is doubtful whether in the days of Napoleon more than a fraction of the people in Europe had ever set eyes on a map of the world; but a century later most of Europe's schoolchildren had seen such a map or a globe and could even recite the names of rivers and mountains in each continent.

It was the last age of global exploration. In almost every decade of the 19th century, a major geographical discovery was made: the finding of the sources of the River Nile; the first ascent of the Matterhorn and other mountains which had previously been seen as unclimbable; the discovery of the sources of the Amazon, Mississippi and Congo rivers; expeditions into the sunburned interior of Australia; the finding in Greenland of the world's largest glacier, the Humboldt; and voyages up the forest-lined rivers of New Guinea. One of the few symbolic landmarks still unvisited was the South Pole, which was to be reached in 1911 by the Norwegian explorer Roald Amundsen – just five weeks ahead of the Briton, Robert Scott, who died in the snow. Many of these remote landmarks now being seen and mapped by people of European descent had long been seen by natives of the regions. The Europeans put them in perspective and printed them on the maps.

New insights into the long history of the world came from some who travelled far. Charles Darwin sailed slowly around the world in a British naval vessel in the 1830s, visiting places as inaccessible as the Galápagos Islands in the eastern Pacific and gaining the knowledge that led to his theory of biological evolution, first published in 1859.

In the straits and islands of South-East Asia, another British naturalist independently discovered Darwin's theory, as well deducing the existence of a remarkable dividing line separating the habitats of many species of plants and animals. Alfred Russel Wallace, teacher and surveyor, was in his mid-twenties when he fell in love with natural history. Deciding to collect exotic birds, partly for the pleasure of those European collectors who wished to stay at home, he sailed in 1848 to the Amazon River to collect and conserve. On his return voyage the ship caught fire, and many of his specimens and zoological notes were lost.

Wallace was not deterred. Setting out for the Indonesian archipelago he moved from island to island, collecting specimens of every living thing that was garish and extraordinary. In 1862, his collecting and observing almost finished, he returned with the first living birds-of-paradise to reach Europe. His alert eyes and powerful memory assembled the facts that enabled him to prove that between South-East Asia and Australia, and especially visible between the islands of Bali and Lombok, was a deep and permanent sea barrier, now known as Wallace's line.

It was not yet realised that a new dimension of the oceans was waiting to be explored. Whereas the human eye can see, at least in clear weather, the highest mountains on earth, it cannot see the chains of mountains lying on the seabed, for the sea blocks out the sun's light. Few educated people knew that the seas occupied more than twice as much of the world's surface as did the land. The existence of ranges of mountains far beneath the sea was not known. A British wooden vessel, HMS *Challenger*, was equipped to sound out ocean beds in remote parts of the world. She set sail in 1872 and systematically dropped overboard a long wire-line to measure the depth of the ocean. Her first major discovery was a winding chain of mountains which lay far below the surface of the Atlantic and ran along the seabed in a north–south line. At no place did this Mid-Atlantic Ridge come close to the continents of America and Africa.

In 1874 *Challenger* ventured far to the south, becoming the first steamship ever to cross the Antarctic Circle. In dredging the bottom of the icy Antarctic ocean her scientists found fragments of continental rock which had been smoothed by glaciers. This discovery, conveying the firm suggestion that a big landmass lay to the south, was the most persuasive evidence so far found for the existence of an Antarctic continent as distinct from a small land or a cluster of islands.

The sea still covered mysteries. Were the continents, now far apart, once joined tightly together? A young German meteorologist, Alfred Wegener, after travelling to Greenland, made a sweeping observation of profound importance. In 1912 he devised the theory of continental drift. He suggested that there had originally existed only one massive continent, that tropical Africa and South America had once been joined but that North and South America had not always been joined, that the Himalaya mountains arose from the pressure of continents slowly colliding, and that present continents were not fixed in position but were either slowly moving apart or coming closer. His brilliant ideas were deemed preposterous and only won wide respect in the 1960s, long after his death.

With the widening knowledge of the globe and the influence of the romantic movement came a realisation that the world was sprinkled with unfamiliar places that could elicit gasps of wonder from lovers of nature. The ancient Greeks had listed their wonders of the world, nearly all of which were buildings created by their own artists and architects within a small radius of the cities of Athens and Alexandria. In 1900, by contrast, many travellers preferred the grand spectacles of nature to the grand buildings of Greece and Rome, China and India. Some pointed to Niagara Falls, the Swiss Alps, the Himalayas, the harbours of Hong Kong and the table-shaped mount of Cape Town, the trees of Yosemite in California, New Zealand's Milford Sound and the muddy Irrawaddy in Burma, while others collected a different set of coloured postcards. The assumption that these marvels could in no way be imperilled was more confident than it is today.

Many fortunate travellers marvelled at the volcanic terraces and rock stairways on the North Island of New Zealand. One wide terrace was a delicate pink with crystals like rosy icicles. The waters of the other terrace were wonderingly described by the English historian J. A. Froude in 1885: 'The hue of the water was something which I had never seen, and shall never again see on this side of eternity.' It was not the colour of the violet or the harebell – the flowers he loved – nor sapphire or turquoise. A master of English prose, he confessed he could find no way of conveying 'a sense of that supernatural loveliness'. One year later the pink and white terraces were utterly destroyed when stones, ash and hot mud poured from the nearby volcano.

In 1901, in the arid centre of Australia and far from the nearest railway, a miraculous thread was tied between the 20th century and the era of the nomads. Professor Baldwin Spencer and F. J. Gillen captured the dances of Aborigines on one of the first movie cameras and recorded their haunting songs on the wax cylinder of a phonograph. As the learned visitors had no battery or electricity, they were forced to crank the handle of the camera continuously to supply the motive power. Moreover they had no alternative but to arrange the heavy camera for long periods in a set position, so that it pointed continuously in the one direction. Spencer decided to direct the camera towards a group of near-naked men performing the dance of an ancient rainmaking ceremony, with the dust rising from their bare and pounding feet. The dancers, wisely not inter-ested in posterity, suddenly began to make 'a wide semicircular sweep' and slowly they passed out of the camera's vision. Thus much of the precious film was wasted.

It was a remarkable occasion and time signal. Here were the representatives of a dying way of life that had dominated the entire world in 10 000 BC, standing face to face with the latest step in technology. The dancing Aborigines retained the sense that they and not the strange intruders held the key to the universe. While they danced, their voices – for they were impressive mimics – imitated the cry of the plover bird. The Aborigines believed that their imitation of its cry would entice rain to fall on the dusty ground, which had long been parched.

In the shrinking of the world, the surviving remnants of the hunters and gatherers, once all-powerful on the face of the globe, were the most drastic losers. Later most of their descendants would probably gain from readmission to a wider world; but the generation which faced for the first time this new, powerful and incomprehensible European way of life – so many years removed from their own style of life – could only feel bewildered. They had occupied their lands for thousands of years, and their future had seemed eternal. In that sense they were exceptionally privileged. They had been able to retain, far longer than all other human societies, a traditional way of life based on the luxury of a tiny number of people possessing vast and often attractive spaces. But in the end the demise of the old nomadic way of life had been spurred by its inefficient and aristocratic monopoly of what was becoming the world's scarcest asset, land on which to grow food and find shelter.

The material advance of the human race and the multiplying of its numbers in the previous 10 000 years had come largely from the skilled and ingenious use of land, plants, animals and raw materials. Much of it had come from the more intense use of land for farms and flocks. Now, in Australia and the icy fringes of the Northern Hemisphere and the arid corners of the southern half of Africa, the last of the nomads were being called upon, with unanswerable urgency and sometimes with violence, to stand aside or join in. How could they join? They lacked the skills and attitudes, values and incentives which would enable them to take part with ease.

THE SEA CARPET

New shipping routes were joining the continents, uniting them with a speed and safety not seen before. Shipping was cheap; the cost of carrying goods was cut. Bulk commodities such as coal and wheat, cotton and pig-iron and petroleum, were carried cheaply from one end of the world to the other: and yet a few lifetimes ago, only precious commodities such as pepper, ivory and gold could afford to be carried long distances in ships. The children of the lighthouse keepers at Cape Horn, if they were curious about the ships passing by, could discern in fair weather a straggling procession of stately tall-masted sailing ships carrying nitrate from the dry coast of Chile all the way to Germany where it was becoming prized fertiliser. They could perhaps see ships carrying bales of wool from Australia to England, or oregon timber to Europe from the north-west coast of America. The Panama Canal, that remarkable short cut across America, was not completed until 1914.

Free or half-free migration had never been on such a large scale, whether Germans and Irish flocking to the United States, Italians and Iberians to South America, Japanese to Hawaii, Britons to Canada and New Zealand,

Chinese to the Malay Peninsula and Java, Welsh to Patagonia, or Indians to Fiji and Natal.

Carriers of culture also crossed the world in unprecedented numbers. Christian and medical missionaries, women and men, poured into China, India, German South-West Africa, French Indochina and wherever they were permitted to enter: in practice they were permitted to enter almost every land during the heyday of Europe. In Africa one of the famous explorers was David Livingstone, a Scottish mill hand who became a Christian missionary, while the Alsace-born medical missionary Albert Schweitzer spent most of his life helping victims of leprosy and sleeping sickness in Gabon. Missionaries such as the Belgian-born Father Damien, who died while helping lepers in Hawaii, were folk heroes in an era when it was not yet thought quite right to acclaim footballers as heroes. Musicians also criss-crossed the world, and at the turn of the century the young Italian tenor Enrico Caruso divided his year between opera houses in Buenos Aires, New York and Europe. Global empires made it easy to lay down professional pathways across the world.

This many-sided process was to be given, at the end of the 20th century, the name of globalisation. It was certainly international and global but it was also rabidly national. While the world was becoming one, it was also remaining divided. The map was fragmented into empires controlled from Europe. Much of the world had been divided amongst European imperial powers by 1850, and the final phase of subdivision took place in the following 50 years when colonies as far apart as New Guinea and East Africa were acquired by Germany, tropical Congo was taken over by Belgium, parts of north-eastern Africa fell to Italy, New Caledonia and much of Indochina were taken by France, a vast area of crag and plain in central Asia was absorbed into the Russian Empire, and a string of islands and large patches of mainland fell to Britain, which was far and away the largest owner of colonies. Even the United States reluctantly entered the race, buying Alaska and capturing Spanish colonies stretching from Cuba to the Philippines. By 1900 most parts of the world were governed by colonial powers.

The coloured maps of the world were dotted and dashed with the red which was widely used by map-makers to symbolise the British Empire. Queen Victoria, who was to die in 1901, ruled an empire that would have made even the Mongols blink. Hers was the first empire on which the sun never set.

THE PALE EMPIRE OF IDEAS

While the Roman Empire in its extent and longevity was a marvel, several empires which were flourishing by 1900 were larger. Russia, the United States and China each occupied an expanse larger than that of the old Roman Empire. Likewise the empires of Britain and France across the seas were vaster in area than the total of Rome's colonies, though Europe's control of daily life in its colonies probably was less pervasive than that of Rome within its empire.

There are two categories of empire. One is the physical, consisting, like the Roman and British empires, of colonies and dependencies. The other category is the pale empire of ideas. In the 19th century, Europe spread in influence even more through its empire of ideas than through the possession of new colonies.

At the same time a pale empire of ideas – much paler – was extending in the opposite direction. Around 1900, a river of powerful ideas quietly flowed from Africa and Asia to European civilisation. In art, French cubism was much influenced by west African art. Famous writers such as Jack London and Rudyard Kipling saw virtues in the Inuits and the Indians. A new respect for nature in sections of western society meant that those so-called 'primitive' people who lived close to nature on the other side of the globe were accorded virtues previously ignored. The founding of the international Boy Scout movement in 1907 reflected the belief that much could be learned from the wolf as well as from the books of Cambridge and Tübingen.

Secular knowledge was in the ascendant, though it owed much to religious impulses. Ever since certain wings of Protestantism had encouraged the idea that everyone should be his own priest, and even her own priest, an ability to read had been vital. Protestant Prussia, Holland and Scotland – each of which was relatively small in population and area – led the way in literacy and so in the general pursuit of knowledge. Scotland's places of learning continued to produce so many talented young men that the country could not use them effectively; and so they trooped south to London where the book-publishing industry, probably the largest in the world, became almost a Scottish home away from home. The Jews also came to the fore in seeking education. Their role in the knowledge industry was far more influential than their small numbers would have suggested. Knowledge was their real estate, their title deed.

Traditionally in most parts of the world the ownership of land had conferred income, social status and political rights on those who owned it. Knowledge was now challenging the economic role of land, though it was not yet making deep inroads into the status of land. By 1900 nearly as many people probably made a remunerative and satisfying living in the USA, France, Britain and Germany from knowledge as were making it from ownership of land, minerals and other natural resources. Knowledge was the new frontier. There was virtually a rush for knowledge just as there had been a rush for gold in California and Australia half a century previously.

An ability to expand knowledge was almost the hallmark of the leading nations; and no other period had seen such an accumulation of useful knowledge. Albert Einstein, the physicist, was widely seen as the genius of the first half of the 20th century; but who could say so with certainty, for the learned theories formulated by this brilliant and unassuming German Jew were understood by few. Each field of knowledge was now the domain of specialists, and few specialists jumped the high fences designed to separate them from outside fields.

Specialisation was the secret of Europe's success but it carried great dangers for the specialists, even more than for the civilisation that gained from their research. It was sometimes complained in a whisper – for the thought was heretical – that if knowledge and indeed wisdom were really so important, why were most of the specialists satisfied with the possession of such a small and concentrated morsel of knowledge?

From this invasion of knowledge no land could hide. Japan had had periods of hiding and yet had retained vitality and inventiveness in its isolation. In the late 1500s, at the close of its first period of contact with Europe, Japan manufactured more muskets than probably any other country in Europe. In the 1850s it put out its hands to the world again, opening its ports to foreign ships. In the 1860s it began to model its army on the French and its navy on the British. In 1876 its ban on the wearing of swords was another sign of the rejection of its feudal past. The building of railways – fiercely opposed by some Japanese – was one more. The reshaping of Japan was brisk and decisive. In 1895 it was victorious in its short war with China and 10 years later it won – to the surprise of the world – its short war with Russia.

China's long and proud phase of self-absorption, in contrast, ended in some humiliation. In many of its ports the Europeans made their own laws, and Shanghai was fast becoming a European city. The throne of China, once all-powerful, was soon to collapse. There was even a prospect that China would suffer the fate of Africa and be partitioned amongst the European powers.

It was an extraordinary somersault in the relations between China and Europe. If such a humiliation of a throne and a culture had been possible in, say, the year 1400, it would have been the Chinese who sent Buddhist missionaries to Dublin, who operated the customs houses in Hamburg and Constantinople, and who threatened to partition Europe if the people did not behave themselves.

Around the world most of the locked gates were flung open, but not those of Mecca. It remained a forbidden city to unbelievers. Even so, many Arabs setting out on the legitimate pilgrimage now liked to wear coloured Manchester textiles.

THE RISE OF NORTH-WESTERN EUROPE

For several thousand years there were only two long-standing centres of innovation and economic power. One was eastern Asia and the other was the Mediterranean, especially the lands near its eastern shores. Of the influential western empires before AD 1500, the Egyptian, Mesopotamian, Greek, Roman, Hellenistic and Byzantine empires lay in this relatively small zone. The eastern Mediterranean was not only the birthplace of the three most influential western religions – Judaism and its offspring, Christianity and Islam – but also the cradle of most of the vital western innovations, ranging from farming and metallurgy to writing, arithmetic and even the state.

The ascent of north-western Europe to a dominance on the world stage, such as was never achieved by the old eastern Mediterranean and Asia Minor empires, could not have been predicted in the year AD 1600. The ascent was not inevitable, but, in retrospect, a few powerful factors were promoting it. With the discovery of the Americas and the opening of the long sea route past the Cape of Good Hope to India, the East Indies and China, north-western Europe held an advantage. Admittedly it shared this advantage because the west coast of Italy and the Mediterranean coast of Spain were in as favourable a position as Amsterdam and London to tap the wealth of the New World across the ocean.

Protestantism was part of the new dynamo of north-western Europe. This religious movement mainly flourished on the north side of the Alps. Almost certainly it was easier for a reformation to succeed when it was far from Rome and from those other Italian cities and princedoms with an affinity to the papacy and an economic and emotional interest in supporting it. Moreover the Reformation in its early years was adopted and promoted by the exponents of that commerce and capitalism, much centred on textiles, which was already vigorous in parts of north-western Europe. With some notable exceptions the Protestant creeds were more sympathetic to the spirit of inquiry which the growing science and technology needed.

Geography promoted the rise of north-western Europe in another way. This cold region with its long winters was a heavy consumer of fuel. As England and Belgium and other parts of the region began to run out of a cheap supply of firewood they turned to shallow coastal beds of coal. It so happened that this region was wonderfully endowed with coal compared to Italy, Greece, Egypt, the Fertile Crescent and all the lands of the eastern Mediterranean and the Persian Gulf. In turn the mining of coal led, though not automatically, to the steam engine and the coke-burning blast furnace. The steam engine was the most powerful agent of globalisation so far experienced, for it led directly and indirectly to the engine in cars and aircraft, and to the age of gas and oil.

So a mixture of major and minor factors helped north-western Europe to supplant the warmer and drier Mediterranean and Middle East. Western Europe exploited its geography with a spirit of intellectual and commercial adventure such as the world had possibly not seen before.

The United States displayed the same spirit of adventure, with even more effect. A vast bowl of resources and a dynamo of knowledge, it was potentially richer than north-western Europe and by 1900 held more people than any two western European countries combined. It was also united whereas Europe was divided. Nothing was to do more to mould the 20th century than the increasing unity of North America and the increasing disunity of Europe.

29

THE WORLD WARS

A history of the world could be so written that it was almost dominated by the wars between clans, tribes, nations and empires. Countless wars, recorded and not recorded, have taken place even in the last 10 000 years. Certainly, peace is the more normal condition than war, but war and peace are linked in their causation. Thus a memorable period of peace can depend on the outcome of the previous war and the enforcement of that outcome. Peace between the nations of a region is often the result of an agreed pecking order which has been arrived at either by war or by the threat of war. In Europe in 1914, alas, there was no agreed pecking order.

Europe's last major war, fought between France and Prussia in 1870 and 1871, had been swift; and so the short war was thought to be the likely pattern of the future. The First World War was approached in the belief that war itself was still a quick and efficient solver of problems. Both sides expected to win. They also expected to win quickly, for military technology seemed to be more decisive than ever before.

A DEADLOCKED WAR

The war began in August 1914 and was expected to be won before Christmas or soon after. When the Germans and their ally, the Austro-Hungarians, clashed with the Russians in eastern Europe, and the Germans fought the French and British armies on the plains of northern France, and the Austrians fought the Serbs, the war seemed to be moving swiftly towards an early conclusion. Germany was the early winner but casualties were huge.

The firepower of the latest machine guns, and of the heavy guns drawn by horses, was so devastating that soldiers advancing towards the enemy were mown down in their thousands, and the thousands who replaced them were mown down. In the space of a few months, on most battlefields, soldiers had to dig hundreds of kilometres of trenches and arrange walls of barbed wire for their own protection. The long battlefield trench, deep enough for a soldier to stand upright and not be seen by the enemy nearby, was really a form of shield.

So the opposing armies ceased to move swiftly as in past wars, and the war became defensive. Any attempt by one army to leave the shelter of the trenches and storm forward usually led to the capture of only a tiny strip of ground – before the rain of shells and bullets from the opposite line of trenches forced a retreat. On such days the deaths were counted in the tens of thousands.

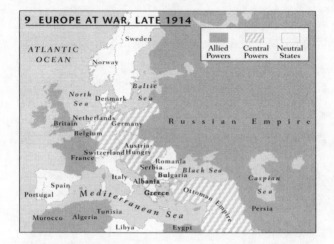

9 EUROPE AT WAR, LATE 1914

On most battlefronts in the last weeks of 1914 the war reached a stalemate. What was intended to be the Great War of 1914 became the Great War of 1914–15; and still the months ticked away. In April 1915, in an attempt to end the stalemate, the British and French with Australians and New Zealanders launched a new front on Turkish beaches near Gallipoli, at the mouth of the Dardanelles. They hoped to defeat Turkey in a few weeks, use the liberated Dardanelles as a sea route to ports in southern Russia and so send arms and munitions which would equip the huge Russian armies. In turn it was hoped that the Russian armies would apply pressure on the Germans on the Eastern Front. The Turks, however, dug trenches as their shield, deadlocked this sector of the war and forced the invaders to withdraw at the year's end.

The military deadlock defied the predictions of all but a few gifted generals and armchair strategists. Nothing like it had been seen in the history of the world. It is common to blame the generals. But in most of the countries at war, even the mothers and wives and girlfriends were initially supportive, believing with the aid of propaganda that the perpetual bloodshed would miraculously terminate in the defeat of the exhausted enemy.

The war, with all its surprises and uncertainties, was spiced with 'ifs'. If Russia could have been propped up in 1915, the tsar and his ministers might have maintained control of their restless country. But failure in three successive years of fighting amputated the leg of the already hobbling tsar. In 1917 two revolutions in quick succession broke out, and Lenin and his communists took control. Russia withdrew from the war.

At the start of 1918, Germany still possessed a fighting chance of winning the war or negotiating a favourable peace. The United States, entering the war late, was not seen as likely to exert a powerful influence. Furthermore, Germany's main ally, the Austro-Hungarian empire, was still holding firm the mountainous front line against Italy. In great heart the Germans commenced an offensive which, in March 1918, won much ground and pushed close to Paris.

Slowly the fortunes of the war swung against Germany. It suffered because the access to food and raw materials, and the power to produce munitions and men, favoured its enemies. Its front lines were dinted by hammer-blows. By September 1918 Germany's allies were about to wilt. The Bulgarians surrendered. The Turks, fighting to hold their old empire in the Middle East, were close to surrender. The Austro-Hungarian empire was about to break into splinters, and in October both Yugoslavia and Czechoslovakia proclaimed themselves republics. In Germany, as winter approached, the morale of civilians and even soldiers was failing. Food and clothing were scarce, the enemy blockade having done its damage. On 3 November 1918, German sailors mutinied at Kiel. On 9 November a socialist revolution captured Munich, while the Emperor of Germany, Kaiser Wilhelm, abdicated in Berlin. Two days later, on 11 November, Germany and its allies signed the armistice.

For soldiers it was the most terrible war the world had known; for civilians the Taiping Rebellion had been worse. Of the 8 500 000 soldiers and sailors who died in the First World War, Germany lost the most, followed by Russia, France, Austro-Hungary and then Britain and its empire. In addition more than 20 000 000 soldiers were wounded, and this list of the slain and maimed did not include maybe five million civilians who died as a direct result of the war. From crowded apartments in Moscow to sheep farms in New Zealand there were millions of mantelpieces on which stood framed black-and-white photographs of earnest or smiling young men, killed in the war which everyone now called the Great War, not realising that a greater war was barely 20 years ahead.

Without the Great War there would probably have been no Russian Revolution and no victory for communism. But for this war, the activist monarchs in all their splendour would have continued to reign in Vienna, Berlin–Potsdam and St Petersburg, and the sultan would have presided over the Turkish Empire – an empire which also vanished. If there had been no war the name Hitler would probably be unknown, for he arose out of the bitterness of Germany's defeat, just as Mussolini arose as dictator of Italy largely because he played on the deep postwar disillusionment of his people.

In the discussions around the tables of the peace conference at Versailles in 1919, high hopes as well as a desire for revenge were present. Many nationalities seized the chance to set up their own nations. It was a map-makers' picnic. In Europe now stood 31 states and nations where, on the eve of the war, had stood only 20. Some of the new states were tiny and some were large, such as Hungary and Poland. Most tried their hand at democracy, not always successfully. Some turned into dictatorships.

The war, much longer than had been expected in 1914, was a jolt to the optimism which had taken root in much of Europe during the relatively peaceful, prosperous and civilised 99 years since the defeat of Napoleon. And yet many Europeans took heart. A permanent round table of diplomacy called the League of Nations was set up at Geneva. A parliament of peace, it was possibly the bravest experiment in the history of all the nations up to that time. The hope of the liberals and idealists of the world, it became just a debating club.

Without the Great War, Britain and Europe would have remained dominant in finance, but during it they had to borrow. So the United States, especially in those war years when it was neutral, became a financier of the war effort. One cause of the approaching world Depression was the new financial power of the United States in the 1920s. Relatively inexperienced as global leader, tolerant of the cycle of boom and setback, and happy to watch the stock exchange in Wall Street acting as a trumpet major, it led an unstable world towards chronic instability. Another cause of the economic downturn visible in 1930 was that Britain tried to restore financially the pre-1914 world and its craving for stable prices. But one should not be too critical of these attempts. After the catastrophe of such a war, a determined attempt to piece together the peaceful jigsaw of the lost past was almost inevitable.

In many nations in the 1920s the unemployment in lean months exceeded 10 per cent. It was partly a result of the dislocations caused by the speed of change. New industrial regions and industries rose and fell, the shift of work from farms to factories continued, but a factory was more likely to suffer from serious slumps than was a farm. On the farm, when prices were low, the farmhands kept on working at much lower wages, or at least they could grow much of their own food. In the car or tyre or textile factories, when slumps came, the workers stayed at home and had nothing to live on. Governments and economists, moreover, were not sure how to cope with a depression. The prevailing principle was that they should do nothing and that the economy, after swallowing its medicine in the form of high unemployment and low wages and profits, would quickly cure itself.

The crash of the share market on Wall Street in October 1929 is now seen as the fire-bell. Financial confidence fell, and people stopped buying and thereby destroyed more jobs. Unemployment grew, exceeding 30 per cent in some industrial nations in the rock-bottom year of 1932. An economic depression on this scale had no precedent. It was a boost to communism and fascism. It led towards the Second World War, which was really the outcome of what was increasingly seen as an unfinished First World War.

Hitler of Germany and Stalin of Russia shaped the coming war. They were the decisive leaders when the war broke out in 1939, a date of their choosing, and briefly they were allies.

Adolf Hitler came from a river-town in Austria where his father was a minor officer in the customs house. A would-be artist, he imbibed some of the anti-Semitism of Vienna and some of the patriotism bubbling over in Munich at the outbreak of the First World War. Enlisting in the German army, he won the Iron Cross for valour on the Western Front. One of the German soldiers who in 1918 were stunned by the collapse of morale at home, when morale was still solid in many parts of the hard-pressed army, he gave vent to his sense of betrayal – on his return to civilian life – by dabbling on the fringes of politics. In 1919 at the age of 30 he became head of a little Bavarian political party, the National Socialist German Workers' Party. His party developed its own private army, which excelled in street fights against the Marxists and other parties of the left.

Hitler knew his Germany. His oratory, magnetic with the aid of astute coaching, warmed the hearts of many Germans who felt their nation and their world had been unjustly torpedoed in 1918. He spoke with such physical and emotional energy that his shirt, after a two-hour speech, would be soaked with sweat. The new outdoor loudspeaker and the radio helped to spread his message. Few party leaders in Europe were quicker to use innovations.

The world Depression in the early 1930s fostered anxiety and a premonition of chaos. On these fears Hitler thrived. Many Germans saw Hitler as the welcome upholder of law and order. Fear of communism won him increasing support from small farmers and shopkeepers. He and his oratory appealed to Germany's pride and exploited the widespread resentment that Germany had been defeated unfairly in a game in which it had long excelled – the game of war.

In the elections of 1930, Hitler's party enlarged its

vote. In 1932 it doubled its vote again, becoming the largest German political party. In January of the following year it joined a coalition of smaller right-wing parties, and Hitler was formally appointed chancellor. Soon he became in effect a dictator. The persecution of Jews, suppression of trade unions and crushing of civil liberties were under way. In 1934 the aged president died, and Hitler, by popular consent, took complete control.

In fact he was ill-prepared for power; he did not like administration or deskwork. Until he came to office his most senior official post had been as a humble corporal in the army.

A DICTATOR FURTHER EAST

Joseph Stalin was not the real name of the ruler of Russia. An organiser and agitator who had served sentences in Siberian prisons as punishment for his political activities, he took the name of Stalin, meaning 'man of steel', soon after the victorious revolution of 1917. As editor of the communist newspaper *Pravda* he was an insider, and increasingly powerful. The head of government, after the death of Lenin in January 1924, he began to eliminate personal and imaginary rivals. He set out to strengthen the armed forces, and for the economy he launched the first of his bold Five Year Plans in 1928. Though the new Soviet Union still suffered from many economic ills and discontents, it experienced no official unemployment, and ensured that virtually all idle hands were put to work. The nation escaped the Depression, and that was a marvellous boost to its prestige.

With clusters of new power stations, factories and mines, Stalin successfully converted Russia into an industrial power. He carried through the most sweeping agricultural change ever attempted by one ruler. He turned the private farms into collective farms – an astonishing and sweeping change, because more of his people were involved in farming than in any other European nation at any time, and most of them had a peasant's possessiveness towards their own land and an abhorrence of Stalin's collective farms. Peasants who resisted the collectivist policy were deported, starved or killed.

Stalin believed that communism would perish, that he himself might perish, unless he was ruthless. In peacetime his police state ordered or sanctioned the death of his fellow citizens on a grand scale. And yet national patriotism was higher under Stalin's rule than under the tsars' rule. The stamina and bravery of the Russian soldiers in the Second World War was to be impressive.

Hitler and Stalin had much in common, including the fact that each came to power as an outsider, Hitler being an Austrian and Stalin a Georgian. They were both virtually unknown and powerless at the age of 35, and both were hopelessly underestimated by their opponents. Hitler's rearming of Germany in the 1930s took France and Britain by surprise, as did

Stalin's rearming of Russia. Both leaders cultivated an aptitude for telling plausible lies to their people and to the world. They were the field marshals of propaganda in an era when its influence was magnified by radio and film.

Stalin, Hitler and the Italian dictator Benito Mussolini, who seized power in 1922, shared a strong determination to rewrite the results of the First World War and if necessary to resume that war. The fighting that began in 1939 was their tailor-made, long-awaited opportunity.

Traditionally in Europe a long and major war usually led to a long period of peace. By setting up a clear pecking order amongst major nations, a decisive war enabled many problems to be settled by diplomacy. Moreover, in the first decades of peace the realities and terrible human losses of war were usually remembered only too sharply: diplomacy was therefore preferred to war as a way of solving disputes between nations. Just as the decisive victory in the long Napoleonic Wars ushered in a long period of relative peace in Europe's far-flung world, so the end of the First World War – optimistically viewed as the war to end all wars – was expected to usher in an even rosier period of peace. The tragedy of this war was that in retrospect it was utterly pointless. The victory was soon lost, and another war was in the making.

Why was the victory so brief? Unfortunately for the victors, and for the peace of the world, the massed

might that won the First World War was soon dissi-
pated. The United States, whose industrial might was
vital even before its first soldiers sailed away in 1917 to
fight, mentally retreated soon after the war was over. It
quarantined itself, closing its eyes and ears to Europe.
Japan, whose sea power had helped during the early
months of the war, also retreated. Thus two major powers, with a strong interest in upholding the victory they
had helped to win, ceased to use their weight against
the defeated powers. This had rarely, if ever, happened
in the aftermath of a major war. In addition Italy, also
on the winning side, was disillusioned because it was
not given the German colonies in Africa and other
spoils it had been promised by the Allies. Italy became
the third victorious nation to undermine the hard-won
peace treaty. Russia became the fourth. It was on the
winning side until March 1918 when, exhausted and
revolutionised, it withdrew from its war with Germany. As a result of the war it lost or surrendered a
vast territory including Latvia, Estonia and Lithuania.
It therefore had an incentive to overthrow the new
Europe that came into being in 1919.

Of the powerful nations which were on the winning
side in 1918, only Britain and France were left with
a strong incentive to uphold the peace treaty and to
disarm Germany and keep it disarmed. Here was an
incredible erosion of a wartime victory.

Then came the Depression, and a sense of helpless-
ness was felt by many of the industrial nations which

had fought in the war. The Depression handed power to Hitler, who was determined to overthrow the peace treaty. When he began to rearm, the League of Nations was too weak and divided to intervene. In March 1936 Hitler thumbed his nose again at the treaty by occupying the Rhineland. If France and Britain together had acted promptly, Hitler's soldiers might have marched out again.

Hitler continued to rearm. The building of the autobahns or motor highways and the recovery of the automobile industry did almost as much as rearmament to abolish unemployment in Germany. German morale and self-respect soared. In March 1938 Hitler's troops entered Austria. In October he suddenly occupied the German-speaking part of Czechoslovakia. Page by page, he had torn up the Versailles treaty. The main loser of the First World War had recovered most of its territorial losses inside Europe.

The new war began in 1939 with Hitler's invasion of Poland. The Soviet Union joined in the invasion. Poland was crushed before France and Britain could give it the aid they had promised. In the years 1940 and 1941, Hitler captured nearly all of central and western Europe except for Italy and Romania, who were allies, and Spain, Portugal, Turkey, Sweden and Switzerland, who were neutral. He caught Stalin by surprise and invaded Russia, and late in 1941 his advance guard reached the outskirts of Moscow. But the further the Germans advanced, the more their supply lines were vulnerable. Hitler's invasion of Russia proved to be the slow turning point in a war which hitherto had favoured him.

The Second World War consisted of two distinct wars, one fought mainly in Europe and the other fought mainly in eastern Asia. The Asian war was earlier. It began when Japan invaded Manchuria in 1932, and became more intense in 1937 when Japan began to occupy the eastern half of China. Hitler's astonishing victory in western Europe in 1940 exposed the weakness of the British, Dutch and French colonies in South-East Asia, and the American bases in the former Spanish Philippines. Japan seized on their weakness. In December 1941 it suddenly attacked territories and bases extending from Burma and Hong Kong to Pearl Harbor.

At once the two wars – the European war and the Asian war – were welded into one, with Germany and Japan fighting on one side and the United States, Britain, China and most of the other nations of the world on the other. This was a world war, whereas the First World War had been primarily a European conflict with ragged edges.

No previous event, in peace or war, had mirrored so much the shrinking of the world. Aircraft and radio jumped across continents. The Pacific Ocean was now as easily crossed as the Mediterranean in the era of the galleys. It was a sign of the new era of mechanical warfare that during the decisive Battle of the Coral Sea, fought close to eastern Australia in May 1942, the fighting Japanese and American fleets did not see one another. They simply launched the aircraft that bombed the warships and determined the victory.

By the last months of 1944, after more than five years of war, the end of the fighting was in sight. Germany and Japan faced total defeat. But it was difficult to forecast whether the defeat would come in six or 36 months. Few human events are as unpredictable as the outbreak of peace.

30

THE BOMB AND THE MOON

Early in the 20th century, physics was perhaps the most commanding of the sciences. Busily unlocking and inspecting the long-hidden physical world, it gained glamour. Part of its fame, however, comes with hindsight. If no atomic bomb had been invented, physics might not be viewed with such awe.

For long the atom had been proclaimed as the ultimate building block. An atom was so tiny that if 10 000 million atoms were placed side by side they would just span 1 metre. In 1704 in *Opticks* Sir Isaac Newton wrote that the atom was so hard and so basic that it could never be broken into pieces, 'no ordinary Power being able to divide what God himself made one in the first Creation'. An even tinier and more complex unit, named the nucleus, was discovered later. The enormous power of the atom and the nucleus to create energy and inflict destruction was not foreseen at the start of the First World War. Only after research by the emigrant New Zealander Ernest Rutherford, Niels Bohr of Denmark and physicists of other western nations was its power clearly glimpsed.

As Germany was to the fore in physics, it could be expected to be energetic in harnessing that science to war. Germany placed racial purity, however, above the search for knowledge. Many of its stars in physics were Jews, and in the 1930s they sensibly found refuge across the seas. The United States belatedly became the spearhead of nuclear research. In December 1942 it achieved nuclear fission in a controlled way but there was still a long path of experiment and research to be followed.

Germany was finally conquered in May 1945, before America was ready to test its first atomic bomb. But America pressed on with its research, for Japan still had to be defeated. On 16 July 1945 the first bomb was tested in the desert in New Mexico. The explosion generated such heat that the surface of the desert for a radius of nearly 1 kilometre was fused into glass. Here was the most extraordinary weapon in the history of warfare. To the question 'Should it be used against the Japanese forces?' there was no easy answer; and the chosen answer has been fiercely debated to this day. Amongst American political leaders was a desire to avenge Pearl Harbor. In the minds of the nuclear scientists was an understandable resolve to test the effectiveness of a weapon for which they had worked so hard. In the minds of American generals was the fear that Japan would fight to the very end, and that perhaps half a million American lives would be lost before Japan was finally defeated.

Soviet Union

Extent of Japanese
control 1942

Mongolia

China

Peking

Korea

Japan

PACIFIC
OCEAN

Tokyo
Hiroshima
Nagasaki

Delhi

Shanghai

India

Hong
Kong

Taiwan

Burma

Thailand

Laos

Bangkok

Cambodia Vietnam

Manila

Philippines

Mariana
Islands

Guam

Marshall
Islands

Caroline
Islands

Ceylon

Malaya

Singapore

Sumatra

Borneo

Jakarta

I n d o n e s i a

Java

New Guinea

Nauru

Solomon
Islands

Darwin

New Hebrides

INDIAN OCEAN

Australia

New Caledonia

Perth

New
Zealand

Sydney
Canberra

10 JAPANESE EXPANSION IN ASIA, 1941–42

Even in July 1945 about five million Japanese soldiers were ready to defend most of their earlier conquests, including much of China, the Indonesian archipelago, the Malay Peninsula, Taiwan and the present Vietnam. The munitions arsenals inside Japan were still highly productive. Japan held more than 5000 Kamikaze aircraft, with brave pilots ready to sacrifice their lives by crashing into enemy aircraft carriers and air bases. Japan was not yet willing to admit defeat.

Today many historians denounce the American decision to drop atomic bombs on Japan as another step in human infamy. They point out that the bomb inaugurated a new era of slaughtering civilians. And yet perhaps the new era had already arrived. Air raids on German and Japanese cities with conventional bombs were already deadly. Thus one raid on Tokyo in the previous May had killed 82 000 civilians – or four-tenths of the number of Japanese who were to be killed by the first atomic bomb. And if the war went on and on and only high-explosive bombs were used, hundreds of thousands of Japanese civilians would be killed by air raids and bombardments and perhaps by the ultimate invasion of Japan's islands.

These arguments were broadly accepted by President Truman in Washington. One crucial factor, however, was overlooked. The atomic bomb, when exploded, would do what no normal bomb could do: its radiation would create genetic damage and so punish unborn children for the failures and sins of the wartime generation of Japanese. But even if radiation had been fully understood by the scientists, they might still have come to the same conclusion – that the atomic bomb must be used against the Japanese. For nearly six years the terrible all-out war had been waged. Victory must not be postponed. This argument is always more persuasive to those on the spot than to those viewing it decades later.

On 6 August 1945 a heavy American bomber flew from the Marianas to Japan and dropped the bomb. Much of Hiroshima became almost a blast furnace, and close to 90 000 Japanese were killed. In nearby Tokyo there was no willingness to surrender. Three days later a second atomic bomb – the last such bomb in the American arsenal – was dropped on the city of Nagasaki. Even then the eagerly awaited message of surrender did not come out of Tokyo. Five days later, the Emperor of Japan personally announced on the radio that his nation had surrendered. It was a sign of the aloofness and majesty of the emperor that his voice was being heard on radio for the very first time. Here was an emperor exercising relics of divine power in an era shaped by Marconi and Henry Ford.

The first formal shots of the Second World War had been fired on the northern European plain, and now the documents of peace were signed in a battleship anchored in the Bay of Tokyo. In the course of the war, more than 107 million people had been enlisted in the armed forces. Perhaps 11 million Russian soldiers were killed – a toll larger than that of the total forces fighting on both sides in the First World War. Deaths in the combined German and Japanese forces reached almost five million. Civilian deaths dwarfed those of the previous world war, and in China they perhaps numbered as many as 20 million and in Russia 11 million.

The Jews, whose prewar population in all of Europe was small compared to the population of Germany, had suffered more deaths in total than did the German armed forces and the German civilians living in the bombed cities. Ironically, many Jews once felt safe in Germany. Indeed a host of German Jews had held honoured positions in the law, universities and medicine. Some had travelled in hope to Germany from troubled lands, and many rejected the opportunity to emigrate to the growing Jewish settlements in Palestine: the state of Israel had not yet been born. But by 1942, if not earlier, the German leaders had resolved, in all the lands they ruled, to exterminate the Jews. At least five million were killed.

To this project of liquidation some Nazi leaders gave the name 'The Final Solution of the Jewish Question'. Later 'the Holocaust' became the simple description. In savagery and hatred this event was not unique. Human history, over the centuries, is peppered with acts of large-scale savagery as well as of generosity and goodwill. But the Holocaust was chilling because of the scale of the slaughter, and the refusal to exempt the very old and the very young. It was a shock to the idea of human progress, for it had been designed and executed by a nation which was seen by many impartial eyes, at the start of the century, as the most civilised and cultured in the world.

The existence of nuclear weapons was also a shock to the idea of human progress. Most people of the world would have felt safe if the United States alone had owned this weapon that was so superior to all other weapons. But the Soviet Union did not feel safe. It had to own a similar weapon. At last in 1949 the Russians secretly tested their first atomic bomb. President Truman responded with an even more powerful weapon, the hydrogen bomb, in 1951.

GLUING THE GLOBE TOGETHER AGAIN

After 1945 Europe was divided into two. Democracies dominated the western half. The Soviet Union controlled the eastern half, including part of Germany. Two other communist nations, Yugoslavia and Albania, formed an isolated pocket in the western half. The tension between communism and democratic capitalism was now called the Cold War, though in retrospect it contained far more peace than war.

Germany, occupied by the victors, had lost most of its power. Even Britain and France and Holland were less powerful than they had been in 1939. Wartime damage was on a large scale, and they had run up heavy debts or sold foreign assets in order to finance the war. Moreover their overseas colonies, which were a source of pride and of potential income more than present income, seemed likely to seek or snatch independence.

Most leaders refused to face the fact that their nation was now considerably weaker in influence. Europe had followed in the footprints of earlier centres of power which, in their confident heyday, had quarrelled internally. The Greek city-states had fought self-defeating wars with each other and collectively they had lost supremacy. Rome's empire had been weakened by internal conflict and civil war. Islam and Christianity too had been weakened by schisms. China and the South American empire of the Incas, just when their own self-confidence was high, had been torn by internal disputes. The postwar clash between communism in Russia and capitalism further to the west was another phase in the long history of European disputes. And yet Europe was saved from decline by a growing unity.

This unity began simply as a proposal for a small free-trade zone embracing the coal and iron and steel industries of the traditional enemies West Germany and France. When the zone was launched in 1952 it had six member nations. By the 1970s, it was the biggest common market in history, involving more people and commerce than that older common market, the United States of America. In 1993, when it became a political as well as an economic union, it embraced 15 nations extending, with only two gaps, from Portugal and Ireland in the west to Greece and Finland in the east. Known as the European Union, it now constituted virtually a new nation.

Europe revived even though it lost nearly all its overseas colonies. In some ways the colonies were a burden, though they had not usually been seen as such during the four and a half centuries when, one by one, they had been acquired. Even in 1945 the possession of overseas colonies carried prestige. They were not easily surrendered.

At the outbreak of the Second World War about one-third of the world's peoples still lived under European colonial rule. The ups and downs of the war, especially the military plight of France, Holland and Britain in 1940 and 1941, shook the European grip. The fighting showed that Europe's colonial powers were not invincible. In many colonies, resistance fighters seized their opportunity. The morality of nations owning colonies was challenged in European parliaments where, after the war, the parties of the left were stronger than previously.

The first large colony to be liberated was India. Its chief liberationist was Mahatma Gandhi, one of the most remarkable politicians of the century. In 1891, in his early twenties, Gandhi became a barrister in London and dressed fashionably and learned dancing and elocution. By the end of the decade he was a prosperous lawyer in South Africa but beginning to live an ascetic life, making his own clothes, and undergoing periods of fasting – a habit learned from his mother. In

1907 the Transvaal parliament compelled Asian residents to carry registration cards, and Gandhi applied his formula of 'passive resistance' for the first time: as a result he spent a total of 249 nights in jail. Returning to India in 1915, he shaped the campaign for Indian independence with a strategy of civil disobedience towards the ruling British. Wearing his white shawl, white loincloth and sandals, and often flashing his toothless smile to news-photographers, he became the most famous of all Indians in the eyes of the outside world. He tried more than anybody to unite a land which could not be united.

When India gained independence in 1947 it was divided into two separate nations, a Hindu India and an Islamic Pakistan; later Bangladesh became a third nation. In the upheavals surrounding the division of 1947, about 15 million people fled as refugees so that they could live safely in the India of their choice. Gandhi himself was a victim of the first stormy year of independence: he was killed by a militant Hindu.

India held its first national elections in 1952 with a vote available to virtually every adult, literate or illiterate. Here was one of the astonishing events in the history of politics. The second most populous nation in the world was implementing a system of government first devised for small democratic assemblies in ancient Greek cities at a time when the entire world held fewer people than democratic India held in this year of its first elections.

China also liberated itself. While it had never lost its independence completely, it had been too weak, during the last 100 years, to fend off the Russians, British, French, Germans and especially the Japanese, to each of whom it made concessions or surrendered territory. It was also weakened by its own civil war. Mao Zedong, who brilliantly led the communists during a long guerrilla war, was finally victorious in 1949, leaving his opponents only the island of Taiwan.

The new People's Republic of China, as the world's most populous nation, was expected slowly to regain the authority it had held some five centuries ago. But the relationship between population and power has often been precarious and complicated. Instead of becoming a major power, communist China for a time was an economic dunce. The countryside was in poverty, and economic progress was more a chanted slogan than a fact.

China's liberating leader, known now as 'Our Great Helmsman', believed that the minds of his people were fortunately 'blank' and that he could inscribe on them an indelible message. In 1966 his nation was the vast setting of a cultural revolution or morality play staged on a huge scale, with death, imprisonment or rural exile imposed on those opinion leaders who were judged to be politically immoral and incorrect. The nation which, five centuries before, probably led the world in utilising its people's talents, now deliberately consigned hundreds of thousands of its teachers,

artists and intellectuals to the humdrum tasks of minding pigs, reaping crops by hand and lifting irrigation
water on the treadmill. Not until the 1980s did China
begin to make that great leap forward which had been
the boast of its party propaganda three decades earlier.

Indonesia was another of the extraordinary nations
that emerged in the decade after the Second World
War. In 1940 the Indonesian islands held about 70
million people, only three million fewer than Japan.
Just over half a century later Indonesia held nearly 200
million people, being exceeded only by China, India
and the United States. It was also the most populous
Islamic nation in the world.

President Sukarno made the nation of Indonesia
and then almost unmade it. Born of a Balinese Hindu
mother and a Javanese Muslim father, he developed
a gift for words and languages. Eventually he spoke
Dutch – in which language he received much of his
education – and English, French, German, Japanese,
Javanese, Balinese and Sundanese. Of course he
learned Arabic too so that he could study the Koran. At
the same time he was more conversant with technology
than most of those who were to lead new nations, and
in 1925 he graduated in engineering from Bandung
University in Java.

Confident, exuberant, a magical maker of speeches,
Sukarno protested against the rule of the Dutch at a
time when colonial uprisings in the world were not
frequent. For 13 years he was either in jail or exiled

from his native Java. When the Japanese occupied the Dutch East Indies in 1942, Sukarno welcomed them and became their special adviser as well as a leader of his people. After Japan was defeated he resumed his fight against the Dutch, winning independence for his nation in 1949. He allowed a parliamentary election in 1955 and, not liking the indecisive result, eventually chose what he called 'Guided Democracy', with himself as guide and with democracy not all that visible. Like many of the founders of new nations he was eventually toppled from his perch.

Between 1945 and 1960, colonies holding a quarter of the world's people gained freedom. Most of the leaders of new nations had no experience of governing. Their bureaucracy was untrained. Their eagerness to borrow money far exceeded their ability to repay it. Wars against neighbours, or preparations for war, absorbed money that might have built railways, dams, hospitals, schools and cities. Few skilled entrepreneurs were available to develop natural resources in the infant nations.

The Third World – the name was coined in France to describe the poor and unaligned new nations – was third on the list in everything, whether average income or level of literacy. In one facet it was first. Its population grew at a speed such as no nation had experienced in the known history of the world. The spread of medical knowledge, the presence of more doctors and nurses, the vaccination of infants, the crusade

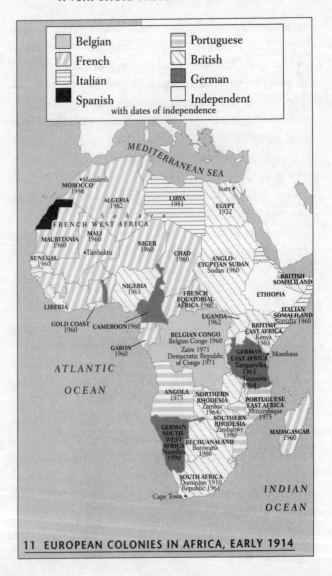

11 EUROPEAN COLONIES IN AFRICA, EARLY 1914

against malaria, and improved public hygiene cut the death rate, while the birthrate remained high. Between 1950 and 1980, during a time when new attitudes and the new contraceptive pill curbed the birthrate in Europe, the population of a variety of poor lands virtually doubled. The main task – as formidable as that experienced in possibly any other phase of human history – was simply how to feed their fast-multiplying people. The so-called green revolution with its new breeds of rice and other food-plants was initially a lifesaver; but the population still multiplied. China already held close to one billion people when, in one of the most unusual experiments in global history, it tried to restrict each of its families to one child.

Africa, the busiest arena of decolonisation, soon possessed too many nations, too many presidential palaces, and too many ambassadors living in luxury in foreign cities. By 1982 there were 54 nations in Africa – more than twice as many as in the whole of Asia. A dozen of the African nations each held fewer than one million people. In no African nation did higher education receive a high priority, and the whole of Africa in 1980 had fewer universities than did the American state of Ohio. Black Africa was impaired by tribalism, and even the white settlers in South Africa devised their own form of tribalism called apartheid. In a typical decade the standard of living of most African nations stood still.

Outside Europe and North America and the other

lands mainly settled by Europeans, economic achievements in the postwar period fell short of initial hopes. Eastern Asia was the spectacular exception. Japan displayed an economic success exceeded by no European nation between 1945 and 1990. Singapore, Malaysia and Thailand, Hong Kong, South Korea and Taiwan, most of which had a large sector of Chinese ancestry, also began to perform impressively. In contrast China itself, by depriving people of economic incentives, barely hobbled along in the space of three decades. In postwar history a remarkable contrast lay in the sluggishness of China itself compared to the systematic energy of the relatively few millions of ethnic Chinese who lived in capitalist lands just across the sea.

In military affairs, Asia could no longer be discounted. No neutral scientists had foreseen, back in 1945, that China and India would test their own nuclear weapons within a quarter of a century, or that nations as small as Iraq and North Korea would pursue nuclear ambitions or that Pakistan would possess its own bomb at the end of the century.

TO THE MOON

The Second World War had spurred a need for new ways of propulsion. In 1944–45 in occupied France the Germans used powerful rockets to launch missiles which flew straight across the sea to London. In peacetime these same rockets offered a way of launching radio transmitters which, from on high, could beam amplified signals to every corner of the earth.

On 10 July 1962, a day as momentous as any in the 20th century, a satellite transmitted television pictures and phone conversations between Europe and the USA. Satellites soon spanned the world. They became vital for the world's communications, and for tasks as diverse as forecasting the weather, searching for minerals, and enabling ships and aircraft to plot their position. In the Persian Gulf in 1991 the United States used satellites to guide weapons to their distant targets, some of which stood on the site of those early valley civilisations that flourished several thousand years ago.

With the new rockets, outer space could be explored. In the race to explore this newest world, the Soviets gained an early lead. In October 1957 they launched their first spacecraft, and it orbited the earth. There was no pilot aboard. In the following year the Russians sent two dogs into orbit in Sputnik III where they rode in cramped glory, 500 kilometres above the earth.

In the expensive contest to send the first person into space the Russians won by 23 days, sending Yuri Gagarin and his space capsule on an impressive orbit of the earth on 12 April 1961. One of the remarkable days in the history of the human race, no subsequent feat in space could surpass it. The brave dream of placing a person on the moon was achieved by the United States on 20 July 1969 when, in front of a huge television audience, Neil Armstrong and 'Buzz' Aldrin, wearing cumbersome suits, stepped from their craft and walked on the moon. In 1976 an unmanned American space-craft landed on Mars. As Mars was 1000 times further away from the earth than was the moon, this was the equivalent of Vasco da Gama's ship finally reaching India instead of Gibraltar.

The exploring of space was a triumph for the Russians as well as the Americans. But in the end the ailing Russian economy could not finance the nation's high military and scientific goals. The cost of the latest missiles, huge armed forces and the space race, and the dint to national morale by a frustrating war in Afghanistan, combined to weaken the Soviet Union. An inefficient economy could not afford these luxuries; and so the standard of living in the Soviet Union lagged far behind that of western Europe. Meanwhile, citizens in Poland – spurred by a strike in the shipyards in 1980 – and in Czechoslovakia began to rebel against communism. From Moscow there came no effective retaliation.

The nations of eastern Europe broke away from the Soviet Union and from communism. Even the states that comprised the Union were permitted to secede. In December 1991 the Soviet Union itself ceased to exist. Its collapse was another step, though belated and unpredicted, in the process of decolonisation. In one swoop, Russia lost its overland empire just as Britain, Holland, France and Portugal, in the period from 1945 to 1975, had lost most of their overseas empires.

When the Soviet Union was riding high, it seemed possible that Russian would become the chief international language. It was already the diplomatic language of the second-largest power bloc in the world. In the 1950s it was the main foreign language taught in China. Seen as the language of the future, it was studied eagerly by young socialists in Africa. By the end of the century, however, the Russian language had fallen far.

The popularity of English as a global language was only one sign of America's increasing influence during the 20th century. During the first 40 years of the century, America's influence on the world was smaller than its size and potential power would suggest. It was not the dominant trading nation, and in foreign policy it tended to be isolationist.

The 1940s and 1950s were the first decades in which the United States exercised both a continuing and profound influence on the world. They could equally be called Russia's decades, for that nation played the larger part in defeating Hitler, in helping communism to win in China, and in winning for itself an early lead in the space race. Thereafter the United States dominated the century. Even the British Empire, when it held colonies in every continent and on nearly every crucial sea lane, did not exert an influence quite comparable to the present power of the United States in economic, military, political and cultural matters.

The power of the United States depended heavily on its pale empire of ideas, attitudes and innovations. Its ideas alighted effortlessly on foreign ground, irrespective of who owned the ground. Much of its influence came from such innovations as the telephone, electricity, aircraft and the cheap car, nuclear weapons and spacecraft, computers and the Internet. Its influence came through jazz, cartoons, Hollywood, television and popular culture. Its influence came from an excitement about technology and economic change, and a belief in incentives and individual enterprise. It was also the most ardent missionary for the creed of democracy. While military and economic might was vital to the success of the United States, the power of its empire of ideas was probably even more pervasive.

The global role of the United States is perhaps the ultimate chapter in that long period of European expansion which had begun in western Europe, and especially on the Atlantic seaboard, during the 15th century. Europe slowly had outgrown its homeland. Its cultural empire eventually formed a long band traversing most of the Northern Hemisphere and dipping far into the Southern. In the history of European peoples the city of Washington is perhaps what Constantinople – the infant city of Emperor Constantine – was to the last phase of the Roman Empire; for it is unlikely that Europeans, a century hence, will continue to stamp the world so decisively with their ideas and inventions.

31

NO FRUITS, NO BIRDS

One profound change in human history is so obvious that it is rarely commented upon: the slow blurring of distinctions which had once been all-important. The seasons were blurred; the differences between night and day, and summer and winter, were blurred. As the night sky became less important, the moon waned in its influence on human activities. Work and leisure, city and country ceased to provide such contrasts.

In the vast time span of the hunters and farmers the seasons had been all-important. Summer and winter, spring and autumn determined what people ate, the ceremonies they performed and the comforts or hardships of their daily life. Most human beings, even in AD 1800, were still farmers and keepers of herds and were deeply affected by the changing of the seasons. Thus in winter, eggs and fruit and even meat – unless it was salted – were luxuries. The summer of plenty gave way to a winter of belt-tightening. It was Thomas Hood, the English poet, who wrote:

'No fruits, no flowers, no leaves, no birds, –
November!'

Religious manuscripts prepared 1000 years ago emphasised how distinctive was each season. For each month they painted a scene or task; and that task flavoured a month in a way in which no work-task can now mark out a typical month.

Today a typical task of the month, if there is such a task, is likely to be a leisure pursuit: the erecting of a Christmas tree or the attending of a football final. In contrast, a Byzantine manuscript of the year 1100 singled out the monthly workday tasks in the Balkans and Asia Minor. In April the shepherd was depicted preparing to take his flock from the barn, where in winter it had lived on stored hay, to the fresh grass of the hills. May was symbolised by the carrying of flowers. June depicted a man cutting lush grass in readiness for the making of hay. By October the summer was ebbing, and a bird-catcher or fowler held on his wrist a small bird which he used to decoy and thereby capture big edible birds before they emigrated. In November the ploughman prepared the land for the sowing of next year's crop. And so, in orderly procession, the working year was dictated by the seasons, though the actual tasks varied from region to region.

Even the fighting of wars was affected by the seasons. In the Northern Hemisphere international wars usually broke out in spring or summer. In the years between 1840 and 1938 a total of 44 wars were fought in those northern lands where winter and summer were clearly contrasted. Of those wars only three were commenced in the winter months but 26 began during the warmer months from April to July. The coming of spring offered a chance to attack and defeat an enemy, for rivers were forded more easily, rural roads were less obstructed by mud and ice, days were longer and advancing armies could steal or buy food in the blooming countryside. In China the traditional time for fighting a quick war was the autumn, for crops had just been harvested, rivers were more passable and dry land enabled troops to march quickly to the locality chosen for their first attack.

Travel was always regulated by the seasons. In Asia the start or end of the annual monsoon signalled the departure of the merchant fleets, whether Arab dhows or Malay praus. In Europe most journeys were postponed until winter storms had passed. In the 16th century most German pilgrims set sail from Venice to the Holy Land in June or July, having left Germany as soon as the snow in the Alps had melted.

In Europe the first day of May honoured that boundary between cold and warmth, between hunger and plenty. Midnight on the eve of May Day was greeted by the beating of drums and the blasts of cow-horns. There was dancing around the maypole – sometimes with such sexual frolickings that the day was denounced by preachers at the time of the religious Reformation. Suddenly milk and cream were plentiful. In parts of England a highlight of May Day was to milk cows directly above a bucket containing sherry or port, so that the squirts of warm creamy milk enriched the drink.

The celebration of the first of May extended to the swelling cities. In London in the 18th century the milkmaids made the day their own. A century later it belonged to the army of chimneysweeps who, with the arrival of warmer nights, systematically brushed away the layers of soot which had accumulated in house chimneys over winter. In continental Europe the social-ists and trade unionists were to commandeer May Day. Their choice was natural, for it had long been a day of hope and renewal. In those regions of China where win-ter was harsh, the sight of fresh flowers in city markets served as the equivalent of May Day. The early yellow peony was the favourite, and even in the eighth century it commanded the high price of 'five bits of silk'.

The coming of May and its flood of milk, meat, eggs, butter and flowers was rendered less exciting by such innovations as the steamship, railway, canning factory and refrigerating machine. To Europe in the second half of the 19th century came a flow of foods from distant lands. As early as 1850, one-quarter of the bread eaten in England came from grain grown in the USA and Ukraine. At the same time, canned food was shipped across the Atlantic to Europe – tins of beef, mutton and fish to be followed by tins of vegetables, fruits and jam. By 1880 refrigerated beef and lamb were being shipped to Europe from as far away as Buenos Aires and Sydney.

In prosperous cities in the year 2000, every large department store displays roses, out of season but flown from afar, and strawberries and pineapples too. But in previous centuries, whether along the Yellow River or the Avon, it was pointless to ask for a fruit or flower which was out of season.

THE BLURRING OF NIGHT AND DAY

For most of human history the contrast between day and night was as acute as the contrast between summer and winter. Darkness kept people inside their cave, bark shelter, hut or farmhouse. Fear of wild animals was also an incentive to stay inside or near the protective light of a blazing fire. Night was linked to the sinister. The devil was said to conduct orgies, and witches rode on their broomsticks in the middle of night. At least two of the major religions saw night as a time when in the silence and darkness God might speak to them. Mohammed received much of the Koran from on high late one night. Early Christians saw virtue in praying in the night because then they could pray in silence. Many expected Christ to return at the hour of midnight.

As towns and cities became important, darkness lost a little of its terror. But even in the time of Columbus and Luther the main streets of cities were only lit faintly after dark. Inside the typical house in Europe the light was almost too dim for the reading of a book; in any case, most households did not possess a book.

In many European towns at a certain hour of the evening the law decreed that the household fire should be extinguished or covered. Before the family went to bed, the fire had to be made safe. This simple rule helped to save many towns, where wooden houses were jammed together, from catching alight. In England William the Conqueror, fresh from France, ordered the ringing of a curfew bell at 8 p.m., after which all fires were curbed. For most of the world's history the advent of night was like the closing of a door. Few occupations were carried on at night. To be a nightwatchman was to follow a lonely occupation.

During the 19th century an extraordinary change reached some cities in Europe, Australia, North America and Asia: the night ceased to contrast sharply with the day. Inside a house, for the first time in history, the artificial light at night was often clearer than the natural light of day – thanks to the abundance of whale oil, the new kerosene extracted from underground oilfields, and the invention of gas and electricity. Many daytime activities could, if necessary, be continued during the early hours of the night. Moreover by 1900 the streets of large cities were lit by electricity and knitted together by trams and trains, and so people could travel a short distance to pursue social activities in the evening.

The new ways of providing light also supplied

heat for winter. Houses could become as warm as in summer. Wool had been the main raw material of warm clothes and blankets, but by the end of the 20th century the heating of houses and offices was so widespread – and synthetic fibres so cheap – that wool was no longer in strong demand for winter clothes.

The blurring of night and day was aided in an unexpected way by new electronic communications. They provided instant contact, and so somebody experiencing daylight could talk to somebody who, far away, was already in the night. It was the Italian engineer Guglielmo Marconi who discovered a way of transmitting messages by electromagnetic waves; and he sent an invisible message across the narrow Bristol Channel in 1897. Experiment slowly improved the radius of the message. Four years later Marconi was in Newfoundland when he received, from a Cornish radio transmitter on the far side of the Atlantic, a faint radio message. It was a procession of sounds more than a clear message, but it was exciting.

While the old-time telegraph did not carry the human voice, the radio could carry the voice a short distance. The first radio or wireless station for the public was founded by amateurs in Pittsburgh in 1920. Many Americans purchased or assembled their own 'wireless' sets and listened, for the radio soon fulfilled an additional function – the playing of recorded music on a gramophone. Rarely is a modern invention born with its wings flapping, and in the 1920s the gramophone transmitted a sound that was eerie and sometimes scratchy. Radio transmission improved, and by 1939 those listening to the radio in New Zealand at night could hear, not always clearly, that morning's news being broadcast from London.

Meanwhile in 1926 an inventive Scot, John Logie Baird, transmitted the first television image, in black and white, from a room in inner London. His invention, while dramatic, was in a sense a dead end. For another quarter of a century few people outside Britain and the United States saw a televised picture. By the 1960s in most of the prosperous nations the television – with the aid of the satellite – was beginning to blur night and day. A viewer in Australia, at night, could watch the Olympic Games being contested in broad daylight on the far side of the world. So night and day changed places.

The moon for long had held a special significance. In Assyria the crescent moon was the symbol of the king as early as the ninth century BC. Israel based its calendar on the moon. The date of the celebrations of Easter and Ramadan were determined by the full moon. The crescent moon became the sign of Islam, and now appears on the flags of Pakistan, Turkey and most of the Islamic nations.

As the night was a prison, the full moon unlocked the gate, allowing important activities to take place. Some crops could be harvested in the light of the full moon. The timing of important military and naval engagements was sometimes influenced by the knowledge that the moon would be bright. In ancient Australia ceremonial dances were usually held under the full moon. In living memory in rural South Africa and Canada, farmers would hold formal dances and Masonic services on the night of the full moon; and then the participants, guided by the moon, could ride or walk home along unmade roads. In that era, rural households possessed an annual printed almanac that told them when the moon would be full.

The dome of the night sky, which seemed to be so near, held an intimacy for generations of people. The stars foretold the future of individuals and nations. For centuries, farmers planted crops according to the stars as well as the moon. On 4 January 1948 the nation of Burma fixed the hour of birth of its republic, and its independence from Britain, after receiving advice from astrologers that 4.20 a.m. was an auspicious time. During the last four centuries, the telescope and radio have dispelled some of this mystery and wonder.

The electricity which enabled day to be prolonged in the big city served also to weaken the majesty of the stars. For countless ages the night sky had been a familiar temple and shrine in the eyes of tens of millions of people scattered across the face of the earth. But in the 20th century, for the first time in human history, the artificial light cocooning a large city dimmed the brilliance of the stars above, diminishing what one balladist called 'the wondrous glory of the everlasting stars'. Indeed, if a prehistoric hunting family could be resurrected and set down in Tokyo on a clear night, they would first be astonished by the tall buildings and the crowds of people and then they would observe with equal puzzlement that the night sky was no longer brilliant.

The day was also transformed. The work of the day followed a new path in prosperous western nations. Even a century ago the hard work needed to produce food, shelter and clothing was a lifelong task for most adults and many children; and the penalty for idleness or misfortune was hunger or even death. But the machine and new techniques of production transformed most jobs. Hours of work were shorter, holidays increased, and fewer jobs required the lifting of heavy weights or the unremitting use of arms and legs.

The increase in leisure, especially for those with money to spare, was now a dynamo of economic life. Many of the booming industries were centred on tourism, sport, recreation, the performing arts or other leisure pursuits. In Europe in AD 1000 the popular heroes were soldiers and saints. In AD 2000 they were more likely, in many parts of the world, to be athletes, actors, singers, artists or other heroes of leisure time.

BIG CROWDS, BIG CITIES

The revival and spread of spectator sport in the western world was a mirror of the rearranging of work and leisure, night and day, winter and summer. England and

Australia were the first to be obsessed with spectator sport. This obsession first arose more in the cities than in the countryside: more in the Birminghams and Melbournes than in the farming villages. It reflected the increased wealth produced in fewer hours of work, thus facilitating the awarding of a half-day holiday on Saturday or Wednesday in commercial and industrial cities.

At first the rise of spectator sport reflected old patterns. It was not played on Sunday, for such activity was banned on the Sabbath day in those Protestant countries which were the first homes of modern spectator sport. Amongst the players themselves were clear distinctions between professionals and amateurs, or between working-class and upper-class participants. The strict seasons allocated to each popular sport mirrored the age-old contrast between summer and winter; and so football was allocated the winter, whereas cricket, tennis, baseball, athletics, bowls and rowing were given the warmer months.

Late in the 20th century, spectator sport was able to discard some of the conditions originally imposed on it by the seasons, the calendar, the Sabbath and nightfall. With the advent of powerful electric light, a daylight contest could become a night game. With the rise of roofed stadiums the contrast between summer and winter was blurred. With the decline of Protestantism, Sunday became secular and was available for sport as well as for shopping. Moreover with the ease of international travel and the spread of sporting culture, professional players could play the same game throughout the year, moving from hemisphere to hemisphere in order to catch the change in the seasons.

It is a mirror of the extraordinary spread of leisure that spectator sport is almost becoming the international language. Whereas in 1900 there were few sporting contests that aroused international enthusiasm – the revived Olympic Games was still a minor carnival – now international sporting fixtures stretch from January to December and show tentative signs of becoming a focus for some of the national pride and aggression that was traditionally poured into warfare.

Throughout human history, nearly all people were close to the soil. Therefore their lives were profoundly affected by the alternation of winter and summer, by the coming and going of the full moon, and by the pattern of rain and drought and the annual harvest. Steadily the ever-expanding city displaced the countryside as the home of most of the world's people; and the big cities now dwarfed the biggest city of several hundred years earlier. In 1995 at least 25 cities each held more than seven million inhabitants. Only four of these – London, Paris, Moscow and Istanbul – stood in Europe. In contrast 13 of the greatest cities were in Asia, and another seven were in the Americas, including four in Latin America. Africa had only one, Cairo, on the Nile. In 2000 years' time, how many of these cities will remain great? The city of skyscrapers seems the most lasting of creations – the skyscraper is almost the sphinx and pyramid of our age – but in some distant era most of these tall cities will presumably go the way of Nineveh and Carthage.

The cities reflect the soaring population of the world. Observers in the 20th century, more than in any previous century, spoke fearfully of global overpopulation, whereas in 1800 even a scholar as learned as Robert Malthus, the population expert, had few means of estimating with any accuracy the population of the world. In his day, much of the world was still sparsely explored and its peoples were uncounted.

As far as is known, the world at the time of Christ did not hold a population exceeding 300 million. In essence the population then was about the same as that of today's United States. By the year 1750, the world held perhaps 800 million people – far less than the present population of China. Then came the dramatic increase. The population of the world passed one billion in about 1800 and then doubled in the next 125 years. The most remarkable increase came between 1927 and 1974, when it doubled to about four billion people. In the next quarter of a century, another two billion were added. More people were added to the population of the world in just the 1990s than in all of history stretching from the origins of humans to the birth of the industrial revolution in England.

Nature was now seen as an old and even a dear ally, to be protected against a soaring population and a powerful technology, but it had long been regarded as an enemy as well as a friend. Since the human race first existed, nature and its extremes of flood and drought, wild beasts, invisible microbes, storms, dark forests and temperamental oceans had often been feared. Nature was capable of inflicting, in just one blow, more damage than humankind inflicted through war and other forms of self-inflicted wound in the course of an entire year. The Black Death killed more Europeans than did the First World War six centuries later. In some centuries, millions of lives were wiped out by cyclones, tidal waves, earthquakes and the erupting of volcanoes. In modern decades, however, human technology was often seen as more devastating than aberrant nature.

NEW GODS AND OLD

Religion tended to flourish most vigorously when daily life was perilous and often painful. Religion flourished when floods, droughts and other catastrophes of nature were more destructive, when starvation lay around the corner and an early death was the expectation of most people. Religion flourished when people lived on the land and knew how easily a long-awaited harvest could be thwarted by pests, drought, soil exhaustion or storms. For most of history, human life was perilous. Religion provided answers to the inexplicable events in the life of a state or a region or a family. Satisfying a deep and sometimes inexplicable yearning, it was also a source of strength and inspiration.

Religion was the cement of numerous societies which otherwise might have crumbled. Powerful monarchs gained by upholding it. The official religion enabled them to proclaim that they were even descended from the gods. Therefore, to disobey the king was indirectly to disobey the gods. The revolutions in France in 1789, Russia in 1917 and China in 1949 set out to overthrow the old religions because they were a prop of the old order.

In the 20th century, religion faced other difficulties. With increased prosperity and a longer life, part of the appeal of religion was weakened. In Europe and some regions of the United States, churchgoing declined rapidly, as did acceptance of whole moral and sexual codes preached by the churches.

And yet in the world as a whole, religion remained powerful. Both Christianity and Islam claimed far more adherents than a century earlier, and their meeting houses traced a dotted line across the whole earth. Buddhism, no longer so powerful in China, retained vitality in many lands. In India the Hindus and Jains, Parsees and Sikhs were far from invisible. Judaism was alive and thankful to be alive. In Africa more people ardently practised religion than had probably practised it in Europe at any one time. Significantly, the very churches which refused to make a truce with rising secular trends – and continued to assert their belief in the importance of the next world – tended to be the most vigorous.

Islam made no truce. There was only one God and Allah was his name. Most of its preachers opposed secularism, consumerism, materialism and what they saw as an increasingly restless and godless culture in New York, Paris, Moscow and Singapore. Within Islam, the evangelical extremists were conspicuous. They were not typical but were made to seem typical because their activities were often in the news. They were stridently opposed to Judaism and Christianity. They denounced the secularised western world as decadent and far too permissive and tolerant. In their turn they were denounced as backward and far too intolerant. Such deep-seated disputes had occurred again and again in human history. Whereas in the west, cultural and religious diversity – for perhaps the first time in history – was hailed by many as the supreme virtue, it was viewed in many mosques as almost the supreme sin.

Predominantly a religion of the countryside and the villages, Islam early in the twenty-first century grew at a rapid pace, partly because it believed in itself and partly because it believed in large families. It was now the religion of almost one in five of the world's people and was growing more rapidly than Christianity though still far behind in its total adherents. Today the truly massive places of worship constructed in the world are more likely to be Islamic mosques than Christian cathedrals. The Moroccan city of Casablanca recently built the tallest minaret in the world, while even in the Catholic nation of Venezuela arose a mosque which astonished devout villagers from the countryside.

Millions of educated people in the western world distanced themselves from those gods to whom, when young, they had been taught to pray. Part of their self-reliance came from the achievements of science and technology. Science itself was a new rational god and was hailed as all-knowing, all-wise and capable of producing materialist miracles. Marxism for a time was a powerful alternative religion: Karl Marx preached that he was the first to find the scientific laws of human history and that those laws would ultimately produce a heaven, even though the heaven would be on earth. While science and communism claimed to dispense with the gods, they almost enthroned the human race, and its potential, into a god. This utopian attitude, even more than traditional religion, was in decline at the end of the 20th century, with the collapse of communism in Russia and eastern Europe. But it might well appear again in new garments.

Science, hailed in the previous century as the benefactor of the human race, was now condemned by many western critics as the wrecker. A vigorous environmental crusade singled out technology and science as the enemy which was polluting sky, earth and sea. Pollution became an all-purpose word of disapproval. This was the first century in which pollution was seen as a global force. The widespread hostility towards science and technology came when their triumphs were still far more pervasive than their threats.

EPILOGUE

The recent history of the human race is like an amazing rebirth. Most parts of the body have acquired a substitute.

Two thousand years ago human legs were indispensable. There was no substitute except a horse or a sailing ship. Elsewhere legs carried people when they worked, when they strolled. People stood on their legs for most of their waking hours, except in a tiny proportion of sit-down jobs. The moneylender and scholar could perhaps sit down while they worked: the rest stood, whether to sow crops or to reap, whether to be a preacher, soldier or cook. Even the act of writing was often performed while standing at a tall desk. But now the aircraft and train, car and motorbike and bus are substitutes for legs.

Likewise, 2000 years ago, arms and their muscles were essential in most tasks. At sea the wind gave help but arms were necessary to hoist the heavy sails or to row the ship in still weather. The strength of the oxen was vital in ploughing but the strength of human arms was necessary to steer the plough. The arm muscles and fingers were vital for producing food and shelter and security.

Then arrived a chain of dramatic changes, with the human arm and hand being helped or replaced by the waterwheel and steam engine, by the wheelbarrow, gunpowder and dynamite, the hydraulic crane, jack-hammer, bulldozer, rivet machine, washing machine and vacuum cleaner, by sewing machine, fruit-picking machines, hole-digging machines, computer keyboards and countless other substitutes. The human arm and fingers have been transformed even more than the legs. The fingers can even send nuclear missiles from one continent to another.

To the human head have also come unimaginable changes. The eyes have been enhanced by the tele-scope, the microscope, television, radar, spectacles, the printing press. The ears hear more, the mouth speaks more clearly and the voice travels far through radio, microphone, telephone, and music cassette. The cre-ativity of the human brain has been aided and mirrored by the computer. Sexual activities have been altered by the Pill. The efficacy of teeth has been prolonged not only by dentistry and the artificial tooth but by changes in diet and in the processing of foods. The knowledge of the human body has been further enlarged by the study of genes.

Likewise the memory of human beings, especially the collective memory, has been enlarged by libraries and archives. Curiously this enlarging of the human memory was significant long before the rise of the Roman Empire thanks to the innovation of counting, the devising of the calendar, the rise of the art of writing, and that ingenious aid to a retentive memory, skill in rhyming. In contrast most of the startling gains in the efficiency of legs and arms, mouth and teeth, eyes and ears and memory, and the diagnosing of human illness, came after the 15th century.

None of these profound changes altered the human will, human restlessness, the human desire either for freedom or for conformity. So many of the triumphs of science and technology were skin-deep. It was easier, in this era of mass production in the countryside and city, to satisfy the stomach than the mind. It was easier to tame diseases than to tame human behaviour and put an end to warfare.

ALMOST ONE WORLD

The advances in technology magnified the potential power of one particular leader or group. Ten thousand years ago, a leader of a tribe was rarely able to wield influence more than 100 kilometres from home. The world was like a pond with space for thousands of small ripples, each ripple reflecting the tiny sphere of influence of one tribe. The radius of ripples became larger after the emerging of bigger empires – the Chinese and Indian, the Hellenistic, Roman and Aztec.

The sphere of influence of each of these empires

was still small. Such was the prevailing technology of war and transport that there was virtually no way of achieving central control of a civilian population spread far and wide. Two thousand years ago, no empire could extend far. Rome in its heyday could have conquered and ruled parts of India and even China but its reign would have been brief. Hitler, if he had been victorious, probably could not have controlled the whole world. The technology of war, communications and censorship did not allow it.

Today, as never before, it is possible for one strong nation to control the whole world. Within the next two centuries, as the world shrinks and its distances are diminished, an attempt could well be made, by consent or by force, to set up a world government. Whether it will last for long is an open question. In human history, almost nothing is preordained.

FURTHER READING

In the unabridged edition of this book, *A Short History of the World*, there is a long list of the sources I used. Covering thirty pages, they can easily be consulted by readers who wish to learn more about the evidence underlying my narrative and interpretation. For readers who wish to delve into other books covering wide aspects of world history, the following are recommended as an entrée.

Barzun, Jacques, *From Dawn to Decadence: 500 Years of Western Cultural Life*, Harper Collins, New York, 2000.

Braudel, Fernand, *A History of Civilizations*, trans. Richard Mayne, Allen Lane, Penguin Press, 1994.

Davies, Norman, *Europe: A History*, Pimlico, London, 1997.

Diamond, Jared, *Guns, Germs and Steel: A Short History of Everybody for the Last 13,000 Years*, Vintage, London, 1998.

Gombrich, E. H., *The Story of Art*, Phaidon, London, 1972.

Hsu, Immanuel, *The Rise of Modern China*, Oxford University Press, New York, 1995.

Hufton, Olwen, *The Prospect Before Her: A History of Women in Western Europe*, 2 vols, Fontana, London, 1997.

Johnson, Paul, *A History of the Jews*, Weidenfeld & Nicolson, London, 1987.

Jones, Barry, *Dictionary of World Biography*, 3rd edn, Information Australia, Melbourne, 1998.

Kennedy, Paul, *The Rise and Fall of the Great Powers: Economic Change and Military Conflict from 1500 to 2000*, Random House, New York, 1989.

Sowell, Thomas, *Conquests and Cultures: An International History*, Basic Books, New York, 1998.

INDEX

ALSO BY GEOFFREY BLAINEY

BLACK KETTLE AND FULL MOON

In *Black Kettle and Full Moon*, master story-teller Geoffrey Blainey takes us on another absorbing journey – a guided tour of a vanished Australia. Covering the years from the first gold rush to World War I, Blainey paints a fascinating picture of how our forebears lived – in the bush, in towns and cities, at sea and far inland. He looks at a host of aspects of daily life, from billycans to brass bands, from ice-making to etiquette, from pipes to pubs. Professor Blainey's evocative text is further brought alive through contemporary illustrations by artists such as Julian Ashton.

This is Geoffrey Blainey doing what he does best – bringing to life for the modern reader the sights and sounds and smells of another time.

'Blainey paints an unforgettable picture of an all-but-vanished Australia ... *Black Kettle and Full Moon* is a joy to read and savour.'
ROSS FITZGERALD, *THE SYDNEY MORNING HERALD*

'It is the richest account yet written of life for the ordinary Australian in the years between the gold rushes and World War I. Its texture is so light and readable that it seems to have been spun without effort.'
EVAN WILLIAMS, *WEEKEND AUSTRALIAN*

SCURVY
STEPHEN R. BOWN

In the days of the tall ships, one dreaded foe was responsible for more deaths at sea than piracy, shipwreck and all other illnesses combined. Cruelly culling sailors and stunting maritime enterprise from Vasco da Gama to Sir Francis Drake, this plague of the seas was scurvy. Countless mariners perished from the disease in agony; their early symptoms included bleeding gums, wobbly teeth and the opening of old wounds.

A cure had eluded doctors and philosophers since the time of the ancient Greeks, but in the late eighteenth century the surgeon James Lind, the great sea captain James Cook and the physician Sir Gilbert Blane, undertook to crack the riddle of scurvy. Their timely discovery, just as Napoleon was mobilising for the conquest of Europe, solved the greatest medical mystery of the Age of Sail and irrevocably altered the course of world history.

This is both a history and a detective story; it is about class, wilful ignorance and ludicrous decision-making, and about how a cure for scurvy was found, ignored, lost, and finally implemented to the great benefit of all seafaring nations.

'This is one fabulous, accessible look at the history of seafaring…Never was a now seldom-seen vitamin deficiency so interesting.'
SHAUNAGH O'CONNOR, *HERALD SUN*